THE FIFTH PARADIGM

The Fifth Paradigm

A Twenty-First-Century Strategy for America

Joel Cawley

Joel Cawley Publications:
Invisible Forces: Modern Strategy Principles from the Aerie of IBM
The Fifth Paradigm: A Twenty-First-Century Strategy for America

Produced by Dan Levine
Cover illustration by Jason Gamber

ISBN-13: 978-1-7332754-2-2 (eBook)
ISBN-13: 978-1-7332754-3-9 (paperback)

Library of Congress Control Number: 2019916649

CONTENTS

CONTENTS

Introduction

SOMETHING IS VERY wrong. We all know it. As the poet Yeats wrote in 1919, "the best lack all conviction while the worst are full of passionate intensity." The adjectives "hyper-partisan" or "polarized" characterize essentially every debate. Not only are those acrimonious debates filled with more heat than light, the only paths being offered are ones that we all know lead to dead ends or create as many problems as they solve. The old paradigm of left versus right has been radicalized into socialist versus fascist expletives, with nobody understanding what those terms even mean these days. I will highlight many insights and answers in this book, and none of them will be based on meaningless and useless debates about "capitalism" versus "socialism."

The list of issues is daunting. Our health care and education costs have been spiraling out of control for almost four decades. Despite costing twice as much as any other developed nation's, the health care we provide can charitably be described as "below average." During that same 40-year period the manufacturing jobs that brought middle-class living standards to millions have dropped by over a third. The communities surrounding those abandoned factories have been devastated in the process. Wages have been stagnant in real terms for nearly 50 years. There are 40–50 million Americans living in poverty who are forced to rely on the worst assistance programs in the developed world. Income disparity has reached levels not seen since the gilded age. Our roads, bridges, tunnels, airports, public buildings, and other vital infrastructure are crumbling. They've been shamefully neglected for those same four to five decades. We've squandered our resources instead on a series of endless foreign wars with zero purpose and no means of withdrawal. Amid all those failed programs, both public and corporate debt has skyrocketed.

If that list of real, concrete problems weren't enough we have an equally daunting list of issues that have become hopelessly twisted through false assertions, alternate facts, and conspiracy-theory madness. Immigrants represent a tidal wave of crime and social burdens . . . Except, they don't. Crime rates are out of control . . . Except, they're at the lowest levels since the 1950s. The freedom for people to sexually identify and associate as they prefer creates an enormous moral burden on traditional families . . . Except, it does nothing of the kind. Globalization and trade are the cause of our economic woes . . . Except, they are absolutely vital aspects of our economy. Climate change is a hoax . . . Except, it's already having major impacts all over the world. We can't even begin debating solutions because we have no shared understanding of what we're even talking about.

Compounding matters, the institutions we rely on to help solve our problems are fraught with their own breakdowns. Trust in government has been in precipitous decline for those same 50 years. The decision by the Supreme Court in *Citizens United* to legalize domestic political bribery has made that bad situation even worse. Trust in business is at an all-time low and, considering the recent conduct of companies like Volkswagen and Wells Fargo, deservedly so. Our sources of information in the mass media and expert commentary have been split into camps living in different realities. Demagogues have seized the day promoting culture wars and social division to solidify their standing with followers. We've been infected by a culture of trolls, bent solely on causing anguish to others. The trolls themselves have been infiltrated by foreign actors and automated "bots," all seeking to split us asunder.

Where did all this dysfunction come from? Why now? What can be done about it? If all the known paths on the map are bad, in what direction should we head? How can we tell what has real promise from simple wishful thinking?

I believe there are real answers to those questions. I spent over two decades as the vice president of corporate strategy at IBM. In that role I dealt with countless issues and opportunities from all over the world. I spent much of my career finding the stories buried in mountains of data, translating economics into actionable insights, and understanding the deep human and technology drivers lurking behind market trends. Those experiences, along with the specific tools and methods of the strategy profession, have given me a unique perspective on the much larger challenges we face as a nation.

Business strategists see the world as a mosaic of complex systems whose behaviors are shaped by a medley of invisible forces. Adam Smith's "invisible hand" is the most famous example, but the full combination is far larger. Our economies and society are driven by the beliefs, needs, and desires of humanity—of people. Those are always evolving, responding to changes in the world around us and our own experiences. Personal identity, morality, and perceptions of truth play a powerful role in shaping the way we see and react to the world.

That world is also in constant evolution. Science, technology, and the innovations from businesses, people, government, and other institutions continually reshape what is possible. The productivity gains arising from all of that activity are crucial to powering our overall economy. They are also highly disruptive, with the potential to dramatically shift employment patterns throughout our society. Strategists search for and focus on the deep structural shifts with enduring influence, the forces that really change the world. Few of us spend time hunting for fads.

The most important of those structural shifts are driven by the enormous spectrum of things we value both as individuals and in society. Every business must create value for its customers that is superior to its competitors. That value must be continually reinvented and defended for the business to endure. Understanding value and all of the forces and influences that surround it is the true heart of business strategy and people are the blood cells that course through that heart. Understood more broadly, our values are both shaped by and reflected in our social institutions including our businesses, governments, churches, and communities. What we value truly shapes our world, and the current shape of our world reflects our current values. And that mirror on our collective souls is not offering a pretty picture.

Our social cohesion as a nation is under enormous stress. The design of our economy is failing the needs of our citizens. We are no longer a society where children can expect better lives than their parents. We are no longer a society in which life expectancy increases from generation to generation. We have not yet reached the level of inequality leading up to the French Revolution, but we are at a level higher than right before the Great Depression. Those economic stresses are intensified by the deep philosophical core of what we each perceive as being "moral" and "true." Our philosophical differences have always existed but have been magnified by the echo chambers of our tribal media and the coalescence of a particular faction with a deep worship of power. Understanding all these "behind the headlines" forces will provide an important layer of insights that are critical for our twenty-first-century strategies.

One of the more distinctive aspects of the perspective that shapes this book is the combination of an ethical compass based on progressive human values with a deep, solid understanding of global economics, markets, and business. Despite violent assertions to the contrary, from all corners, those values need not be in conflict.

Strategists know that people don't behave the way economists assume and build that reality in their thinking and analyses. While economics and economic theory will feature strongly in the pages ahead it's the strategic insights that will point to our answers, not economic theories. Key to those insights is recognizing that the modern world simply doesn't work the way our established ideologies and pundits assume. The deep conceptual flaws of our existing socioeconomic paradigm are increasingly inescapable. Not only do those beliefs fail to reflect modern realities, but the data indicate it probably never represented any reality.

Before we can begin defining our strategies we must first escape those conceptual traps. The first half of this book is dedicated to that purpose. We need a new socioeconomic paradigm, our fifth as a nation. From our founding up through the Civil War we were governed by an agricultural paradigm with two distinct variants—the slavery culture of the South and the family farms in small communities throughout the rest of the nation. After the Civil War and up until the early 1930s, our second paradigm was one aimed at enabling monopolists to exploit immigrants, citizens, and smaller businesses. Our government resources were deployed to arrest or kill anyone who fought for a living wage or to resist the demands of those monopolists. When that system inevitably collapsed we set out to design a new socioeconomic paradigm that fit the enormous opportunities across the nation and around the globe, while also working for the benefit of all our citizenry. That paradigm, our third, was the most successful in our history but was replaced in the late 1970s by our fourth paradigm, known to academics as neoliberalism. Neoliberalism has endured for the last 40–50 years and sits at the root of the four decades of decline noted earlier. It's not a coincidence. That paradigm has dominated the beliefs of both parties and carries much of the blame.

This history plays several important roles in understanding all the issues and possible strategies on our plate. First and foremost, history is not passive. It is an inexorable propulsive force driving our economy, shaping our social and political beliefs and relationships between races, classes, and tribes. It is also the source of endless lessons that are critical to understanding what's happening and assessing possible strategies.

Many of our debates and ideologies are rooted in beliefs about the relative roles for government, markets, businesses, and other forms of social governance. It is here where so much of what is assumed is so badly disconnected from modern reality and the lessons of the last 200 years. Many of the historical events shaping business, society, and economics have either been forgotten or rewritten to obfuscate the insights that are most critical to developing solid strategies for the future. That process has been driven by ideologies rather than the clear observation of what works, what doesn't, and why. These are complex systems whose emergent behaviors are shaped by governing rules that are under our control. Piercing the ideological fog will reveal clear, manageable interventions that have worked in the past and that provide patterns we can draw from for our future.

When our national history is viewed through this multifold perspective the insights are revelatory. The issues we face are deeper than most people realize. Data that are rarely in the public eye point to problems that are eerily similar to the years preceding the Great Depression, the rise of Fascism, and World War II. Not only are the data patterns nearly identical, the social and political behaviors currently emerging are as well. We're treading a path fraught with peril.

As we look to the future there are further changes under way that will challenge many more core beliefs. Modern businesses simply don't operate the way they did in the nineteenth or even twentieth centuries. The very nature of innovation, so crucial to the development and growth of society, is undergoing a shift as profound as that of the late nineteenth century. Both what people value and how the innovation process works have taken radical turns. One of the things we value is the health of the globe and our need to shift to a green future has become urgent. Digital technologies have also permeated everything we do in ways that are deeper than most realize. Even those who are familiar with technology trends are often unaware of how many core economic principles are turned on their head in the digital realm. Finally, the reality of global forces, particularly the rise of China, is shifting the dynamics of economic power in ways our nation has never had to face.

All of these insights will provide essential guidance for the solutions to our current challenges. I believe the path that emerges is remarkable. It uses strategies we've used before or that other nations have proven can work. It's a path with enormous promise for everyone in our society. It's one we can all embrace and celebrate. It is a path based on knowledge, insight, and the firm belief that our best days are in front of us, not in our rearview mirror.

It's not enough to change our path for the twenty-first century. We must also change the entire belief system, the entire socioeconomic paradigm, of our society. We've had four in the course of our history. On average they've lasted 40–60 years so this latest is due for replacement, just based on longevity. As we will see in the pages ahead, our fourth paradigm has also been a spectacular failure both in its assumptions about the world and the results it has delivered.

It's time for our fifth paradigm. Let's go explore what that might be.

PART 1

A Strategic Economic Tool Kit

1

STRATEGIC CONCEPTS

BUSINESS AND ECONOMIC DESIGN

I JOINED IBM in June of 1981 as a very junior programmer. A few months later the company introduced the original IBM Personal Computer (PC). That product launch triggered an absolute explosion of economic activity throughout the world. Over the following decades literally thousands of companies would be formed. Some would remain quite small. Others would thrive for a while and then go out of business. A handful would grow to become among the largest and most profitable companies on earth. My career would take me through many jobs in product development, planning, and sales and from hardware to software to services. By the time I reached the corporate-strategy organization in the mid-1990s, IBM had been in the PC business for over a decade and a half. It was a business that brought in more than $10 billion in revenue every year. Those who tracked the company closely knew that the 15-year aggregate profit IBM made from all those billions in revenue, over all those years, was basically zero.

There were lots of other companies making money in the PC business. IBM had launched the entire economic tsunami. Why didn't the company make any money? Dozens of books have been written over the ensuing decades to answer that question. The accepted wisdom is that it had to do with the level of technical market power held by Microsoft and Intel. That wisdom became an entire strategic ideology in the industry. But that isn't the whole story. There were substantial profits captured by Dell and many others that had nothing to do with those two behemoths. Those simplistic answers were incomplete.

I spent the next 20 years developing and mastering methods and tools to examine these kinds of situations. What are the things that trigger large-scale economic activity? What are the real keys to making money from all that activity? How do those answers change from one industry to another? What are the structural forces that endure strategically?

The bottom line for the PC was that the business was poorly designed for IBM. Not the product—the business. The company had outsourced all the enduring sources of value. The places where IBM had market power were applied to capture lots of activity but none of the value. Senior leadership consistently failed to grasp that these devices were "personal." They may have been bought by businesses, but the real market dynamics that surrounded them were driven by people, by individuals. The primal economic forces of value, power, and people had been arranged in a business design that consistently generated activity and revenue, but no profits. Nor would that design ever do so. It wasn't a lack of effort. It was a bad business design.

I saw these same three factors at work again and again over the years— value, power, and people. My team and I learned how to organize these elements, along with a handful of others, to develop a variety of business designs. Some designs worked, and the businesses flourished. Some were flawed, and the organizations struggled. The higher I rose in the executive ranks the more I would come to appreciate the deep importance and subtle dynamics of people and culture to the whole process.

I also realized the same design issues and structural forces were at work throughout the economy. Economies have a structural design. Value, power, and people can be aligned in ways that produce a thriving economy or they can be poorly designed leading to a wide variety of socioeconomic failures. The ideologies we rely on to navigate these choices are quite clumsy and hopelessly out of date. The traditional dichotomy of "free markets" versus "government controlled" is pretty much useless. Neither extreme is real. The nuanced design choices we need to assess in the real world get no help from the loud voices out in the ideological wings. In fact, that conceptual frame is one of our biggest single impediments to real progress.

As we sit here in the early stages of the twenty-first century our socioeconomic paradigm is suffering from a poor design. It needs an overhaul. As was the case for IBM in the PC business, no amount of "working harder" will fix the problems. We need a complete redesign.

To do this we need to probe deeply into our socioeconomic core to find the real strategic design elements and choices. Some of that exercise will be historical. Some requires a new conceptual foundation. Before we delve into those topics let's start the process by getting a better understanding of the basic building blocks of value, power, and people.

VALUE CREATION, CAPTURE, AND CONCENTRATION

Every business strategy begins with a value proposition. As a result, strategists spend a lot of time trying to understand the various dimensions of value. One of the conceptual tools in that process that's particularly relevant when we scale up to a full economy is the distinction between "value creation," "value capture," and "value concentration."

Value *creation* is the fundamental driver of the economy. This is true regardless of economic or political models or philosophies. Value creation can take many forms, some of which we will explore in more detail later in this book. For now, we will focus specifically on *economic value creation*. Economic value can be rooted in (1) innovations, (2) accurately understanding and delivering what customers want, or (3) the efficient production of goods and services. While it may seem there should be many other sources of value creation, there's actually a body of academic work that asserts all economic value creation can be decomposed into those three factors. Whether this assertion is completely true isn't critical to this book. Those three pillars are broad enough for our purposes and will be used in several instances. (As a side note, the business design for the IBM PC had outsourced all three of those value creating roles.) The crucial aspect of any socioeconomic strategy is supporting and enabling the *creation* of value.

This is distinct from the *capture* of value—getting paid. There are countless instances where the source of value *creation* is *not* where, how, or who is able to *capture* that value. In some cases, the value capture is mainly by customers in the market, not by suppliers. In other instances, value is captured at the point where money exchanges hands, which may be far removed from the original source of value creation. This might be intentional within a firm, or it might be due to other factors or other players in the market. In some cases, entire businesses have been built with the purpose of extracting or capturing value they had no involvement in creating. Ideally, the *capture* of value is associated with the *creation* of value and serves to motivate and enable additional value *creation* which is the crucial factor to economic vitality. However, that is not always the case. When value capture is disconnected from value creation it may or may not be problematic. The crucial factor to understand is that *value capture is not the key to economic vitality—value creation is.*

The third distinction is value *concentration* which is the accumulation of large amounts of economic value, essentially capital. Those individuals, firms, organizations, or governments that have large concentrations of capital may or may not have any connection to the original value creation or subsequent value capture. There is nothing inherently good or bad about value concentration. Once again, the real key is whether that concentration either helps or hinders the value creation processes.

There are many instances where large amounts of capital are absolutely essential for the value creation process. A great example from our modern world is the production of the semiconductor chips that power practically all modern devices. A single at-scale semiconductor facility can easily cost close to $10 billion to build. The chips it produces may sell quite cheaply, even as low as pennies in some cases, but all of that is only possible once the massive capital investment is in place. The principle purpose of the stock markets around the world is to enable the distribution and assembly of capital on the scale needed to support the industrial economy. Value concentration often plays an essential role in that process.

However, one of the economic risks from high value concentration is to reduce the effective liquidity in the economy. We usually assume concentrated wealth gets invested in productive capabilities like the semiconductor example. However, that's not always the case. It is also frequently placed in speculative financial instruments that amount to little more than gambling in a casino. In other cases, it's simply "parked" in long-term holdings like real estate which are essentially illiquid. None of that concentrated capital is actually flowing through our real economy. Capital that doesn't flow doesn't contribute to our value creation processes.

These distinctions will help us diagnose economic conditions for their long-term health. Substantial accumulations of private capital aren't inherently bad but cannot be used as a sign of economic health. We must look deeper to see whether the core value creation engines are thriving and whether adequate value capture is flowing to those creators. As we will see, this is a common problem and a frequent source of conflicts and breakdowns.

Yin and Yang of Value and Power

Good strategies begin with a value proposition, but they must also include a formula to sustain that value creating position in the face of competition. This introduces the next key concept which is the relationship between value and power. In the domain of business strategy this is a deep and subtle topic. It is far more nuanced and complex than most people who have not plumbed its depths would realize. Winning value propositions always attract competition and can only be sustained through some form of market power. This is sometimes built through the creation of "barriers to entry or exit." It's also what drives companies to seek monopolies. In modern business strategy discussions, the phrase that's often used is how to "control" the market. This is the "power" dimension. Both of these elements are present in every winning strategy. The key is which is primary and which secondary. When businesses, economies and governments *use power to support and sustain value creation*, that's healthy. When those same entities *use power to divorce the capture of value from the creation of value*, that's unhealthy and, ultimately, destructive.

This also introduces a critically important correction to a widespread set of beliefs. Many will assert that markets operate based on a free exchange and are therefore inherently free from any form of coercion. This is one of the foundational planks of the neoliberal ideology which places markets in a pristine, exalted state. And it's wrong to the core. *Every* business strategy contains a power component and in *every* transaction there are power imbalances. Every single one. No exceptions. The power component is always in play. Every good strategy *also* includes a value dimension. Value and power are intertwined in every exchange. It is the inclusion of value, *not* the exclusion of power, that is the distinguishing characteristic of markets. This error is one of the two or three deepest flaws in the entire neoliberal paradigm. It's an obvious mistake to anyone with any real business experience.

In some exchanges the value dimension can be the dominant factor. In many others, however, the power dimension is the dominant factor. One of the debates in the modern world of business strategy is which of these is more important. While I personally disagree, the majority of modern venture capitalists believe strategies based on power are preferable to strategies based on value. They believe a company that can "lock in" a set of customers can refine and improve its value proposition over time. I've always felt this put the cart in front of the horse.

Many of the neoliberal faithful will grant those points but argue those forms of power are not coercive. This is another falsehood. Having personally negotiated countless business deals I know all too well the differences between deals where both parties are balanced versus those where one holds the upper hand. The coercive power of that upper hand can be considerable. Those deals are also backed by the courts and by strong property rights. Governmental power is always part of the equation. On a more human level, when one party is working on finding their second billion in wealth while the other is struggling to find enough work to feed and clothe a second child, the coercive dimension is deep and soul wrenching. Economic power is power, not value.

One of the key lessons from history is that *in the absence of outside intervention, wages and working conditions are market exchanges that are consistently dominated by the power dimension, not the value dimension.* The simplest proof of this is the observation that once unions are allowed to intervene, balancing the power dimension, wages always go up. The true economic value of people can only be determined through the intervention of an external factor to address the power imbalance. *Markets on their own always understate the true economic value of people.*

— 8 —

The interplay between value and power will be developed much more throughout this book. For now, lets' close with an important observation. Ultimately, value creation always grows. People everywhere will naturally build on things of value, creating more value as they do. In contrast, when power is put in the lead, it will always be resisted. No matter how strong the power or its source, it will eventually be expelled or overthrown. Always remember Ozymandias.

PEOPLE ARE PEOPLE

Value and power are intertwined forces that power our socioeconomic systems. The third elemental factor is people. Understanding the true importance of people and all of the motivations that drive them is a central focus of the strategic perspective and, as we will see, rediscovering the importance of people, as people, will be at the core of our fifth paradigm and our twenty-first-century strategy. One of the first steps in that process is to recognize that the very terms used by economists, businesses, and governments are themselves part of the problem. When we speak of "labor" and "capital" as factors in a production equation we have conceptually blinded ourselves to the fact that "labor" are not production factors, they are people. We perpetuate this in modern times with the phrase "human resources," or "resource actions," which makes it sound like people are interchangeable with stock in iron ore and that layoffs have no human impact.

This is much more than a point of verbal gymnastics. Economists quite consciously make a huge number of "simplifying" assumptions in their models. There's nothing inherently wrong with that. When we learn the laws of motion in high school physics, the role of friction is routinely dropped out of the equation to help students better understand the fundamental forces. Similarly, economists usually assume a "free flow" of goods, labor, and capital in their models. They all know these "perfect markets" are a fiction—they're just a useful fiction. That fiction does, however, introduce a few dangerous blind spots. One of those is that goods and capital are *much* freer-flowing than labor, precisely because labor is not a "production factor"—it's people. This means during periods when goods and capital are being fluidly rearranged by market forces, people have a tendency to get chewed up in the process. Economists tend to ignore this reality. Strategists do not.

When we examine the core drivers of value creation in the economy the role played by labor, by people, becomes critical. As our various sources of value creation become more productive they generate more value with fewer resources, fewer people. That's an unequivocally good thing for our economic health. It powers growth and can lift society. When that happens slowly and in narrow segments, people, communities, and society can adapt. They can flow. However, when it happens quickly, at large scale, and in the heart of the value creating core of the economy, it can bring disastrous human consequences. When that happens the "simplifying assumption" of free-flowing people is not equivalent to leaving friction out of the early lessons in physics. It's more like leaving the very laws of motion out of those lessons. People with their passions and needs are central elements to everything and their motivations and behavior are far more complex and resistant to change than economic models reflect.

Those three elements, value, power, and people, are at the central core of the business strategy perspective and of any economic design. There are other factors as well, but the combination of these three provides a powerful and unique way of seeing the world. Most economists focus solely on the value dimension, treating people as simple mathematical abstractions. Unfortunately, ignoring people isn't helpful if you want a well-designed economy. Most investors focus solely on the combination of the value and power dimensions. We want our businesses to thrive so that's not necessarily bad, but it still does nothing for the people side of our economic design. Social scientists tend to study people with a secondary focus on power. That perspective does bring people into play, but it loses economic focus and is frequently hostile to our economic health. Political scientists are primarily driven by the power dimension. They may seek to root their power in either people or economics, but their focus is on power, not the underlying sources of value. Each of those disciplines will be helpful, but none of them holds the complete set of answers. The fifth socioeconomic paradigm we seek must bring value, power, and people together in a structure that will thrive and endure.

2

IDEOLOGIES AND CONCEPTUAL TRAPS

THAT THREE-PART STRATEGIC framework sits alongside the far more familiar collection of ideologies which will be lurking behind the scenes all the way through this book. In some cases, ideologies serve simply to shape our thinking, but in other cases they represent tangible movements with specific agendas to shape and define our society. These are tricky beasts we're about to grapple with and while we can't completely tame them we do need to bring them to heel.

Political ideologies are a specific class of what are generally referred to as conceptual frameworks. We all have them. They shape what we see, where we focus, and what we value. Even those who think of themselves as "nonideological" have some form of conceptual framework that guides their thinking and perceptions. They are cognitively inescapable. However, we can choose among them and those choices matter. Some choices lead us to all kinds of productive possibilities while others lead to nothing but dead ends.

One of the major disciplines in the world of business strategy is the study of decision making. When we consider any decision in any context we are constrained by the range of alternatives we think are realistic or possible. That range is determined by how we "frame" the situation. A narrow frame always leads to an equally limited range of options. A larger frame introduces many new possible paths to consider. Decision makers often find themselves "anchored" to a specific path and can quite unconsciously narrow their frame until that path is the only one that is even conceptually possible. This is known as a "conceptual trap" and it is probably the single most common cause of decision failures. These traps have a powerful and often invisible impact which is only magnified and intensified through the groupthink that occurs when everyone comes from the same background and belief system.

In the socioeconomic domain of this book the relevant groupthink is vast and deep. "Left" versus "right" tends to define almost everything. There are nuances and variations, but the core structure is deeply embedded. Every reader is enmeshed in some fashion. It's not just a national conceptual frame, either; it's global. It is derived from hundreds, if not thousands of years of philosophy, history, politics, economics, literature, and even poetry. Families have been divided, children estranged, and siblings cast away based solely on the power of this frame to cleave us apart. Literally millions have died for one "side" or another. While the roots of this frame are ancient, most of the stories that shape our modern thinking come from the last 200 years. They are based on tales describing the late nineteenth and early to mid-twentieth-century world. Most of those stories, including those that are putatively nonfiction, are hopelessly romanticized and almost none of them are relevant or helpful going into the twenty-first century.

Our fifth paradigm is neither "left" nor "right." It ignores that conceptual structure completely, as did most of its predecessors. Not only is our shared conceptual framework useless to understand the path to the future it's also useless to understand our history.

Unfortunately, the framework we all share is actually a deep and profound conceptual trap.

We need to escape, and it won't be easy.

The tribalism most of us abhor actually assumes the frame. It's part of the trap itself. For the most part the important choices we need to see and evaluate aren't one tribe versus the other. We need to step out of the looking glass and emerge into a different world. Indeed, the stories of Lewis Carroll illustrate how deeply our perceptions and even logic can be affected by our hidden assumptions about reality. Every one of us is lost somewhere down the same rabbit hole. Whether you're currently consorting with the murderous

Red Queen or the hash smoking blue Caterpillar isn't the important point. The important point is getting out of our shared trap.

Before we dive into that ideological rabbit hole we must first reflect on the difficulties we all face when our imperfect conceptual frames run into implacable reality. These are incredibly insidious traps and we need to examine the different ways they manifest themselves in our perceptions and thinking. Unfortunately, jumping directly into the left-right debates will just drop us straight into the rabbit hole. To illustrate the dangers, I will draw from a period with equally deep passions, but a bit more historical distance, which is the American experience in Vietnam.

THE DANGERS OF CONCEPTUAL TRAPS: LESSONS FROM VIETNAM

Our history in Vietnam was filled with examples of leadership failures whose roots can be found in the flawed frames of our conceptual traps. There were many of these frames at the time, but for our purposes I will focus on three of the most important:

- We saw Vietnam as an effort to contain communism instead of a struggle for freedom from colonialism.
- We believed our containment strategy was akin to halting the fall of a series of dominos instead of a specific national conflict.
- We believed the war was strictly a "win/lose" scenario that offered no opportunity for any other possible outcome.

As is always the case with a widely held belief system every aspect of that conceptual framing is reasonable, defensible, and understandable to any rational and informed adult. None of this is "crazy." Deeply held conceptual frameworks rarely are. The same can be said about the various flavors of the left-right frame down in our rabbit hole. This is part of why they are so difficult to shed.

That simple frame led to four distinct and specific conceptual traps. This is also what happens more generally. These four traps show up again and again and have direct parallels to the failures of our current ideological frames. Bad conceptual frames don't just lead to poor decisions; their impact is much wider, deeper, and insidious. Let's look at those four traps.

Blindness to current and future realities. One of the most cited frames at the time was the notion of a war against communism being fought over a series of adjacent dominos. It was a war, or more likely a series of wars. It involved countries that were lined up like dominos. If one fell to communism, then the next would fall, and the next and the next. President Johnson actually said at one point, "once you let one go, before you know it they're in your kitchen." The conceptual dominos ran from Vietnam to Thailand to Malaysia, to Indonesia—and, then I guess to Australia, to Tahiti, to Mexico, and finally to Johnson's kitchen in Texas.

Obviously, none of that ever occurred. Instead of a series of "domino wars," we could have seen the larger conflict with the Soviet Union as a battle of economies and focused our energies on rapidly expanding our incredible global success in trade. Or, we could have seen the world through the lens of developed versus developing nations and built an agenda to assist nations emerging from colonialism all over the world to find their own paths to sovereignty, dignity, and prosperity.

Neither of these were even remotely conceivable frames in the mid-1960s even though either of them is a more accurate frame for understanding how history actually unfolded. Not only are they more accurate, they would have led to far more effective decisions and strategies. It's important to recognize how this form of frame blindness works. It's not that we thought about those alternate frames and rejected them. They were never even seriously *considered*.

The left-right frame in the rabbit hole is as overly simplistic and blind to reality as our earlier faith in dominos. We find ourselves in constant struggles over the false dichotomy of "free markets" versus "government control." In debate after debate, our ideologies offer only those choices even though neither is real. They're fictions found only in Wonderland. One of the core challenges of this book is to enable all of us to get far enough out of our shared ideological rabbit hole to actually be able to see the possibilities for new twenty-first-century strategies. From the depths of the rabbit hole those possibilities are nearly invisible.

Narrow range of options and repeating failed strategies. In addition to not seeing the world accurately, and not being able to even consider alternate interpretations, a narrow frame always brings a very narrow range of possible strategies. In Vietnam that came down to "escalation" or "humiliation." Those were the only options anyone could see. An important side effect of this narrow range is that decision makers keep resorting to strategies that have already been proven as failures. It's precisely the behavior Einstein used as his definition of insanity.

The depth of the conceptual trap in Vietnam stemmed from the combination of both the domino frame and the win/lose frame. If all we were thinking about were dominos, we could choose where we wanted to make our stand. We could have created a clear list of which countries we thought would fall and in what order and then carefully picked our fight. None of that was ever really considered because the second frame assumed that in every contest there is only a winner and a loser. There are only two possibilities. For us to be a winner, North Vietnam had to be a loser: they had to surrender.

These two frames created the conceptual trap that left us with only two options—escalation or humiliation. At every critical juncture in Vietnam, Johnson and his team would confront that choice. In every case they chose escalation even as the odds of that path producing anything at all positive dropped in their own minds from one in three, to one in ten, to zero. Before long, escalation itself was seen only as a way of avoiding humiliation, not as a path to any positive outcome.

In our modern rabbit hole, a clear equivalent is the strategy to cut high end tax rates with the expectation that added economic activity will generate enough growth to pay for the cuts and that that same growth will "trickle down" and improve the lives of most citizens. It's a proven failure, but from certain corners of the rabbit hole is the only *conceivable* economic strategy. As a result, it's a strategy that gets called again and again, not because those doing so are insane, but because their conceptual frame literally doesn't include any alternatives.

Leadership failures, losing sight of what's important. Effective leaders define conceptual frames for their followers. When those frames are flawed and inconsistent with reality those people struggle to be effective and find themselves in one hopeless quandary after another. Nothing works the way it should because everything about how they see and interact with the world is impaired by their deep conceptual flaws. One of the most crucial aspects of the conceptual frames articulated by leaders is defining what's important and what is not. It's such a central, even primal, function we often literally cannot perceive things our frame categorizes as unimportant.

In the case of Vietnam, the Vietnamese knew what was important. They were fighting for their freedom and independence. We Americans were fighting over a conceptual "domino." The South Vietnamese leaders were hated by their own people. When South Vietnamese generals tested the waters, the United States gave tacit support for a coup. The coup followed, the former leaders were executed, and the people cheered. And then another coup. And, another. And another. In a short period, there would be eight different coups, none of which produced a truly viable administration. We were fighting over a domino in support of puppets who were falling like dominos.

Meanwhile, Buddhist priests were kneeling in the streets, dousing themselves with gasoline, and setting themselves on fire. The South Vietnamese leaders laughed it off, offering to light the matches themselves and claiming it was a phony protest because the monks used "imported gasoline."

We lost all contact with the deep desire people have for freedom and independence. There was simply no place for that in our frame. No matter how provocatively the human dimension was shoved in our face it simply led nowhere. We had no place to put all those truths, so they simply dropped away from our perceptions.

Down in the rabbit hole we find Wall Street, the Dow, GDP, and other misleading information in bright, flashing, neon lights. The realities of Main Street, burned out factories, shattered communities, and, most of all, people, are buried down side alleys few ever explore. Our leaders of both parties have adopted a set of conceptual frames that are devoid of any human content. We've truly lost touch with what matters, what's really important for the health of our nation. It's been a complete failure of leadership arising from their collective immersion in the neoliberal subdivisions of the rabbit hole.

Forced into consistent lies. When frames are broken, when they don't accurately help interpret the world, the facts of the world are the first casualties. That shouldn't be the case. When the facts don't fit it should be a signal to abandon the broken frame. Unfortunately, we usually do the opposite. Rather than abandon the frame we ignore the facts. This is particularly acute for the leaders who have defined or endorsed the broken frame. What they end up doing is lying. The more badly the frame is broken the more lies they have to tell.

This was certainly the case in Vietnam. Kennedy and his administration lied about our purpose, our chances, our activities, our strategies, and our results. From the moment they took over, the Johnson administration was no better. LBJ confided in private that the United States had absolutely nothing to gain in Vietnam, but he also said there was no way to leave. All of that had to be covered over with lies. The Nixon administration would do the same. The government leaders of both parties systematically lied about everything.

The simplistic notions of ideological dominos and one-sided victory were simply inadequate to contain, let alone explain, all of what was happening in the real world. Rather than abandon those flawed frames our leaders chose instead to abandon truth. This would be a defining feature of Vietnam and a major contributor to our loss of confidence in government in the 1970s.

Down in the rabbit hole the enormous and growing world of "alternative facts" is a clear indication of a completely broken and defunct conceptual frame. Unfortunately, so too is the assertion that "hope" is an adequate strategy for what ails us.

Three simple frames led to four conceptual traps that led to 58,000 American deaths along with 250,000 South Vietnamese troops, 1 million North Vietnamese and Viet Cong, and approximately 2 million civilians on both sides. It was a war that was fought because of deep flaws in strategic thinking and those flaws were hidden by decades of lies by members of both political parties.

Conceptual traps—ideological beliefs—are powerful, insidious, and deeply dangerous. They are also inescapable. Part of the insidious danger of these ideological beliefs is that they often go unstated. They lurk behind the actions and positions people take without revealing themselves. They are ghosts in the machine of society. Before we can cut our way out of all the embedded conceptual traps in our shared rabbit hole we must first examine a few of the more noxious such spirits.

We will begin this exploration with communism. Fears about communism were major drivers of individual and national behavior for most of the twentieth century. Those have faded in large measure because communism has been such an evident failure. For many, those same fears have now been shifted to socialism though that term has little to no consistent meaning across our society. Even those who assert they are "socialists" have different definitions of the term. Other than a fairly common list of progressive policy objectives none of them really share a consistent socioeconomic framework.

The second focus will be on the libertarian movement and its association with the now global ideology of neoliberalism. This is probably one of the most pervasive socioeconomic conceptual frames in the world. Every President of both parties in the last 35–40 years has believed in its veracity and relied on it for governance and policy directions. It's no coincidence that so many of our current problems can be traced to roots put down over the past 40 years. Many of the most traveled pathways in the rabbit hole have neoliberal street signs.

Our third focus will be on a true ghost in the machine. This movement emerged from neoliberal thinking and has the profound and dangerous goal to eliminate democracy itself. This particular ghost has become a powerful hidden threat to the nation.

FADING FEARS OF COMMUNISM

For most people, fears about communism are more rhetorical than real these days. Nonetheless, its ghost still looms large and there are some useful insights to be found in its history. By the early 1930s, with the Russian Revolution and the formation of the Chinese Communist Party (CCP), the long-feared moment when communism would become a reality had arrived. All of Europe was dealing with the painful aftermath of World War I and the horrific working conditions of the early twentieth-century industrial economy. Those societies were being pulled apart by the conflicts between the extreme positions of the Communists and Fascists. The fears of communism were so deep that Germany would eventually decide the Communists were the far greater danger of the two and chose Fascism, Hitler, and then World War II.

Russia suffered enormous devastation and loss of life during that war. Along with an estimated 30 million casualties, some estimates suggest that roughly 25 percent of Russia's economic infrastructure was destroyed. In the aftermath of the war they seized vast territories across Eastern Europe as well as the Baltics. This adventurism was accompanied by a substantial build out of heavy industry. The factories seized in East Germany became models for elsewhere in their dominion and were used to provide machinery and raw materials for Russia.

By the mid-1950s they had not only restored their heavy industries, they had expanded them dramatically. Steel production, for example, was twice the scale it had been before the war began. There was, however, no interest in building a consumer base, nor any consumer goods. Consumer goods production had not only not returned to prewar levels, they were actually operating closer to the level of the early 1920s. There was no expansion in the quality of life for the average citizen. I have a European friend who frequently uses the phrase "like a Soviet supermarket," where there's only "one brand of bread and it's both stale and moldy." As we will see, the contrast between postwar Russia and what unfolded in the United States and Europe could not be more stark. The supposed "ideology of the people" was doing nothing for actual people while the "ideology of capital" was generating fabulous improvements in living standards for most of its citizens.

Not only were the Russian people's lives not improving, they would be stricken with drought, famine, epidemics, and Stalin's infamous "purges." Any hint at infidelity to the Party could be fatal. The gulags were real places you did not want to visit. Thousands lived in hollowed-out crevasses in the rubble that had once been the beautiful city of Stalingrad. The idealistic notions of a "brotherhood of workers," or "providing to each their needs" were laughable. This was all about power. Value and people were not priorities.

The communist ideology can sound appealing for some. Indeed, in many intellectual circles across Europe there was a fascination with the writing and ideas that were at the heart of communism. Karl Marx had correctly identified some of the chronic failures of capitalism. He specifically noted the same point highlighted in this book, that systemic power imbalances meant people aren't paid their true economic value and that means aggregate economic demand doesn't keep pace with supply. Marx believed these and other flaws were sufficient reason to reject the entirety of capitalism rather than highlight points of necessary intervention in the design. This "revolutionary spirit" was highly appealing to those who felt left behind and who had no desire to even attempt capitalism's repair.

The attraction also stems from the superficial interpretation that it is an ideology oriented toward the needs of people. However, when viewed through our strategy lens there's an interesting and glaring flaw. The ideology itself refers to people as "workers." It's not an ideology about people as people, it's an ideology about people as economic production factors.

This is one of the major blind spots of this ideology and recognizing it as such is crucial to a proper understanding of its utter failure. This is not a trivial flaw. People are not workers. They are people.

The second superficial interpretation is that the ideology provides a vehicle for those workers to hold the reins of power. Nothing could be further from the truth. Communism does always bring a seizure of assets and the deposing of the prior regime, but what follows are new leaders with no more interest in supporting the needs of people as people than their predecessors.

Furthermore, since people at the most basic level of this ideology are simply production factors, those new leaders almost always assume they can move them about as they need. When people don't respond well to being managed as a free-flowing production asset, they have to be forcibly moved. Like any good business, those "assets" need to be maintained, but only at the minimum expense needed. Many of the horrific consequences of the various communist regimes around the world stem from this simple but profound conceptual defect. People are people, not economic production factors.

Setting aside the specific political trappings there is a remarkable similarity to the economic power abuse found in the slave economy. In both cases, the business model assumes that people are not people. They're production assets to be managed accordingly. There were many, though not all, nineteenth-century industrialists who held the exact same mind-set. The men with guns those industrialists placed at their factory gates were not there to protect the physical assets inside. From the perspective of the slave/worker (human being) it doesn't really matter whether the overseer with a whip or gun considers themselves part of a genteel society, a company hired goon, or the government. It's truly the same at some primitive level. This observation would deeply trouble those wedded to the notion of the antebellum as an ideal society or the romanticized version of unfettered nineteenth-century capitalism. The actual realities of communism were a close cousin to both because in all three cases the real focus is power, not value, and people are regarded as production assets not people.

The conceptual frame in which the "ideology of people" is represented by communism and the "ideology of capital" is represented by capitalism is simply inaccurate. Almost all of the capitalist societies in the West have democratic dimensions and those have all chosen to intercede in markets for the benefit of people. It is the communist societies that have consistently ignored the interests of people on behalf of those in the new positions of power. After all, it was the democratic capitalist societies who banned slavery and child labor while it was the communists who rounded up and ultimately starved people in forced mass relocations. However, we must also note that all these efforts on behalf of people were fought ferociously by individual capitalists who actually labeled those efforts as "communist."

It is actually *democracy* that has addressed the needs of people, not communism and not capitalism. The traditional ideological frames get everything backward and obscure the underlying reality. If it were not for the direct intervention of democratically empowered governments, our Western societies would be little better for the average person than that of the communists. The working conditions of nineteenth-century industrial Europe and America provide ample proof of that assertion.

The communist reality becomes even more crystal clear with the strict compliance demanded by Soviet authorities of the time. The actual "compliance" being demanded had nothing to do with communist ideology. The real demand was simply surrendering to power. And, the power in question made little pretense to behave in ways that had any connection to the purported "ideology of people." That ideology was simply a pathway to power. Once they had the power, the ideology itself became utterly irrelevant to the leaders.

This introduces another useful dimension in understanding the blind spots in almost all ideological frames. The yin-yang of value and power is central in every case. For any ideology to gain the support of large numbers of people it must have some central, defining dimension of value. Whatever that is will bring its associated dimension of power. Over the course of human history, it is those power dimensions that have almost always proven to be the dominant aspects of ideological reality. Ideologies are sold on value but manifest themselves in power. In the case of communism, the "value" of an "ideology for people" has never been real. That has always been a sham. In reality, it has consistently been about putting tyrants in power and then exploiting people as workers.

Neoliberalism and Ayn Rand

The ideology that effectively defines our fourth socioeconomic paradigm suffers from a deep name problem. Some think of it as "libertarianism." Others view that as merely a specific branch of the philosophy and not a very complete one at that. The broadest, though also "wonkiest," term is neoliberalism. While that's probably the best term and is the one I'll use in this book, it struggles with two issues. The first is the philosophy behind this paradigm has absolutely nothing to do with what any average American thinks of as "liberalism." In fact, it's closer to the exact opposite of that more familiar term. Its second problem is that the followers of the philosophy themselves don't like to use that name, specifically because it has been so thoroughly discredited by a wide variety of observers and analysts.

This ideology has roots in the crisis that gripped the globe in the 1930s. As we will see in the chapters ahead, government played a central role in resolving that crisis. That success struck a deep fear for those whose conceptual frames were centered on the myth of market perfection. They needed and built a philosophy that would reject all forms of government activity as evil intrusions on freedom. Early developers and champions of this ideology included the Mont Pelerin Society, Friedrich Hayek, Milton Friedman, and many others. Those thinkers laid the basic economic foundations of the ideology but had only modest success outside academic circles. In large measure what propelled the movement to fame and eventual domination of socioeconomic thinking around the world were the writings of Ayn Rand.

Ayn Rand called her ideas "objectivism" though almost nobody uses that term. Most just use her name—either as an expletive or in hushed worship. There are definite flaws in her thinking. She wrote a number of nonfiction books that are rarely read by any other than the true die-hards. Her fame comes from three fictional books, *Anthem*, *The Fountainhead*, and *Atlas Shrugged*. Those novels allow her to depict her ideas and beliefs in a fictional world context. Her stories provide a colorful and powerful way of conveying her thoughts without the messiness of the real world intruding. Unfortunately, her fictional format also allows a proliferation of blind spots and illusions.

She is probably most famous for the phrase "greed is good." At one level, in typical Ayn Rand fashion, that is no more than an inflammatory expression of Adam Smith's original observation that self-interest actually leads to healthy, functioning markets. That is definitely a core part of what Ayn Rand means. However, she actually wants to mean something a bit stronger as well. And here is one of the first places things get a little dicey.

The unstated Adam Smith formula is that pure greed in and of itself may not be *morally* good, but the beauty of markets is that it doesn't matter because good things will happen. The slightly less certain element of Adam Smith's concept is whether good things happen *in spite of* greed or *because of* greed. In either instance, greed is a perfectly fine and acceptable element of the market. Ayn Rand wants to go further, claiming that greed, in and of itself, *is morally good*. She goes to great lengths in her novels to attempt to illustrate this point, with extended passages in which her characters espouse that claim. She is quite effective in punching holes in the notion that "from each according to their abilities, to each according to their needs" is a viable and coherent wage system. However, that's not the same as her desire to assert that greed in itself is good. The actual behavior of her heroes, particularly when their friends are in need, does *not* reflect that assertion. In fact, it is her villains who consistently operate from a platform of pure greed while espousing the opposite. So, did she really believe greed is good?

Certainly, many of her modern fans would like to believe so, but this is one of the many places where her flawed or inconsistent exposition leads to dubious interpretations. A closely related idea is around compassion for others. Ayn Rand's heroes are almost always viewed by other characters as cold, aloof, disinterested, and lacking in compassion. A superficial read could cause one to think that's the belief and behavior she advocates. However, the exact opposite is the case.

Here again we get into tricky territory. Her heroes are always in reality deeply passionate and concerned about what they and their fellow companions are doing. The concerns they care about are their businesses. Again, the superficial interpretation is that caring about business is good and caring about people is misplaced. However, when we unpack the notion of "business" using our conceptual tools around value creation, value capture, and power, a very different picture emerges. All of her heroes are value creators. All of her villains focus solely on using power to capture value they have not created. She calls these people the "looters." Ayn Rand and her readers conflate all these concepts under the umbrella of "business" in ways that lend themselves to misinterpretation, but when cleanly pulled apart her actual position is very clear. Her greatest passion is to focus on aligning the capture of value with those who are the creators of value. Her vilest oaths are against those who use power to distort this process, using political power to seize value from its creators. Far from being aloof or disinterested, she held a deep passion and commitment to the creation of value, in whatever form that takes.

This is the core of her economic belief and is certainly a noble cause. Value creation is what matters and value capture should flow to those who create it. Here again, however, her modern fans get this all twisted up. They don't distinguish value creation from value capture and therefore conclude all that matters *is* the capture of value, which plays back into the notion of simple greed.

This is an enormous blind spot for many champions of this ideology. Value capture is *not* synonymous with value creation. In fact, value capture, even in her novels, is often driven by the power dimension. Just as we saw with communism, the "value" aspect of the ideology brings a "power" dimension which in practice is what dominates.

An ironic aspect of this is that her modern champions frequently support exactly the kinds of power abuses Ayn Rand rails against. Her books are filled with examples of greedy villains using government power to funnel money into their businesses. Those are absolutely villainous practices in her philosophy, yet they are often precisely the things advocated in her name by her modern fans, often under the guise of freedom.

Her notion of what makes up a company also leads directly to deep blind spots. In her world, a company is a single smart innovative executive with some organizational fluff around them. There may be a few occasional subordinates tossed in just to provide narrative illustrations of the leader's vastly superior knowledge and his ability to give orders, but that's it. It's a heavily romanticized version of a nineteenth-century command and control firm and has no bearing at all on modern reality. None. This can't be stated too strongly.

One of the direct ramifications of this particular blind spot is to automatically assert that whoever sits at the top of an organization is the source of its value creation. There are situations in our modern world where there's some tiny grain of truth to that belief, but it's frankly quite rare. A far more accurate generalization would be to assume literally nothing of any substantial value in the modern world is created by any individual. Modern value creation is almost always a collaborative process involving many different contributors. As an aside, there is an equally problematic tendency for some to assert the opposite, that all value comes from those at the bottom of the pyramid. As an a-priori belief this is every bit as flawed.

Finally, the scope of humanity and human experience included in her range of discourse is severely limited and narrow. The world is full of things like slavery, child labor, speculative market disruptions, monopoly behavior, violent conflicts over wages and working conditions, and ideologues of all types. That's not to mention the great mass of people struggling to survive amid bigotry, misogyny, and racism. Her personal experiences growing up in Russia before, during, and after the revolution certainly gave her direct exposure to those realities. However, those human sufferings are not really reflected in her fictional worlds. This massive blind spot for her entire ideology is one of the more common causes for people to conclude her thinking is just too simplistic for the real world. Nonetheless, her devoted followers do willingly live with this morally repugnant blind spot.

What she did carry from that awful Russian period is a deep distaste for the power of government. In fact, one of the most prominent aspects of her books is that all aspects of government are depicted as evil. Pure evil. Evil incarnate. Her business people come in both heroic and villainous guises, but government is always evil. In fact, when good people go into government they are transformed into evil demons. This is a somewhat understandable response for someone who endured the power-mad ideology of that early Russian period.

This is another deep flaw in her frame. She sees the power dimension of government all too clearly. However, the entire value dimension of government is a complete blind spot. Followers of this system must either rationalize or ignore all the countless examples in history where government has been the true source of value.

Over time, this deep flaw has grown far beyond a simple blind spot. It has become a central feature of a complete retelling of history. Modern neoliberals, along with many more mainstream conservatives, have created two broad collections of stories that serve to define their alternate tribal reality. The first of these is that the "New Deal destroyed America." This is an old and deeply inaccurate story that was widely shared by the early founders of the movement. Some of those loud voices proclaimed the New Deal to be the introduction of "fascist agriculture" and the "end of Western civilization." Neither was true, of course, but the voices were and are quite loud.

Those specific negative stories abated for a while but came back to life in support of the second narrative that "government is evil." This is the camp that believes government power is coercive and bad and that there is no economic coercion. As you might expect, the loudest voices proclaiming the impossibility of economic coercion are those who rely the most on economic coercion.

At its heart, this is a frame centered on the power dimension associated with economic value. In this case the ideology calls for economic power to reign supreme, regardless of the impact on people and society. In this frame, people have no intrinsic human value. None. Their only value is in the economic value they create for the wealthy few. Their literal value as human beings is defined strictly by their economic net worth. Not only are they not valued as people, they aren't really valued as workers either. They are simply cogs in a wealth generating engine supporting America's elite.

THE ANTI-DEMOCRACY MOVEMENT

One of the offspring of the neoliberal ideology is a movement that is almost completely centered on power and goes without an official name. It is deliberately intended to operate below the radar, to be a "ghost in the machine." Its point of origin was the desegregation of schools arising out of the *Brown v. Board of Education* decision. The effective intrusion by the federal government into local customs and practices raised alarms for those wedded to the power behind those local customs. The federal acts were aimed at creating value for those who were being effectively excluded from our national educational franchise. For those who resisted that shift it was not about value; it was about power. And the federal government had just proven it had a stronger hand.

This led to a movement to directly curtail that power. The power they want to curtail was and is the power of people, the power of democracy. There were and still are three primary dimensions of this "anti-democracy" movement. The first is aimed at delegitimizing any government that is principally based on serving the needs and interests of its citizens. That is, specifically, to delegitimize democracy itself. This is sometimes done by claiming anything that serves citizens is a prelude to communism. As we saw, real communism has nothing to do with serving people, but down in the rabbit hole their claims trigger fears for some.

The deeper argument is that left to vote for anything they want, people will vote to "take" things they have not earned and do not deserve from those who "make." Their language is filled with references to "makers" and "takers." In our language, they fear government will use its power to *capture* (and redistribute) value being *created* by others. Even after over 50 years, nobody in this extensive movement has ever identified a single instance where their claims were real. That absence of fact has been no hindrance to their growth. This set of philosophies is almost always portrayed as being about "freedom." The actual freedom they seek is the unfettered right to use their political and economic power to repress the freedom of the rest of the people, specifically the majority.

The phrase "voting for bread and circuses," which was used frequently by the science fiction writer, Robert Heinlein, is close to their claim. One of the anti-democracy movement's primary targets is government programs that the majority values. It started with the desegregation of the schools. These folks felt they wanted to leave schools segregated the way they were. The clear national and moral consensus was to reverse this course. When they realized that democracy ensured the national will of the people was powerful enough to prevail, they declared war on democracy.

This leads to the second dimension of the anti-democracy movement which is to remove the government from any role in society other than national defense, judicial, and police forces. Furthermore, the specific focus of the judicial arm should be ensuring that the freedoms of the democratic citizenry are sacrificed to the license of the powerful and wealthy. If the will of the people is allowed to intrude on society, that is viewed as an unacceptable introduction of a source of power larger than the narrow economic and political interests of the movement. These arguments always rely on the near religious belief in markets as a superior answer to anything and everything. They completely, and quite deliberately, ignore all the coercive power imbalances and abuses found in every market.

It's important to distinguish this movement from those who simply want as small a government as possible. The two may seem the same, but that's a superficial reading. They're actually quite different. The true small government faction can be a healthy and needed voice in our ongoing civic debates. Government programs are as subject to the laws of diminishing returns as any other major activity. Governments are also as guilty of overreach as any other large organization. Those who are constantly on the watch for these errors play an important and valuable part in our society. None of them are taking that posture out of a "rejection of democracy." Quite the contrary. They take those positions with the objective of making our democracy as fair and efficient as possible while maintaining its effectiveness.

This highlights the third dimension of the true anti-democracy movement which is aimed at rendering democratic government ineffective in any nonde-fense or nonpolicing roles. The original movement against public education was and remains a pillar of the strategy. An uneducated and disenfranchised citizenry will lead to poor and ineffective democratic government. This is also the reason for the consistent focus on defunding government as much as pos-sible. An integral element of that strategy is to ensure public officeholders get less pay than their commercial counterparts. Less honestly, but every bit as deliberate, there are efforts to hamstring government programs with so many checks and conditions that the services fail to deliver on their intentions. In recent years this dimension of the movement's strategy has reached a stage of outright corruption and sabotage, including directly and deliberately risk-ing people's health and their very lives. The true believers have come to the conclusion that achieving the ends of eliminating democracy now justifies any means at all.

The early days of this anti-democracy movement were fairly ineffective, but it has grown to enormous power and influence. They began getting real trac-tion in the early 1980s as the nation's trust in all government institutions plum-meted. It was not their efforts that had discredited those institutions. It was the failures, ineptitude, corruption, and outright deceit by those institutions that were the cause. Those failures gave the movement ample raw material. They also had refined and developed their messages into a far more comprehensive and compelling ideology. Part of the refinement was keeping their explicit rejection of democracy hidden. That reality is camouflaged behind a curtain created by redefining the word "freedom."

What they mean by "freedom" is the absence of any balance to estab-lished social or economic power. They mean power, ultimate power primarily through wealth, and preferably in the form of "old money." You can substitute the word "freedom" with the word "power" pretty universally in their materi-als. Here are a few specific examples.

They want the "freedom/power" to avoid paying taxes. One of the many tools used is to hide assets and earnings in overseas tax shelters. Here's a great quote from the Cato Institute from their presentation on *The Moral Case for Tax Havens*. "Tax competition is greatly beneficial in the battle for human rights and personal freedom. Low tax jurisdictions or tax havens are a safe refuge for oppressed people." Those "oppressed people" seeking refuge are not starving Somalians. They are billionaires and the "moral" practice they are promoting is a felony. Note how the laws against tax evasion are portrayed as a form of "oppression" and the felonious act of tax evasion is part of the "battle" for "freedom."

They want the "freedom/power" to spend unlimited money to bribe political candidates. There are several tools used to accomplish this objective. One of their key wins was the *Citizens United* case. This gives them the ability to drown out the voices of regular citizens. It has also opened several more doors. By getting the Supreme Court to decide that companies have equivalent rights to citizens, the entire structure of protections for people built into our political system can now be turned against us.

They want the "freedom/power" to forbid people access to their legal rights. The specific way they accomplish that trick is to force people to accept arbitration clauses in all employment and license terms. The arbitrators are selected by corporations and will only consider cases one person at a time. This denial of legal rights for American citizens was challenged in the Supreme Court in 2018 and the anti-democrats won yet again. They now have unlimited power to deny people access to the legal system. The only "legal" system Americans can now use with companies is one that has been paid for and rigged by those same companies.

In a related move they have been systematically populating the federal judiciary with judges who will consistently rule for wealth and against people, particularly vulnerable people. Those moves are always done under the banner of freedom and in all cases what that really means is denying people access to the balancing power of the judicial branch of government.

One of the tragic ironies of the anti-democratic movement is that many people have concluded the very government designed since its founding to ensure and protect the freedom of its people is in fact the primary threat to freedom. This is where the anti-democracy crowd leverages a collection of "government is evil" stories and their claim to the word "freedom." The twisted logic of these stories helps them position government as the antithesis of freedom instead of being freedom's guarantor. As a result, the true national value of freedom for all is replaced with an unyielding power demand by a wealthy few.

3

PIERCING THE IDEOLOGICAL FOG

GOVERNMENT AND THE ECONOMY

THESE LATTER TWO ideologies, with all their attendant blind spots, reflect the long human history of the tension between the power of wealth and the health of society. This is not about good versus evil. After all, our drive to form societies arises from our pursuit of the value we find in groups. From the dawn of man, we have come together to defend each other from stronger predators and other tribes. We have organized hunting parties and divided our labors to more effectively gather food. We come together to sexually reproduce and because we are simply genetically social creatures. These are all things we value, and each of those sources of value brings its own associated power dimensions. Defense capabilities bring judicial and military power. Developing and acquiring goods and services brings wealth and economic power. Social relationships bring leaders and political power.

None of these are bad. The strategic key is realizing that when any form of power is elevated to an *ultimate* level, value creation will suffer. This is equally true whether the power in question is political, economic, defense, or any other category. It's equally true for communist dictators, plantation slavers, and wealthy industrialists. The trick is to keep power in balance which is what enables the full breadth of value creation and people to flourish.

The democratic republic crafted by our Founding Fathers was based on this realization. They also realized there was a very specific power imbalance that has repeated throughout world history. When a concentration of wealth gets aligned with political power, the "few" always manage to gain ultimate power over the "many." The solution was to create a formula for political power that was not rooted in heredity or wealth, but rather in the interests of all citizens. A crucial, even defining, aspect of that sociopolitical design is the use of political power to balance economic power. The complete system then includes limits and checks on that political power as well, putting everything in balance, but the crux is enabling the political power of the many to balance the economic power of the few.

So how does this design manifest itself in our economy? What role does the government play? How does it actually achieve the balancing role sought by our founders? In the *Alice in Wonderland* trap we seek to escape there are only two answers. Either the government does nothing at all or it plans and controls everything. Like Vietnam we have only those two choices. From the strategy perspective that's just silliness. Once we emerge from the rabbit hole a completely different spectrum of vitally important roles become clear.

CURRENCY AND THE GREAT INFLATION

One of the most crucial roles the government plays in the economy is its stewardship of the nation's currency. This is a complex process and one that often falls victim to the simplistic intervention of shortsighted politicians hoping for a quick fix. Chile in the early 1980s, along with Mexico in 1982, Finland in 1992, and then most of Latin America in 1994 are just a short list of examples of these kinds of failures. In every case, hyperinflation and the total devaluing of the national currency has wrought havoc on the overall economy.

One of the most spectacular recent failures has been in Venezuela. This is a nation with enormous oil resources that enjoyed a partially successful economy while oil prices were high. The level of corruption, crime, and outright theft of national wealth was staggering, but there was enough loot to go around.

Instead of using all that wealth to build up a functioning national economy it was used to buy necessities from abroad and to nationalize one industry after another. When the oil dollars began to ebb, the United States set out to magnify that financial impact by freezing Venezuelan assets held abroad and imposing restrictions on access to western oil company resources. This combination drove down both the price the state-run oil company got for its crude as well as the volume they were able to extract. The Maduro government responded by printing money. Which, of course, was then worth less and less. The inflation rate has recently hit 80,000 percent per year, a level at which an economy simply cannot function. And it no longer does. A handful of corrupt politicians and their cronies have maintained their wealth by keeping it in a separate "special" currency. For everyone else, economic desperation and starvation have been the result.

As in this example, this kind of "hyperinflation" has almost always been caused by corruption, industrial collapse, war, or similar extreme circumstances. I know of no situation where true hyperinflation arose from simple errors made by central banks. But those kinds of errors do exist and can cause great hardships even if they avoid the extremes of hyperinflation. One of those situations in the United States was the period from the late 1960s up until the early 1980s which economists refer to as the "Great Inflation." Most of us who lived through it remember it as the period of "stagflation." It wasn't good. In fact, it was a government management failure almost as bad as the decisions leading to the Great Depression.

This was a situation caused by a flawed conceptual frame that ran into a perfect storm in the real world. In this case, the central conceptual belief was that inflation and employment were tightly and inversely linked. This meant that allowing inflation to grow would cause unemployment to drop. The real-world storms were a series of dramatic price shocks by OPEC, an equally large shock to food prices, and the imposition and then release of wage and price controls. Each of those shocks drove inflationary spikes we had practically never seen before. None of those real events had even a remote link to structural unemployment but policy makers were steadfast in their beliefs. As a result, rather than interceding, the Federal Reserve acted on their belief that rising inflation would reduce unemployment . . . by not acting. The Fed fiddled while America burned.

This had a brutal effect on the overall economy. The high inflation levels destroyed the value of savings, drove investors into increasingly speculative instruments, and starved productive uses of capital. Instead of falling, unemployment grew, and production fell. Prices remained high and growing. As in the Great Depression, mismanagement by the Federal Reserve was a major factor in a "broken" economy. This is not a role we can ignore, nor can we allow it to be driven by political desires. It's a government role that is central to and must be driven by the needs and realities of our economy.

It is also a role very few really understand, and unfortunately that includes many of those who are directly responsible. The problem arises because we all think about budgets, income, and spending as if we were managing our own household. From that deep conceptual frame, everything begins with income and spending is based on what fits in a budget whose envelope is defined by that income. Despite what every politician of every stripe has told you, that's *not* how things work for a nation that controls its own currency. Government spending, the collection of tax payments, and the issuance of government treasuries are all connected but that connection isn't really constrained by some sort of government budget envelope. In many ways the more relevant envelope is not government activity, it's the economy. In fact, it's actually all of the dollar denominated economic activity around the world.

When it comes to currency management there are three key objectives. The first, as noted above, is to ensure the total amount of currency in circulation is in balance with the total amount of goods and services being bought and sold using that currency. That balance is what keeps inflation in check. The second is to ensure the economy is operating as close as possible to full capacity. The usual metric used for that is employment. Those two can be inversely related, but not in the tight fashion assumed in the 1970s. The third is to avoid wild swings that disrupt markets, people, and society.

As long as those three objectives are maintained, when the economy is growing we want more money injected into the economy on a regular basis. If our $20 trillion economy grows 3 percent in a year and we did *not* inject an extra $600 billion into the economy we'd actually be starving the economy of the liquidity it needs. The vast majority of that dynamic is handled by the commercial banking system. Probably 90 percent of the actual money supply is generated through that means. However, government spending, specifically deficit spending, also injects new money into the economy. And, here's the real head shaker, any government spending that flows directly into the economy, such as infrastructure building, generates exactly as much economic activity as it costs. That means a currency-issuing country like the United States can basically issue whatever money is needed to fund any such program without risking inflation.

TAX CUTS: AN ACT OF FAITH

Systematic government mismanagement in the 1970s was a major factor in the election of Ronald Reagan. His administration set out almost immediately to "starve the beast." On August 4, 1981, Congress passed the first of Reagan's several tax bills, the Economic Recovery Tax Act. This bill has achieved near legendary status in the minds of many conservatives even though the actual details bear little to no resemblance to the legend. They believe those tax cuts triggered decades of growth and represent the pinnacle of government strategies to stimulate economic activity. It's a "story-based reality," and is so deeply, almost religiously, believed it's one we need to peel apart in layers.

The 1981 act had tax reductions for essentially everyone in the country, but the largest were for corporations and the marginal rates charged to higher income citizens. During World War II the United States had set the top marginal rate at the staggering level of 94 percent. After the war it dropped, but only to 91 percent where it remained until 1964 when it was dropped to 70 percent. This level of undeniably confiscatory taxes existed only in the United States and Britain. No other country has ever set the top rate anywhere near those levels. That reality played strongly to the "taxes are theft" narrative of the Reagan program. As noted at the time, when marginal rates get that high it basically becomes an incentive to stop working, producing, or investing. The basic logic was that lowering the rate would increase investments and that would fuel growth in the economy. Or, so the Reagan team believed. It was a "supply side" argument that claimed production was more important to stimulate than demand.

The administration boldly claimed these cuts would actually generate increases in tax revenues by virtue of all the growth they would stimulate. Based in part on that set of assumptions, Reagan expanded the defense budget substantially and demanded Congress find spending cuts in every other area of the budget. The defense spending increases happened quickly. The budget cuts never really materialized.

In the two quarters following the tax cuts the economy went into recession, declining by 5–6 percent each quarter. After one positive quarter the economy declined again.

Instead of going up, tax receipts were way down, and the deficit was exploding. In September 1982, almost exactly a year after the cuts had been enacted, Congress passed the Tax Equity and Fiscal Responsibility Act, which *raised* taxes by about one third of what had been cut the prior year. Over the next five years, Reagan would pass another seven tax related bills almost all of which raised taxes in different areas. When all was said and done two thirds of the original cuts would be restored through various tax increases.

The economy would begin a strong recovery in the middle of 1983, a year after the tax *increases*.

The recession had not been caused by the tax cuts any more than the recovery was caused by the tax increases. The missing piece of the story is what was happening with the Federal Reserve. Inflation was wreaking havoc on the US economy and the Fed had been utterly ineffective in dealing with the problem. When Paul Volcker took charge, he set out to tame the beast. He raised interest rates to 20 percent in the middle of 1981. By 1983 inflation had dropped from a high of nearly 15 percent to 3 percent which allowed the fed to finally begin dropping those sky-high interest rates. Those actions were the direct causes of both the recession in late 1981 and the recovery in 1983, not the famous tax cuts nor the "never mentioned" tax increases.

However, that's still not the whole story. What many fail to understand is how all of these actions operate in conjunction with each other. The key thing to track is the notion of liquidity. Tax cuts increase the liquidity in the economy. Deficit spending increases the liquidity in the economy. Raising interest rates decreases the liquidity in the economy. High levels of inflation effectively destroy the liquidity in the economy. In the late 1970s and early 1980s the United States was facing a severe liquidity problem, which was caused by the destructive power of inflation. Volcker's interest rate increases solved the inflation problem, but at the potentially disastrous risk of making a bad liquidity problem far, far worse. Reagan's tax cuts and defense related deficit spending offset that danger. Once inflation was tamed and interest rates came down, the enduring tax reductions did indeed provide an economy that was structurally more "liquid" than before.

The added liquidity of this tax cut, along with its many later siblings, have not worked the way any of its advocates intended or even claim to this day. As often happens when a conceptual model is deeply flawed, the economic logic of high-end tax cuts stimulating economic growth has actually backfired. Not only have they not "paid for themselves" nor created any "trickle down" value, they also have not improved business dynamics. The first two failures have been consistently and widely reported, but the third is rarely mentioned. There are a set of metrics economists use to track what they refer to as "business dynamism." These include things like new business formation, business exits, and employment shifts between firms. All of those metrics have been declining since the early- to mid-1980s. On at least one key metric, dynamism is actually down by over 40 percent. This fact is all the more startling when you consider the enormous growth and innovation in the technology industry over the same period. In fact, if you control for industry mix shifts there should have been a dramatic increase in business dynamism. What's actually happened is the opposite.

When the economy faces a liquidity crunch, tax cuts and deficit spending can be useful tools. However, when the economy is awash in liquidity as it was in 2017, tax cuts do very little and the increased deficits they bring can actually put the overall economy at risk. Equally problematic is where the resources from that particular cut have flowed. We may have hoped they would end up in higher wage growth, but the evidence shows very little has gone that direction. As for investments in new capital equipment most of that has gone into the fracking industry. Unfortunately, while that does produce oil and natural gas none of those investments have ever consistently returned their cost of capital. Most of the corporate cuts of 2017 actually ended up fueling acquisitions, stock buybacks, and dividend increases. None of that provides any real US stimulus effect.

In fact, stock buybacks basically take money out of the economy. We'll cover the business motivations behind this practice in a later chapter, but there's a crucial insight we need to cover in the context of the tax-cut strategy frame. When a company executes a $1 billion stock buyback, they take $1 billion in cash and use it to buy $1 billion in their own stock from Wall Street. They then take the stock out of circulation. Before they execute that transaction, there's a total of $2 billion in assets in the market—the $1 billion in cash they have on their balance sheet and the $1 billion in stock held by Wall Street. Afterward, there's only the $1 billion in cash which is now held by Wall Street. The other $1 billion has been removed from the market. It's a process that is quite akin to central banks managing the amount of currency in circulation.

The 2017 tax cuts led to roughly $1 trillion dollars in stock buybacks which means we basically took $1 trillion out to a virtual parking lot and burned it all up. It did *not* flow into the economy. It was removed. It was destroyed. We could have used that to repair infrastructure, eliminate student debt, or any other national priority. Instead we just removed it from the economy. It's an underreported financial tragedy of gargantuan proportions.

When corporate executives are asked why they do this they almost universally respond by saying they see no better use for the funds. Which really means they just don't know what to do with all the money in their coffers. Using it to increase wages would lead to profit erosion and a higher cost basis so that's never on the table. In the end, they effectively just throw it away. And, to be completely clear, I participated in all of this during my tenure at IBM. When you hear conservatives pronounce their faith that the "market knows best how to use the nation's financial resources," it's worth keeping in mind that the executives they are counting on are saying both explicitly and through their actions that they didn't know what to do with $1 trillion in 2018.

What's also important to consider is that none of us knows how much of that tax cut actually left the United States entirely and went into overseas investments. There can be little question a fair amount of the cut went into the Chinese economy which offers much stronger growth potential than our own. In the twenty-first century we can expect more and more of the liquidity generated by tax cuts to flow to other nations. As that trend grows, tax cuts will be less and less useful as a national economic policy tool even when we do face liquidity challenges.

INVESTMENTS IN INFRASTRUCTURE, SCIENCE, AND INNOVATION

In addition to managing overall fiscal and monetary policies, government is also the primary source of investment for some of our economy's most important productivity drivers. This begins with building and maintaining our national infrastructure. Probably the largest examples of this sort of investment were the Works Progress Administration (WPA) and Civilian Conservation Corps (CCC) programs of the 1930s. People often focus on the employment aspect of those programs but let's not forget what those millions of people built nor lose sight of how much impact that had on our national productivity. Those 1930s-era jobs are long gone, but the highways, bridges, power, and water systems they built serve our nation to this day. Another famous example, dating from the mid-1950s, was the planning and funding of America's Interstate Highway system. That program took over 35 years to complete, built over 40,000 miles of roadways, and has been estimated by economists to have contributed 20–30 percent of the annual productivity boost the economy enjoyed from the mid-'50s to mid-'70s. That's a pretty substantial positive impact. The fact that such large-scale infrastructure programs are basically nonexistent today is a non-trivial factor in our declining productivity improvement rate.

The next critical government investment category is for basic scientific research. Basic research is fundamentally different from applied research. It includes every area of science, specifically at the stage where the eventual commercial value is completely unknown, unknowable, and may not occur for a lifetime. Private industry doesn't spend a lot of time on that kind of work. In fact, Bell Labs and IBM Research are the only two institutions I know of with sustained commitments to a basic research agenda. In recent years, Google has been slowly building a basic research program and Microsoft has as well, but that's about it. This type of work is mainly done in academe and by the government labs. All of that is funded out of government spending. Even the work done by AT&T, IBM, and other private institutions often taps into government programs to supplement internal investments. Absent those investments we simply would not live in the society we do today.

The other substantial government contribution to commercial innovation has been the side effects from defense spending. One can argue about just how much commercial economic impact really comes from those expenditures, but there's a long list of technologies whose early developments are all rooted in defense programs. This would include nuclear power, lasers, fiber optics, satellites, and the microwave oven. Defense programs were also crucial to the early stages of the transistor, semiconductors, computer and communication systems, geopositioning systems, and the internet itself. And it was the evolution of military aviation that gave birth to the commercial jet industry. There can be little doubt that these defense-funded innovations transformed the world and have shaped the modern age.

These are all government investments and activities that are vital to the health and growth of our economy. They don't get a lot of headlines and have certainly had their share of boondoggles and pork barrels, but our modern society simply would not exist were it not for all these foundational investments. Other than defense spending, they have also been sorely neglected for decades and are badly in need of modernization and renewal.

When we speak of government "fiscal responsibility," one of the first things we need to examine is whether government is doing the jobs for which it is the primary responsible party. That's not what most politicians mean by the phrase which is a classic example of the neoliberal rabbit hole gibberish that has become all too common. The reality of the last 40–50 years is that our government has been failing in many of its critical roles and our whole economy is suffering as a consequence.

RULES THAT SHAPE MARKETS
Where the rabbit hole frames really break down is where it comes to the rules that govern how markets function. This is more than a bit ironic. Some of the

staunchest conservatives from the 1960s and '70s felt this was one of the most important tools available to government policy makers. I agree with them. Understanding this concept is essential to understanding many of the policies in this book.

Let's start by observing that regulations and regulatory processes are inherently slow to form and evolve, often complex to administer, and prone to attracting bribery and corruption. It's also quite awkward to fine tune them for all the dynamics and local variability we see in the world. When people talk about the failures of "central planning," this is what they have in mind. In contrast, well-functioning markets provide a dynamism and flexibility that becomes almost self-regulating and is far better at managing all those real-world complexities. Unfortunately, they too bring their own failings. In many cases there simply is no market-making formula other than a complete abdication of our common good. Markets are also ripe with fraud, speculative excesses, and the rampant abuse of people arising from the inherent power imbalances. Both extremes are basically impossible in practice and, as a direct result, exist only in fiction or the fevered imaginations of ideologues.

Less obvious, but every bit as important, markets also fail to function properly when costs that are directly associated with certain activities are not captured in business accounting and recovered through market prices. The simplest example would be a factory that dumps its waste on a nearby property. All that waste will eventually need to be cleaned up and removed. When those costs aren't paid for by the factory owners and accounted for in their business operations, that's referred to as an "externality." Because those externalities aren't included in operational costs, they don't factor into market prices and that means the market allocation that results is fundamentally flawed.

Because of their dynamic flexibility, we'd like to use markets to manage economic activity as much as possible, while being cognizant of all the ways markets fail. In that spirit one of the most basic functions of government is to define the rules that determine how our markets function to ensure we reduce or eliminate those failures. Property rights and contract laws are some of the most basic aspects of this role. Our laws prohibiting slavery and child labor are other examples.

That's on the national level, but the same thing happens globally. The modern global economy has its roots in the Bretton Woods conference in 1944. This led to the equally important General Agreement on Tariffs and Trade (GATT) in 1947. The core vision was a world of open markets to be jointly managed by the major Western powers emerging from World War II. The lynch pin was the establishment of fully convertible currencies and a set of foreign exchange principles all to be overseen through a newly created International Monetary Fund (IMF). Along with the World Bank, these interrelated institutions are the heart of the global system of capitalist economics. They define the rules that make global trade actually work.

The key is realizing that it is the establishment of boundaries and rules that define the playing field that enables well-functioning markets to form and flourish. This point is often counterintuitive to those who feel any regulatory rules impede free markets rather than enabling them. After all, if there are rules then there are limits on what one is free to do. However, in the absence of foundational rules there simply is no market to begin with. Think about a large field with a few dozen people standing around. If they agree on one set of rules they can play baseball. A different set of rules will allow a football game to be played. With no rules at all, everybody wanders away. The field itself with its attendant lines and boundaries only means something in the context of a set of rules.

As important, our economy and society are both examples of what are known in mathematical circles as "complex dynamic systems." Understanding how these systems work and the approaches available to strategists and policy makers to affect them is a major part of the strategy tool kit. These kinds of systems are designed so that nothing is "hard coded" in a deterministic fashion. When there are independent entities interacting with each other amid continuous feedback loops, which is exactly how markets work, you get complex behaviors. What happens in these systems is often described as "unpredictable," but that's a bit misleading. The systemic behavior arises out of the interaction of all the participants in the context of a fairly simple set of shared rules. In strategy circles this is referred to as "emergent behavior," and different sets of rules will generate different emergent results. One set might cause the economy to steadily weaken and collapse while another can lead to strong sustainable growth. The differences between the two may be quite subtle which is where the policy challenges arise, but those core rules mean everything.

This leads to a key principle:

Regulations make markets. In particular, government institutions that address the needs of people and society and that avoid or minimize systemic economic failures are critical to making sustainable well-functioning markets.

This is an "out of the rabbit hole" concept that is obvious from the strategy perspective but utterly foreign to our traditional frames. The shock for those on the right is that governments actually are the institutions that make markets. The shock for those on the left is that when governments exercise that power they must do so not to "control" the market but to ensure it thrives. The shock for both is that there is nothing contradictory about a thriving market designed for the needs of people and society. In many ways, understanding this core principle is a "lifeline" out of the rabbit hole, out of our shared conceptual trap.

Regulations per se aren't a problem. They become problems when there are dozens or more and they're all *slightly* different. When that happens, instead of making markets they fracture and destroy them. The essential keys are standardization and consistency. When 50 states and the federal government all decide to create slightly different regulations that shatters the market. Standardization is the key to transforming regulatory activity from uneconomic cost drivers to market-creating policy tools.

The problem also scales beyond our borders. As markets become global, regulations that are globally consistent can create markets that are global. In the absence of such global coordination, global businesses will design for the highest standards in the largest markets so that they can operate anywhere they choose. One of the key changes unfolding in the world right now is a shift in this important role from the United States to the European Union (EU) and increasingly to China. In the coming decades the standards that are either legislated or emerge in China are likely to end up determining the standards for the entire world.

The insight that policy makers can define standard rules that will enable the complex dynamics of markets to address a wide range of issues was a central feature in the thinking of Milton Friedman and many other leading conservatives in the 1970s. Their focus was specifically on addressing the various market failures that emerged through the 1960s and 1970s. Some of those ideas would prove to be completely unworkable, but many had and still have great promise.

One of the most basic sets of rules are those related to consumer and public safety. This includes everything from the food we eat to the medications we take to the products we buy. In our modern world "caveat emptor" has considerable limits. None of us has the knowledge or testing equipment needed to inspect every salad we eat or appliance we plug in. Even with safety standards in place we still encounter bacterial outbreaks and fires caused by faulty electrical equipment. Setting regulations so that consumers and society can acquire goods and services that won't kill us is a good thing for the economy, not a bad one. When people have confidence, they will buy. When that is lacking, when there's a failure of trust, they will not. This can be seen today in the commercial dynamics around Genetically Modified Organisms (GMO) in the food industry. The lack of trust in both the commercial suppliers and their regulators has severely undermined whatever potential might exist in those innovations.

Like many such things, there are limits on what makes sense and there is room for healthy debate on where to draw those limits. There are countless examples over the years when an unnecessary and unwanted "nanny state" has intruded to the detriment of all. In addition to the undesirable limits of personal freedom, this kind of overreach almost always leads to fragmented regulations and a lack of consistent standards. When there isn't sufficient consensus to establish a clear standard on where to set such boundaries we're often better off waiting until such consensus emerges. However, even in those situations, establishing standard regulations on consumer disclosure can definitely facilitate the development of the market.

Probably the most important field where effective regulation has enormous untapped socioeconomic potential is the environment. There are deep historical threads behind the environmental movement including the American Transcendentalist writings of Thoreau, Whitman, and John Muir. The trigger for the late twentieth-century version is usually attributed to Rachel Carson and her book *Silent Spring*. That book brought attention to the role pesticides played in altering an ecosystem. It would eventually lead to the ban of DDT, but just as important, it made people realize there actually was such a thing as an "ecosystem." It can be almost impossible for people to perceive all of the subtle interactions that cause our world to work the way it does. Rachel Carson's writings began the process of providing that understanding. What she also achieved was an effective challenge to the hegemony of economics in society.

This challenge opened a door for the thinking of Aldo Leopold. His book, *A Sand County Almanac*, went a step further than Carson's introduction of the concept of an ecosystem. Leopold argued we needed an actual system of ethics around the environment. He believed there were rights and wrongs *directly and intrinsically* related to the environment. He rejected the notion of saying "helping the environment is good *because* it does XYZ." We need not claim goodness by virtue of being profitable, or healthy, or good for tourism or any other economic benefit. His assertion was that helping the environment is good, full stop. He articulated the insight that we as people value, deeply value, many things. We are not solely economic animals driven by barter and exchange. The range of values that engage and motivate us as people is far larger than that narrow aperture. This is a profound insight and one that can and should inform far more of our debates about what we want in our society. The failure to see humans as more than just economic creatures is one of the more grievous errors of neoliberalism. Our fifth paradigm needs to explicitly include the socioeconomic "space" to hold those debates and to embrace their conclusions.

Regulating markets to reflect these deep values is akin to abolishing slavery. In all these cases, society is asserting there are values we hold distinct from any commercial value. In the case of slavery, we concluded that form of human exploitation was morally unacceptable and had to be excised from our markets regardless of its economic value. The environment is more complex. There are situations, within certain limits, where the economic impact *is* relevant. There are others where, like slavery, the economic impact is off the table and our environmental ethics take over. There are places in this country where tearing up the land for a pocket of minerals or natural gas is as inconceivable and immoral as tearing down the Sistine Chapel for the same objective.

For those areas where economic trade-offs *are* relevant, the key is to ensure the environmental and safety limits are well defined and all the environmental externalities are properly accounted for. This needs to include capturing all environmental costs and expenses in corporate income statements as well as accumulating liabilities on their balance sheets. These kinds of deep business accounting rule changes need to span the full range of market participants. As long as everyone plays by the same rules we are creating a fair and well-defined market. In the twenty-first century that means those rules need to be developed and implemented through global collaboration. In the absence of that global harmonization, US corporations can find themselves competing on a badly tilted playing field.

To summarize, our government actually has a number of vitally important roles to play in our economy. It starts with fiscal and monetary policy and includes direct investments in infrastructure and basic science as well as defining the rules that make our markets function in a sustainable fashion. Critically, those rules include the full range of economic *and noneconomic* values and needs of our citizens. It's actually quite a large and important role.

Unfortunately, our track record on most of these is weak and our accumulating failure to act responsibly is creating real jeopardy to the nation. Most of these irresponsible failures can be traced back to the ideologies outlined earlier. Other than currency management every one of these critical government roles sits squarely in the conceptual blind spots of those ideologies. The notion that American tax cuts could result in capital being removed from the economy either through stock buybacks or investment shifts to China is utterly unfathomable in those frames. Ayn Rand and the neoliberals literally assert that "government research" is an oxymoron. The value of roads, bridges, and our electrical infrastructure seem equally beyond their grasp. They just assume those things exist through magic, not government investments. Finally, the understanding that standards, rules, and regulations are the tools that *make* markets would be regarded as outright blasphemy.

Our other source of failure comes from the cynical corruption of those who sit in regulatory roles. Some of this arises from the sabotage efforts of the anti-democracy movement, but most of it is more mundane. When the fracking industry and EPA try to assert there are no environmental dangers associated with pumping high volumes of neurotoxins into the ground, releasing carcinogenic gases into the air around schools, and creating waste water that is so toxic it must be pumped into deep underground reservoirs, we all know something isn't right. When the governor of Michigan poisons the water of an entire town and refuses to correct the problem, that knowledge quickly becomes anger. When there is no accountability for these failures the cynicism of the perpetrators becomes the cynicism of their victims.

This unfortunate pattern of irresponsible and cynical behavior by those put in crucial government roles has been going on for decades. It's the primary culprit behind the loss of faith in the ability of our society to cope with the challenges in front of us. That faith can only be restored when the enormous army of those who truly care about public service are given voice and direction from a new generation of public leaders.

Those leaders will fail if our fourth paradigm endures. One of their central leadership challenges is to usher in our fifth. Each of our prior paradigm shifts occurred amid crises, and the leaders who guided us to our next paradigms are among our most revered. Our first paradigm was born through revolution as a result of the leadership of our Founding Fathers. Our second emerged from the Civil War through the leadership of Abraham Lincoln. Our third came from the failure of the second paradigm, the Great Depression, and World War II. It was led by Franklin Delano Roosevelt. Our fourth emerged from the litany of failures around Vietnam, Watergate, oil embargoes, and a decade of stagflation. The leader who pulled us out of that mess and into the unfortunate neoliberal disaster zone was Ronald Reagan. The next true leader, the one who guides our nation out of the neoliberal rabbit hole and into our fifth paradigm, will join Washington, Jefferson, Lincoln, Roosevelt, and Reagan in our shared national pantheon of presidential heroes.

We've done this throughout our history. We can do it again. Conceptual paradigms create deep and powerful traps but leadership matters. Those leaders need a crisis to help them motivate and drive change along with insights to guide them forward. We have all that. What we need now are leaders with the ability to communicate, inspire, and lead a shift in paradigms. The nation is ready and waiting. With bated breath.

PART 2

THE ROAD TO THE
TWENTY-FIRST CENTURY

1

THE NINETEENTH CENTURY: FROM RURAL AGRICULTURE TO URBAN INDUSTRY

O UR JOURNEY THUS far has been focused on theory, with history used to buttress our insights and conclusions. Those lessons will continue in the chapters ahead, but history is not only a source of useful lessons, it is also a powerful force driving us forward. We need to turn our attention back to the nineteenth century and begin using our growing conceptual frameworks to better understand the underlying forces at work and what they imply for our twenty-first-century endeavors.

The nineteenth century encompassed the early stages of our evolution from rural agriculture to urban industry. Those were the nation's first two socioeconomic paradigms. The evolution wasn't planned, and the paradigms weren't "designed." In fact, they each emerged amid crises that drove deep and seismic changes throughout the country. The shift from agriculture to industry would be a central factor in the Civil War and would eventually lead to the Great Depression, the rise of Fascism, and World War II. We are currently in the midst of a similar shift of comparable proportions so it's essential we learn what we can from the last time a socioeconomic shift of this scale unfolded. The concepts of value creation, value capture, power, and the needs of people as people provide a distinct perspective on the major forces that shaped this tumultuous period. We will also see a troubling inconsistency in our application of the various government roles and responsibilities we've highlighted in our ideological musings.

RURAL AGRICULTURAL BUSINESS MODELS

In addition to the propulsive force of the economic shift from agriculture to industry, this period offers powerful examples of the dynamics unleashed when value creation is forcibly separated from value capture and when market power is used to suppress the needs of people. The government interventions to correct those socioeconomic flaws were extreme, but essential, and illustrate the enormous importance of using that power when markets fail the needs of people.

In the early 1800s the United States, like most of the world, was almost completely an agricultural society. Records from the period are often conflicting. One official count had roughly 72 percent of the working population of free men on farms. However, that record did not include women or slaves, which would raise the number to over 90 percent.

Within that larger paradigm there were, at the time, two competing socioeconomic models for agriculture. One model featured large farms, with wealthy landowners, worked by slaves. The alternate model featured small, family-owned plots worked by individuals in local communities and towns. These two models could be found everywhere around the world and both models were present in America's early nineteenth-century economy. Most of the farms in the North and West followed the small family and community strategy. In contrast, the South had larger plantations, particularly cotton, and were heavily dependent on slave labor to work the fields. While both were prominent, the US government would intervene specifically to enable the growth of the family farm and bring the economic model of slavery to an end.

In 1862 the United States passed the Homestead Act which allowed any adult who had never borne arms against the United States to file a claim for land. Over time, the US government would give away 270 million acres, or 10 percent of the total area of the country. Approximately 1.6 million Americans would become landowners as a result. It's noteworthy that these were simple claims, not organized auctions. The act was not aimed at enabling existing wealthy landowners to expand their domains. There were no "bidding wars" where wealth held the winning hand. Much of it was driven by the government's desire to incent people to move into the territories in the West. Those lands were opened to settlement through the displacement of Native Americans. In that sense it definitely was a "redistribution," just not what is usually meant by that word.

Variations on this sort of land distribution scheme would be central features of every socialist and communist movement of the next 100 years. Unlike the Homestead Act, few of those really did what they claimed in the end, but they all made the same promises to their citizens. What those regimes actually did was usually the opposite of what they claimed, a pattern found throughout history. The United States was one of the few nations that actually delivered the dream of the family farm to many of its citizens. Not only was this model more humane than that of slavery, but it also aligned value capture with its creation and was therefore inherently more sustainable. It did not lead to substantial value concentration, but there was more than enough economic activity to support the small towns and communities that sprung up in the process.

In contrast, the alternate business model was both based on and dependent on substantial value concentration. The large plantations worked by slaves were not unique to the American South. They were also prevalent throughout the Caribbean, South America, Africa, India, and East Asia, thanks to European colonization. In fact, the European colonial model was itself an expansion on their older feudal system. In place of lords, lands, and serfs you had governors, territories, and slaves. In both models the fruits of the enslaved labor flowed upward and were heavily taxed. Government forces, either judicial or military, kept everything in line. Whips and starvation diets took care of the rest. This was how the gentry achieved concentrated wealth in the preindustrial era. In the early nineteenth century that was the state of affairs across most of the globe and had been so for generations.

The slave-based economic model was ubiquitous because it worked. Economics care nothing about people or morality, only people do. When all forms of production were heavily dependent on manual labor there were strong economic interests in being able to "own" the labor. The slaves created the value that was then captured by their owners. The owners relied on their concentrated capital to purchase slaves and on their political power to maintain that economic formula.

While the economics of the slavery model were favorable to the wealthy, the inherent deep inequality and misalignment of value capture with its creation made the model socially and economically unstable. It was also morally repugnant from a human standpoint, which we'll come to in a moment. But, first let's note the inherent instability of the model.

The French colony of Saint Domingue, which would later be known as Haiti, illustrates the core dynamics at work. In 1791 it was the wealthiest holding in the entire French empire. That economic wealth was based on the work, the value creation, of slaves. The colony consisted of approximately 40,000 white and mulatto plantation owners, shopkeepers, teachers, etc., and 500,000 slaves. It was the labor of those half a million people that supported the island and provided a steady stream of profits back to France. In return, the slaves got a subsistence living under harsh and often cruel conditions. Value capture went to France, completely disconnected from the value creation of the 500,000 slaves. That imbalance was made possible by the relative economic power of the French owners over the slaves. Those economic interests were deeply embedded within the political and therefore military powers of the French government.

In August 1791, Toussaint l'Overture led a massive slave rebellion to challenge all that power. That sort of resistance is just what happens when power is used to systematically sever the capture of value from its creators. When the dominating power also resorts to physical violence and abuse, as the slave owners had done for ages, its resistance will inevitably do the same. The former slaves managed to stave off repeated military excursions from both the French and British, eventually achieving full independence in January 1804. In the end, it was their power that prevailed.

Slave rebellions were not uncommon. They were an integral aspect of slave-based economies everywhere in the world. That was the reason behind the Second Amendment to the US Constitution. The militias referred to in that passage were not to defend against foreign incursions or "hostile" Indians. The entire purpose of those militias was the suppression of slave revolts. The phrasing of a "regulated militia being necessary to the security of a *free* state . . ." is ironic but will not be the first time we see the word "free" being used to mean "power to suppress." Our Constitution was specifically crafted to enable key practices essential to the institution of slavery.

One of the earliest examples of global cooperation to outlaw a harmful or immoral business practice was the World Anti-Slavery Convention of 1840. It included several nations, though it was mainly attended by British and Americans. Britain had outlawed the slave trade in 1807 and had officially abolished slavery throughout its empire by 1834. The convention sought to establish this as a global principle. While eventually successful, it would take another fifty to sixty years before it was eliminated in most of the world. The shared moral agreement to reject the economic model of slavery was a global stand for human rights over markets. Each nation applied their own specific tools, but in every case government power was used to eliminate an economic practice that was morally unacceptable to society.

In the United States, this exercise of federal government power obviously led to the Civil War. Part of the resistance from the South was based on racism, but there were deeply entrenched economic drivers as well. Slavery was not an incidental aspect of southern economics and society. It was central. In the slave states of the South, slaves represented 40 percent of the total population in 1800 and would grow to 50 percent by 1860. From a business mindset, "investments" in slaves actually dominated the capital structure of the economy. The capital investments of most agricultural economies center on landownership. In the southern United States, the land was relatively cheap, and the bulk of the commercial capital was used for the purchase of slaves. The entire structure of the economy from the overall business model to the labor and indeed capital itself were all completely driven by slavery. The economic value created by the slaves was all captured by their owners and that's what enabled the romanticized social environment of the time. The antebellum society could not have existed otherwise.

Nor was that economic impact limited to the South. In addition to exports to Britain, the Southern plantations provided the raw materials essential to the newly constructed textile mills in the North. The earliest days of the looming

Industrial Revolution would owe their existence to the tons of cotton flowing out of the back-breaking labor of Southern slaves. The business, organization, and financial methods that would later be associated with the railroads were also first deployed and developed on Southern plantations whose sheer size required a level of sophistication not seen before.

Every aspect of that socioeconomic world would be rejected as our society decided that the moral repugnance of slavery along with its inherently unstable social violence made it unacceptable. This was without regard to the economic value it enabled the powerful in both the South and North to capture. We decided people were more important than the deeply entrenched economic power of the wealthy few. Unfortunately, hundreds of thousands of Americans would have to die to eliminate that immoral economic practice.

The government interventions that enabled the family farm and ended the slave plantations did nothing to halt the growth of agriculture. The absolute number of Americans working in agriculture would grow right up to the 1920s. However, while the total number continued to grow the percentage was dropping rapidly. The United States was beginning the transition to its second major paradigm, the industrial economy. Unlike other countries, this was not primarily driven by people leaving farms for urban areas. There was some of that, particularly for black Americans fleeing the still oppressive environment of the South. However, a great deal of the actual urban, industrial workforce was coming in the waves of immigration from Europe. It was largely immigrants who built and manned the factories of the early US Industrial Revolution.

THE NEW URBAN INDUSTRIAL BUSINESS MODEL

This early stage of the industrial economy is filled with examples of successful value creation and healthy, well aligned value capture. However, it was also filled with massive abuses of market power and an outright assault on the needs of people. While the government intervened on behalf of people to abolish slavery in agriculture they did the opposite on the industrial side of the economy. Instead of supporting the needs of people, our government conspired with industry to sustain employment practices that were nearly as hostile to people as that of the Southern slavers. In the process they were magnifying the socioeconomic stresses that would erupt in the years to come. Government also began to step up to its role in our national infrastructure, an early harbinger of the much larger responsibility to come. This second paradigm was far more complex than its predecessor. Our society had not yet learned how to manage all the emerging stresses and challenges that arose. It was also a period riddled with power abuses that slowly, but surely, caused our value creating capabilities to collapse.

The period from 1850 to 1929 was one of the most prolific in Western history for developments in science, philosophy, art, and culture. The amount of intellectual and cultural creativity was staggering. All the contributions to basic science and the world of ideas were joined by a roster of incredible inventors. Thomas Edison might be the most famous but let's not forget Karl Benz and the Wright brothers. It wasn't just new products being invented. The assembly line manufacturing innovations by Ford changed forever how things are built at scale. A bit earlier in the period Cyrus McCormick completely changed the process of harvesting. This was a period where innovations were truly driven by passionate and motivated individuals. All of these men had compatriots and employees who participated in the process, but it really was an era where the inventor in his garret did indeed change the world.

So how did those innovators do? Did the economy reward them for all the value they were creating? Did their personal value capture align with their value creation? How well was this new industrial economic paradigm performing?

Eli Whitney's cotton harvesting innovation completely transformed the textile industry. The vast bulk of the textile market shifted from wool to cotton. Practically the entire economy of the southern United States ended up depending on his innovation. Cotton exports to the mills in Britain, which dominated the world at the time, went from 2 million tons in 1800 to 1.8 *billion* tons by 1860. Whitney had successfully filed and secured a US patent on his invention. However, the invention was so trivial to copy he ended up spending all his time unsuccessfully attempting to enforce his patent. He didn't die penniless, but he did die poor. The enormous economic value he created was almost all captured by others.

Thomas Edison, in contrast, did fairly well. At the young age of 22 he secured his first major patent license for a stock ticker. That fee enabled him to quit his job and devote himself to his inventions on a full-time basis. After numerous other successes he founded the Edison General Electric Company. This company merged several other electric related businesses he had launched into a single entity. It was financed by Drexel, Morgan and Co., a firm that had been founded by J.P. Morgan and others. J.P. Morgan and the Vanderbilt family had been longtime supporters of Edison. Edison was undoubtedly one of the greatest inventors in history, but he was not the best manager or executive. In 1892 Drexel and Morgan orchestrated the merger of Edison General Electric with the Thomson-Houston Electric Company to form GE. In the process, they gently nudged Edison to the side.

There are countless other examples from the period. What they almost all represent is the relatively loose connection between the sources of *innovative* value creation and the actual financial rewards associated with those inventions. There are straightforward success stories, like Edison's, but there are also many who struggled until their deaths. Innovation is critical to economic growth but aligning the associated value capture with its creation can be very inconsistent. That was true in the nineteenth century and remains a critical focus in the twenty-first.

How about the other forms of economic value creation, specifically understanding markets and efficient production?

The Sears catalog business is a great example of value creation rooted in a superior ability to understand markets and align goods with buyers. Richard Sears started in the watch and jewelry business. He originally hired Alvah Roebuck to handle watch repairs. Not long after, he sold the watch business and formed his catalog mail-order business in partnership with Roebuck. Sears himself focused on writing the famous catalogs which were phenomenally successful. As the railways and postal systems spread throughout the country the Sears catalog became ubiquitous and Richard Sears became quite wealthy.

The very role model of efficient production was Henry Ford. He was committed to building a car cheap enough for every American to buy. The United States had long been a primary source of innovation in production processes. In the 1850–1900 period, Europeans often spoke about the "American Model" of production with envy. Ransom Olds had created a mass-production model for his early cars that was the gold standard at the time, but still not efficient enough to meet the cost level Ford was seeking. What Ford did was to take many aspects of the Olds process, but then augment that with conveyor machinery to produce a moving assembly line. That enabled each worker to remain in place with all their tools and parts right at hand. The result changed the world of manufacturing. It also enabled Ford to meet his goals, an incredible example of value creation for all of his customers, and revenue and profits for Ford.

The inventions from this period also led to the creation of an entirely new category of national economic investment. Before this period, a nation's "infrastructure" included ports, canals, and dirt roads. Now there were efforts all over the world to build railroads and lay telegraph lines. Those resources completely changed the dynamics of location and time. When the United States completed its transcontinental railroad at noon on May 10, 1869, the news was flashed all over the United States, Canada, and Britain almost instantly.

This seminal national infrastructure event was not paid for by the US government, but it was explicitly planned, coordinated, and managed by the government. Routes were mapped out, land rights secured, often through eminent domain, and then given to the railway companies who were also granted effective monopoly rights for carriage.

These examples, and countless others, are American economic success stories. The market was creating ample new value and, for the most part, those creating value were also enjoying the fruits of their endeavors. The top-level economic metrics, such as they were, all looked pretty solid. There were also real estate and commodity bubbles that rose and burst, all of which eventually contributed to the popular story of the "roaring twenties." In certain corners of the rabbit hole, this paradigm is viewed as the absolute pinnacle of man's achievement on earth.

Unfortunately, that's only part of the story. There were no restraints on the economic power associated with that value creation and that power was abused in ways that were destructive to the economy and devastating to people and communities. To see the details, we need to examine the story of the railroads more closely as well as the creation and leverage of monopolies and the specific treatment of the people working in all of these companies. Under those rocks are all manner of ugly truths, power abuses, rampant greed and corruption, and deep human struggles and tragedies. This was a deeply flawed paradigm as a whole that remained ignorant of its own flaws right up until it collapsed in utter ruin. Unfortunately, the same pattern of arrogance, frame blindness, and corruption are characteristics of our modern age.

Let's begin unearthing those abuses with the railroads. A railroad, particularly in the late nineteenth century, is a natural monopoly. There are almost never two sets of rails owned by two different companies traversing the same section of geography. When the only alternatives were horses or barges on canals those with needs to ship substantial goods had no other options. In the early stages of our national build-out there were many different companies owning various sections of track, but for each specific region of the country there was only one major provider of transport. They were regional monopolies. Over time, the larger companies bought up others which made it easier to arrange transport over larger distances, but also extended their monopolies to wider sections of the country.

Large size is also a characteristic that's inherent to railroads. By the early 1900s there were over 200,000 miles of track laid all across the United States. That had not come cheap. The US government may have played a substantial role in the planning, but the financing was raised by the railroad companies themselves. This was primarily done through the issuance of railroad bonds, many of which were purchased by European investors. In 1882 one estimate put the total value of outstanding railroad bonds at $4.6 billion. In that year the railroads were generating revenues of approximately $490 million. To put those numbers in perspective, the entire US federal budget at the time was $274 million and the national debt sat at $2.2 billion. The railways were literally twice the economic size of the entire nation's government.

Another factor contributing to this size was the business strategy of vertical integration. There are many considerations that drive corporate structures. Some favor the tight coordination and elimination of middlemen that comes with deep vertical integration. Others favor the reduced capital, improved flexibility, and reduced bureaucracy that comes with extended supply chains. Changes in this business strategy will be a central factor in understanding why the twenty-first-century economy is so deeply different from the nineteenth century. During the industrial build-out of the late nineteenth century, the dominant strategy was extensive and deep vertical integration. Railroad companies built, bought, and controlled mining companies for their coal and steel companies for their supply of rail, trusses, and the like. Many also built grand hotels and lodges to house their passengers on their journeys.

Raising capital and building the large, hierarchical organizations needed to manage these complex companies became organizational hallmarks of the nineteenth-century industrial paradigm. The other hallmark of the age was the pursuit of industrial monopolies and the exploitation of the power those conveyed. The railroads used their monopoly positions in several nefarious ways. First, they kept their rates secret and charged different shippers substantially different rates. In some cases, one shippers could be charged twice the rate of another. This obviously provided direct profits, but the secrecy also gave them negotiating power they could use when striking deals with their customers.

The most famous example of this monopoly leverage were the deals struck between the Pennsylvania Railroad and Standard Oil. Standard Oil was able to get the railroad to make it economically impractical for their oil competitors to ship their products. In most cases, that was done simply by charging exorbitant rates. In others, it was denial of service either outright or through severe limits on volume. The railroads literally had the power to determine which businesses would thrive and which would be choked off. They could offer this gangster-like "service" to whoever gave them the best offer in return. In the oil business that was Standard Oil. In the earliest stages of the developing oil market, Standard Oil had many competitors in western Pennsylvania and New York which at the time had the largest oil fields in the country. With the explicit help of the Pennsylvania Railroad most of those companies would eventually be forced out of business.

As you would expect, the companies enduring these monopolistic practices raised heated complaints with the government. There were numerous attempts by the state of Pennsylvania to get to the bottom of all these shenanigans. One early contract uncovered by the legislature included a scheme in which all oil shippers would have their rates doubled, but secretly the railroad would provide a kickback to Standard Oil of $1 on every single barrel they shipped regardless of its source. When this was revealed, both companies vowed it had been abolished. From that point on, they would successfully thwart all efforts to uncover the details of how they worked their secret manipulations. The Pennsylvania government was sufficiently corrupt and hampered by the courts that there was no progress in stemming these illicit behaviors. When economic and political power are combined there is nothing to thwart the destruction of other economic entities or social values. Ironically, we are in the process of repeating this exact mistake today with our rules around net neutrality. Once again, we are allowing companies with monopoly positions to control the success or failure of every business that depends on them.

This wasn't the only maneuver used by the railroads either. With their power to determine who would succeed and who would fail, the railroad companies had "insider knowledge" that could be exploited in the stock market. Once they had decided who they were going to favor and who they were going to suppress, they created financial instruments that combined direct investments in their chosen winners and short positions on those they were attacking. None of these plans were public, so the whole process was shrouded in secrecy and only select top executives were allowed access to these money-making engines. It was one of these financial instruments that enabled Andrew Carnegie, who was working for the Pennsylvania Railroad, to begin amassing his fortune. When he was offered the opportunity to join one of these investment pools he took out a 90-percent mortgage on his mother's house to do so. The returns on that investment allowed him to begin his journey to dominate the steel industry.

The steel industry was another that was guided toward monopoly status. The direct participants, like Carnegie, certainly wanted that economic power.

But, behind the scenes, J.P. Morgan was the "guiding hand" that sought to create monopoly positions throughout the economy. As the leading banker of the time, his touch shows up in many industrial stories of the period. He would orchestrate and fund acquisitions to "rollup" a specific category, and then use his social and economic influence with buyers to steer sales to his chosen winner. His efforts made a mockery of Adam Smith's notion of an invisible hand. There certainly was an invisible hand at work in this paradigm but it was J.P. Morgan's, not the market's.

This is also the point to dispel the myth of "glorious risk-taking entrepreneurs" building our great industrial economy. They existed, and some did reasonably well. However, with a few notable exceptions, the giant fortunes were mainly built through insider trading schemes, monopolistic abuses, labor practices only slightly less detestable than slavery, and crony capitalism. This was an era where economic power was allowed to run rampant, destroying true entrepreneurs and whole economic sectors, as well as people, families and entire communities.

There are many different ways to wield economic power. J.P Morgan, Andrew Carnegie, the railroads, and other industrial titans were quite creative in exploring all their options. All of those maneuvers created substantial distortions to the underlying markets. Power is always present, but when it becomes too strong and too concentrated, value finds itself in the backseat. The market distortions created by the crony capitalists were not just endangering other business interests, they were systematically squelching the entry and growth of healthy activity throughout the economy. This made the phrase "free market" laughable and was far from any sort of economic ideal.

What Morgan, Carnegie, Rockefeller, Vanderbilt, and most other industrial titans also shared was a deep antipathy toward labor, particularly any form of organized labor. Karl Marx had written his Communist Manifesto in 1848 and it had struck a deep fear in the leading capitalists throughout the growing industrial economies of the world. Both European and US industrialists and governments were extremely wary of the dangers that could arise if the workers of the world actually did stand up and unite. Labor efforts were fought intensively. Not by improving working conditions or wages. They were fought with violence and armed forces, including hired goons, local militias, national guardsmen, and in some instances the US Army. This was not always done with an explicit "anticommunist" focus, but that ideological ghost was never far from the surface.

Unions were not common in the late nineteenth century and were treated as either illegal or un-American organizations in most parts of the country. Working conditions in heavy industry were extremely unsafe. Working 12-hour days five to six days per week was quite common. And, wages were constantly being cut with no notice or justification. Many people struggled to survive. Just as we saw with the slavery model, when the power imbalance between the wealthy few and the working masses is overexploited, social instability becomes unavoidable. Compounding matters, over half the workers in these industrial enterprises were immigrants who were ripe for exploitation. I will not go through all the uprisings and strikes, but I do want to illustrate a few of our strategic concepts in the story around the great railway strike of 1877.

A series of small strikes and disturbances in 1876 culminated in a large-scale strike launched on July 16, 1877 against the B&O Railroad in West Virginia. The railroad had cut wages three times in less than a year to the point where the average worker was making less than 75 cents per day. In their case that was per 16-hour day. For those doing the math that means just over four and a half cents per hour. The people working for the railroad were not part of any formalized union. They were just unanimously past their breaking point. The third wage cut was a third strike for the company—pun intended.

The flip side of the monopoly leverage enjoyed by the B&O business was the impact caused by the strike. Once work stopped in West Virginia in a matter of hours all shipping came to a halt in Chicago and Baltimore, as well as most of Maryland, Virginia, Ohio, Indiana, and Illinois. Sympathetic workers took up the cause in other railroads as well, spreading to Pennsylvania, the Erie and NY Central Railroad, the Great Western lines, and others. Manufacturing operations across Ohio began shutting down. Petroleum exports from the harbor in Baltimore ceased. The rolling mills, foundries, and refineries throughout the great cities of Cleveland, Chicago, St. Louis, and Cincinnati all ground to a halt. The shipments of grain and cattle from the Midwest to cities like New York also came to a halt, generating fears of urban famine. It was estimated at the time that over 1 million people were thrown out of work and that the economic damage was greater than that of any military blockade in the history of the young nation.

The president of the railroad called for help from the US Army. State Governors and President Rutherford B. Hayes all issued proclamations calling for an end to the strike, all to no avail. The US Army was called on to intervene, dispatching troops from all over the country to the beset cities and towns. General Winfield Hancock was placed in overall command from a base in Baltimore while General Sherman and General Schofield took charge of key sectors. Military barricades were erected in Baltimore, New York, and Philadelphia. The Philadelphia operation included 24-hour patrols of every access point to the Pennsylvania Railroad by over 6,000 soldiers and 8 artillery batteries. That's right, artillery batteries. In city after city railroad cars, grain elevators, depots, and hotels, not to mention stores and private homes were looted, burned, and gutted. Years later a writer in *The Atlantic* magazine described it as an American Reign of Terror.

Eventually, the federal troops began to restore order, bringing the strike to an end after about 45 days. Afterward, the union movement around the country was emboldened by the glow of power that had been demonstrated. Government and business also reacted to the event. Laws were passed to forbid "conspiracies" against economic interests. Local armories were built and stocked with munitions to prepare for future uprisings. Those armory buildings you see in towns throughout the Northeast and Midwest were not built to fight invading armies. They were built to fight and kill Americans who sought better wages and working conditions. It was the industrial version of the military force used to suppress plantation slave rebellions. We substituted the slavery of African Americans on plantations for the exploitation of immigrants in factories, mines, and foundries. Those weren't equivalent, but they were both morally bankrupt. When a socioeconomic paradigm requires the deployment of military forces to suppress and kill citizens that is prima facie evidence of its utter failure.

The ability of the railroad to unilaterally reduce wages three times in a year is a reflection of the disproportionate economic power between the company and the people who worked in it. Their repeated exercise of that power with no value offered in the process generated predictable resistance. There were no options for the people working there other than their own exercise of power. And that in turn brought out the power of the US military to resist the resistance. The resulting struggle created no value for anybody, only destruction and the loss of lives. The reactions of the government afterward made it abundantly clear that the value of the property destroyed in the event was vastly more important than the lives of the people involved. Hidden beneath the surface were a set of ideological beliefs justifying the violence against US citizens by US troops. The entire process is centered completely on power and its ability to destroy property and lives.

Entirely lost in the process is any shared agenda for the creation of value and the pragmatic needs of both the company and the people who worked there. This emphasis on power over value is one of the deep flaws of traditional labor movements. It's understandable, and as the example illustrates, has been unavoidable, but it's never constructive. Similarly, the unrestrained exercise of power by companies and capital interests is equally ineffective in the long run. However, since the power imbalance exists, it will almost always be exploited.

The overall assessment of the nineteenth and early twentieth-century industrial paradigm is decidedly mixed. There were many solid examples of real value creation that were amply rewarded. However, there were also many examples where economic power was abused to the detriment of other market participants and to the well-being of people and society. The industrial abuse of people was so extreme that it caused social upheavals requiring armed intervention. From a human standpoint, conditions were certainly better than actual slavery, but economically, not by much. As we will see, the economic foundations were loaded with many other hidden fault lines all of which had their origins in the failures of the paradigm. Unregulated, rampant economic power is not only destructive of people and society, at the end of the day it destroys itself as well.

TAMING THE ECONOMIC BEASTS

The government interventions to address the failures of the industrial paradigm relied on a mix of military and judicial powers. As illustrated by the railroad strike, military power was used to suppress the needs of people who were being abused by the market power of industry. Unbeknownst to all at the time this was not only a moral failure, it would lead to a deep economic failure as well. While government did not intervene on behalf of people, it did take actions to assist those businesses who were being abused by the excesses of the growing monopolists. Those regulatory efforts were intended to ensure the markets were driven more by value than the abuses of power that were so prevalent at the time.

There were two major legislative acts in the period aimed at reining in the worst commercial abuses. The first was the Interstate Commerce Act of 1887. This act was specifically aimed at controlling the secretive monopoly pricing games employed by the railroads and included the creation of the Interstate Commerce Commission. They were charged with investigating complaints of unfair shipping rates and were empowered to generate cease and desist orders accordingly. They had some success, though it was far from uniform. In fact, by 1906 they had lost 15 out of 16 cases that the railroads had managed to appeal to the Supreme Court.

The second major action was the passage of laws to restrain monopoly practices through the Sherman Antitrust Act in 1890 and the Federal Trade Commission Act in 1914. Both acts outlaw any "contract, combination, or conspiracy in restraint of trade" and any "monopolization, attempted monopolization, or conspiracy or combination to monopolize." There are many gray areas, but the courts have been emphatic and consistent that any arrangements to fix prices, divide markets, or rig bids are illegal. It's no coincidence that these are all practices that were rampant in the late nineteenth century and had led to the destruction of countless businesses at the hands of those who truly deserved to be called "robber barons." Unfortunately, just as was the case with the ICC, almost every Sherman Antitrust suit brought to the Supreme Court failed to achieve any result. Perversely, the act was most effective when used against the growing unionization movement. Those were deemed to be "conspiracies in restraint of trade," which was not at all what the Sherman Act was intended to address.

It would take another 20 years before this travesty of justice was fixed. Legislation to support the needs of people has been devilishly difficult to establish in this country. It took a civil war to abolish slavery. The next major focus was around child labor. Once machines were doing much of the "heavy" work, companies began to realize they could use children for much lower wages than adults. In the industrial paradigm of the mid-1800s in both Europe and the United States it was common for children as young as seven to begin working 12 or more hours a day, six days a week. They toiled in factories and deep in coal mines. The British began fighting this through the passage of child labor laws, though it would not be until 1878 that comprehensive protections would be established. It took even longer in the United States. Congress made two attempts to create child labor laws, in 1918 and 1922. They succeeded in passing new legislation on both occasions, only to have the new laws struck down through Supreme Court challenges. It would not be until 1938 through the development of our third paradigm that the United States successfully managed to outlaw this practice. There are those in conservative circles even today who feel the loss of this exploitative tool is a major hindrance to their economic freedom. One of their strategies is to reconstitute the Supreme Court so that court could once again strike down this most basic protection for America's children and the attendant erosion of adult wages.

One of the other keys to understanding the interventions of the late nineteenth and early twentieth centuries is the distinction between *productive capital* and *speculative capital*. Think of "productive capital" as the actual investments needed by businesses and their operations and "speculative capital" as all the rest. Industrial economies are heavily dependent on ready access to capital. This means there *must* be an excess of capital beyond what is needed by businesses in the market at any given time. There must also be differences in investment risk profiles ranging from highly conservative to "riskier" or more speculative. Therefore, a certain amount of speculative capital, above and beyond what is immediately needed by businesses, is actually essential to ensuring that the real needs of business are met. However, beyond a fuzzy, indeterminate level, there's a point where speculation takes over and the productive value of capital can itself be jeopardized.

An interesting example of this phenomenon is the dynamics around the Chicago Board of Trade. CBOT was formed in 1848 as a nonprofit entity by 25 individuals in the Midwest agricultural business. Trades through this market exchange established prices for grain and other commodities and enabled the creation of a futures market. These are vitally important business tools for those in agriculture. In that business, crop prices are always high at planting time when supplies are low and then drop when the harvest comes in and supplies are robust. In that environment it can be nearly impossible to get a consistent return on one's planting investments. Hence the creation of a futures contract that guarantees a farmer a set price on his eventual harvest.

The CBOT was successful, growing to roughly 150 members by 1856. In addition to the trading exchange they also established standards for both quantities (exactly how much is a bushel of wheat) and quality, which greatly improved operational efficiencies and expanded the market of buyer and sellers. It also brought in speculators. That wasn't necessarily a bad thing. Their participation greatly improved liquidity and enabled some riskier ventures to be explored. These are some of the good things that come from free-flowing capital markets.

However, it also began to attract individuals who would attempt to corner the market for certain commodities. Wheat was a particularly favorite target at the time. The number of people with sufficient capital to play this game was small, but there were still countless attempts. In many instances, they succeeded in driving up commodity costs, in some cases by greater than 50 percent. This created artificially inflated costs for buyers and heavily distorted incentives for farmers to produce far more than the market actually wanted. By the early twentieth century the "true" underlying market prices were collapsing, and production was soaring far beyond what was marketable. The "free" as in "unregulated" market was badly distorting the "free" as in "true" market, destroying economic value for all but the speculators. In the context of the enormous, long-term, structural forces that had been reshaping agriculture for over a century, as well as the immediate problems of excess capacity and falling real prices, these distortions wrought havoc throughout the agricultural sector.

There were numerous efforts to establish a regulatory intervention that would retain the healthy aspects of speculative capital while eliminating or reducing its harmful dimensions. A few of the more chronic bad actors were banned from the market altogether. Still, it would not be until the mid-1930s, as part of the third paradigm, that these efforts began to be effective. Figuring out how to set regulations so that free markets are in fact true markets isn't easy, but it is essential. In fact, as this example illustrates, unregulated markets usually become little more than gambling halls, rendering their primary market-enabling purposes utterly ineffective.

This combination of government interventions had some success but none of them dealt with the core underlying economic shifts from agriculture to industry nor the real needs of people. We would not see that until the 1930s, the pivotal period for the shift to our third paradigm. Out of the horrendous economic collapse of the Great Depression we would finally begin getting our economy on a sustainable path that was consistent with the nation's social contract.

2

THE TWENTIETH CENTURY:
FROM COLLAPSE TO GLORY

WHAT WE DID and what happened in the 1930s and 1940s provides a perfect case study of both the challenges and opportunities we face in the twenty-first century. Going into the period we had used government power to eliminate slavery and had passed legislation to prohibit child labor and to curb the exploits of monopolies. These were our first halting steps toward ensuring that markets worked as society wanted. Unfortunately, there's little else good that can be said about these efforts. Abolishing slavery took a civil war that caused massive American casualties and the legislation, while reflecting the will of the people, was consistently being overturned by the courts who reflected the will of wealth. Not only was the will of the people being violated, there were deep and growing fault lines throughout the economy that were about to trigger a seismic socioeconomic collapse. That collapse was devastating. What followed is one of the greatest examples in world history of the power of government to reshape and redirect markets, to create an entire new paradigm, all for the benefit of the entire nation.

We face the same situation today and need the same collective courage and will to form and deploy our fifth paradigm. That may seem hopeless today, but the challenge was far greater back then and we did it. With the right leadership, this is well within our powers.

HIDDEN FAULT LINES

The sixteen years from 1929 to 1945 did more to impact the world than probably any other period in the twentieth century. There are economic statistics that have only regained their 1929 level as recently as the early 2000s. Many people, particularly in the United States, describe this period with the shorthand of "the 1929 crash led to the great depression which was resolved by World War II." This is often accompanied by the phrase "the New Deal created America's safety net." This description has elements of truth but ignores the most important parts of what actually happened.

It was the decisions made during this period that defined the socioeconomic paradigm that would lead to the greatest improvements in economic productivity and shared prosperity in the history of the world. This was not about creating a "safety net." It was about redesigning the basic structure of the economy to ensure the new economy would work for the country on a sustainable basis. In a deep and profound way this represented the replacement of a failing nineteenth-century capitalism originally centered on agriculture with a new twentieth-century capitalism centered on ensuring that the growing industrial economy worked for society. As we contemplate the socioeconomic paradigm we need for the twenty-first century it is vital we understand the details of what was done, what worked, and what didn't.

This is a well-trod topic with deeply embedded conceptual grooves. Whole libraries could be assembled with nothing but books on the Great Depression. Most of those are rooted in some specific frame and see the entire period through that lens alone. All of those lose the dynamics essential to understanding the underlying complex systems with their emergent behaviors. The more recent sources on the subject are so twisted by various ideological frames it can be hard to even settle on the basic facts of what happened. In writing this book I discovered I needed to go all the way back to studies published in the late 1930s and early 1940s before I could find solid data that were free from "spin." In addition to the challenges of getting the facts straight there are other problems as well. The very nature of "work" was different from what we now experience. In many cases, people did not have "jobs" so much as they had "trades" with work being sporadic and unpredictable. This deeply stressful employment practice has been steadily returning in recent decades.

Having sorted through these data issues I will cover this period in five stages: the lead-up to the crash, the crash itself, the crash becoming a depression, the recovery process, and, finally, the years of World War II. Let's start the examination of the lead-up period by looking at agriculture. As we've noted, the US, and indeed global, economy was shifting from agriculture to industry and from primarily rural to primarily urban. As one would expect in that context, the agricultural sector was experiencing a prolonged period of deflationary pressures. The value of farmland itself dropped by almost 50 percent from 1910 to 1920 and then another 15–20 percent throughout the 20s. This was the largest decline in farmland value since the 1770s. In the aftermath of slavery, for most farmers, the land itself was far and away their largest and most important capital asset. The enormous decline in the value of their land put many farmers in a negative asset position. Credit was cheap and could be used to buy grain and fertilizer for planting, but this needed to be recouped through the harvest. When the prices of agricultural commodities began dropping steeply in the 1920s, they were placed in a difficult squeeze. Rural bankruptcies were an early indicator of what was to come.

The industrial sector was growing strongly with productivity rising at rates that had not yet been experienced anywhere in history. The diffusion of steam power, electric lights, and tooling and the widespread adoption of leading production processes were integral and crucial drivers. With unconstrained exuberance, production levels were soaring. However, wages were not increasing, and the overall level of consumer demand was showing distinct signs of weakness. Henry Ford was so alarmed at the danger of inadequate demand that he actually doubled the wages of the people working in his factories. He was the exception. Overall, the surpluses being generated by the tremendous growth in productivity were being held at the top.

This lack of real wage growth was slowly undercutting the level of aggregate demand in the economy. This was offset to a degree by people spending on credit and accumulating debt. By 1929, the overall level of debt in the United States, both consumer and industrial, was at 300 percent of GDP, a dangerous level. Some put the blame for this on the low interest rates set by the Federal Reserve and that undoubtedly was a major contributor. However, when the overall economy is growing strongly and wages are not expanding, there's a completely natural tendency to spend a bit beyond one's means.

Adding to the demand pressure was the simple slowing of population growth. One of the ways of representing an economy is that GDP is equal to the size of the workforce multiplied by the productivity of that workforce. Productivity was growing as was GDP, but the workforce part of the equation was slowing. There were two main causes of this. First, there had been a long-term slowing of the birth rate since 1910. That drop can be almost directly tied to the shift from a rural, agrarian society to more of an urban, industrial society. On most family farms children contributed to the chores that needed to be done. In contrast, in an industrial work setting, they are additional mouths to feed. The family ethics and desires are no different. After all, people are people. It's just that the economic pressures work differently. The second growth-eroding factor was the severe government-imposed limits on immigration enacted in the 1920s. Immigrants had made up over 50 percent of the industrial workforce and the sudden loss of that growth driver was material.

While demand was weakening, factory production levels were soaring. This caused companies to begin slowing their capital investments in tooling and new construction. With all the productive uses of capital slowing at the same time that the overall capital pool was growing, the excesses flowed into speculative areas, particularly the stock market. This led to a soaring market, with valuations steadily exceeding any underlying business fundamentals. Superficially, all was fine. GDP growth seemed solid and the stock market was booming. As events were about to demonstrate, at a deeper level it was a totally different story.

The first stage of the stock market collapse happened on Thursday, October 24, 1929. There had been growing concerns about demand-related earnings weakness across the economy. The initial sell-off moderated slightly the next day as J.P. Morgan and other major financiers attempted to shore up stock values. The following Monday it was clear those individuals and institutions did not have enough resources to stem the tide. On Tuesday, October 29, 1929 the rout ensued. While the initial drop was dramatic, both in absolute amount as well as percent, the level it reached by the end of the year was still almost 50 percent higher than the market had been in 1926, only three years earlier. It was a major event, but there had been major "corrections" before. The real trauma to the market would occur over the next two years as the market drops actually accelerated, eventually reaching a level roughly 10 percent of its absolute peak.

It was the panic that followed, along with the government reactions, that transformed what might have been a "correction" into a wholesale depression. The weaknesses throughout the economy were substantial. Consumer income had been stagnant for well over a decade and their debt burdens were high. Bankruptcies were spreading through the agricultural sector. Many of the rural banks were small and began going through bankruptcy themselves as the land mortgages they held went underwater. The market crash created a crisis of confidence in all financial institutions. People began streaming into the banks to withdraw funds that the banks were unable to provide, adding to the panic.

The early policies enacted by the government did nothing to address these issues. If anything, they actually magnified their impact. One of the key ideologies was the belief in the importance of the gold standard, limiting the money supply to real assets on hand. Because of this belief, the government refused to provide the kind of cash liquidity the banks needed to forestall the bank runs that were happening throughout the country. They also felt it was crucial to maintain a balanced budget. As tax receipts fell, they raised selective taxes and cut government spending, further weakening the overall demand environment. Then they passed the Smoot-Hawley Tariff Act, over the signed objections of literally 1,000 economists. Those tariffs backfired resulting in a further dramatic drop in demand, particularly in agriculture. The rural bankruptcy tide became a tsunami.

With demand dropping everywhere, businesses stopped investing and began laying people off in substantial numbers, which served to further weaken demand. Banks, particularly in rural areas, were failing by the thousands which drove the banking panic to epic proportions. Still, the government held firmly to its austerity policies, and the steadily reinforcing downward spiral continued to wreak havoc. Given what would come next it's natural to wonder why so little action was taken to address the severe toll being taken on the country. This is one of the many examples in this book where a deep faith in ideology took precedence over the direct observation and empathy for the economic, social, and human tragedy playing out throughout the country. In addition to a deep monetary faith there was also a belief that this whole set of events was "normal" and "healthy." The theory was that the economy needed to rid itself of all that inefficient use of resources in the agricultural sector and in uncompetitive companies. In fact, the belief held that any intervention would just prolong the agony. This faith in ideology over reality exists to this day and there are many who believe that the US auto industry should have been allowed to collapse completely in the 2008 recession. Not many of those people live and work in Detroit.

Government Redesigns the Economy

With the election of Franklin D. Roosevelt all of this would begin to change. His actions and the beneficial impact were almost immediate. The steadily collapsing banking industry was the first priority. He started with a four-day "banking holiday" to allow time for him and the new Congress to pass the Emergency Banking Act. This law allowed the Federal Reserve to open the fiscal spigot and allow banks access to cash to meet the demands of depositors. Within a month money began flowing back into the banks. They also passed the Glass-Steagall Act that established boundaries between the banking industry and the vastly more speculative securities firms. That assured people their savings would not be intermixed and subjected to the risks associated with the world of speculative capital. That act also established the Federal Deposit Insurance Corporation (FDIC) providing further assurance against risk. The near constant failure of banks throughout the 1920s came essentially to a halt. Finally, the Securities Act in 1933 and the creation of the Securities and Exchange Commission in 1934 brought an end to many of the corporate financial excesses and abuses of the prior decades. Companies were now required to disclose details about their balance sheets, income statements, and officer compensation. They were also now forbidden to indulge in insider trading schemes.

Collectively, these regulatory frameworks would bring an end to the failing "wild west" stage of US capitalism and set a solid capital foundation essential for the health of the new industrial economy. The deployment of our third paradigm had begun.

This was a crucial start, but there were still several other structural problems that were vital to address. The entire agricultural sector of the economy was a disaster. The productivity improvements that lay behind the century-long shift in the role of agriculture in the economy were still growing strongly. With improved automation, seeds, insecticides, fertilizer, and crop management, volumes were soaring and prices collapsing. Farmers were dumping excess corn into lake Michigan, letting wheat rot in their fields, and having livestock slaughtered and left for buzzards to feed upon. All while other areas of the country were grimly facing the risk of starvation. The miraculous invisible hand of the market seemed to have failed utterly. Economic theory asserts that when prices collapse producers will cut back, reducing supply and leading to price recovery. That might make sense in an ivory tower, but when you're a dairy farmer with debts to pay and prices collapse, your only option is to produce more milk, not less. As bad as the situation was in 1933, nobody knew that the farms throughout the Midwest were about to be hit with drought in 1934 and 1936. The Dust Bowl was just over the horizon. A perfect storm of economics, technology, and nature herself had become unavoidable.

In a partially doomed effort to prop up prices, the government created the Agricultural Adjustment Act of 1933. This was intended to restore agricultural prices to pre-WWI levels by drastically reducing supply. The haphazard crop destruction by farmers would be replaced by government-planned destruction coupled with subsidies to *not* plant land. This did stem the collapse, but it left the government in a role of trying to manage agricultural production which was unprecedented and fraught with risk. Indeed, none of those plans included a forecast for the Dust Bowl, so while the intervention helped, in many instances it was highly problematic. It may not have been perfect, but the use of government subsidies to reduce supply and boost prices did work and continued to do so right up to the mid-1990s. Ironically, this "government managed" economic pillar of the third paradigm would be one of the last to be replaced.

With the benefit of 80 years of history we can see the underlying long-term shift that was under way. The productivity of agriculture over the next several decades would continue its sustained explosion enabling the sector to feed the country, indeed much of the world, even as the number of people involved declined radically. Thanks to ever more efficient markets, like the CBOT, the goods and capital to fuel this process would flow freely and powerfully. What would not flow easily were the families on their farms—the people whose work was no longer needed. None of this was evident at the time. What everyone could see was the havoc being inflicted on these families, their communities, and whole sectors of the country. The underlying structural shift was absolutely inexorable. The capital shifts had not been easy, and had not been "absorbed," but capital itself doesn't suffer in the process. People do.

As we will see, the exact same pattern is playing out today across our industrial sectors and their communities. The same pattern, to the same degree, and with the same community devastating results.

If agriculture was the structural "problem child" in the 1930s how was the "prodigal son" of manufacturing doing? Not well. In fact, it was in need of as much intervention and help as agriculture, just in a very different form. As in the case of agriculture, productivity was booming. Prices were also in a dangerous deflationary spiral. More important, industrial wages had not progressed with productivity. If this continued and the nation became a workforce paid at levels insufficient to support a family, this "industrial revolution" would become an armed revolution. There were many contending factions and ideas. The US Chamber of Commerce proposed the creation of legal cartels to enable industries to begin fixing prices. Congress proposed limiting the work week to 30 hours. What emerged was the National Industrial Recovery Act which was later struck down by the Supreme Court and then followed by the National Labor Relations Act. Both of these laws set minimum wages and maximum working hours in place. Both also allowed industries to voluntarily establish "codes" that would include price floors. The Labor Relations Act added to these a set of laws enabling the formation of unions and establishing rules for collective bargaining. The 40-hour work week became standard quite quickly. Within a year of the first of these acts industrial production was up 45 percent.

It took longer for the union-driven debates about wages and working condi-tions to sort themselves out. Eventually, these would become what we think of today as "good" jobs, with good wages and benefits. For probably the first time in history a socioeconomic paradigm unfurled where people saw their true economic value reflected in their paychecks.

These were major steps on a path to a great American future. However, unemployment was still far too high. Rather than just give people money to get by, Roosevelt decided to put them to work building America through the Works Progress Administration (WPA), Civilian Conservation Corps (CCC), and related programs. There were certainly boondoggles in the pro-cess, but the results stare us in the face every day. They're so prominent we forget their origins. Over 8 million people would build over 600,000 miles of roadways, and 125,000 public buildings. The Lincoln Tunnel, Triborough Bridge, and LaGuardia airport all came from those hands. Millions of acres of farmland were restored through flood and erosion control. The Tennessee Valley Authority electrified and rebuilt much of Appalachia, enabling an entire region of the country to expand industrial production. The CCC planted liter-ally billions of trees, built lodges, trails, and facilities in more than 800 parks, and established forest fire fighting techniques and infrastructure throughout the nation. The great dams including Hoover, Grand Coulee, Bonneville, and Shasta provided the electric and water infrastructure to support our growing western populations and industrial activity. The impact on the country was huge. The impact on the morale and pride of the nation incomparable.

The seemingly endless death spiral stopped, and the economy began to grow. We had found the new combination of "rules," the new paradigm, that would generate the complex emergent behavior we needed as a society. That included the work rules, union, and capital regulations, but it also included directly dealing with the nation's infrastructure as well as the human and com-munity toll arising from our massive economic transition from agriculture to industry.

Which brings us to the eve of World War II. As noted at the beginning of this section, one version of this story is that the country was just bum-bling along until we had the "good fortune" to get into a war and that made everything better. It's as if killing people en masse and destroying property on a historic scale in some way restores economic growth. The country was far from "bumbling along." Economic production, employment, and productivity growth had all rebounded. We had not reached pre-crash levels, but we were back on track.

World War II did have a dramatic impact. It was not the death and destruction of war that changed our trajectory. In some profound ways, it was the same formula we saw in the early 1930s. Instead of dealing with the 33 percent productivity impact of workmen shifting from a 60-hour work week to a 40-hour work week, they were just gone. Many of their replacements were women who lacked the physical strength to perform tasks men had done before, at least without automation and equipment. The necessity to innovate in tooling and production processes took on a whole new urgency.

All of a sudden it was no longer just the shareholders worrying about needed capital investments. It was the US government. Just as they had aided US workers with programs like WPA and CCC, the government began providing businesses with the capital they needed to overhaul production facilities, processes, and machinery—on a huge scale.

Back in 1932 the Hoover administration had created a government agency called the Reconstruction Finance Corporation (RFC.) This agency was basically a bank that worked with the rest of the private banking industry to extend loans that those entities were unwilling or reluctant to provide. The tools used by the RFC to mitigate those risks were wide ranging and included things like enabling the organization of rural cooperatives in support of electrification projects. Their scope of projects remained quite small under Hoover but expanded significantly under FDR. That expansion went into overdrive on the eve of World War II.

To support the war effort the RFC provided $50 billion in government backed loans to build and capitalize literally thousands of factories across the country. That's literally an order of magnitude larger than what had been spent on the WPA programs. In most cases they were leased to companies for $1 per year and given to them for free after the war. Machine tools in US factories doubled from 1940 to 1945. The providers of those tools felt the demand was infinite. Most estimates conclude that well over 50 percent of the total capital equipment stock in the United States by the end of the war had been paid for by the US government. Nobody referred to any of that as "corporate welfare." It was a shared commitment to enable our nation to create more value than anyone else on earth. And, all of that was before the orders started flowing in. The government placed orders for over $100 billion in goods in the first 6 months of 1942 alone.

All of this investment drove government debt substantially. It would peak in 1945 at 113 percent of GDP. However, almost half of that was in the form of "War Bonds" that were pegged at a 2.5 percent interest rate. When the war ended and the wage and price controls that had been put in place were lifted, inflation began to grow. The combination of pent-up demand and strong union pressure on wages both contributed. The net results were negative real returns on war debts, while postwar investments in industry generated fabulous returns. By 1955, the government debt to GDP level had dropped to a perfectly healthy 51 percent, without having to impose any drastic austerity measures that would have choked off growth.

THE NEW DESIGN WORKS!

The economic success that emerged from the deployment of our third paradigm is unrivalled in history. There are those who wonder how this could be. How could a reduced work week, increased wages, and competing with the government for labor lead to improvements in economic growth? There's a complex answer to that question and a simple one. The complex answer starts by noting the change in capital incentive arising from increased labor costs. There was now a much stronger incentive to substitute capital equipment for labor. Those investments had certainly existed before the legislative changes, but once labor costs went up, the capital intensity of one industry after another began rising steeply. The resulting productivity increase more than made up for the increased labor costs. After all, that was the exact basis of the business case for every single one of those investments. The companies who provided these innovative tools began to grow strongly. Entire industries of production machinery providers began to grow. And, most important, because of higher wages, the consumer demand for the goods being produced was both restored and put on a growth path that now mirrored industrial growth instead of diverging from it. The failed divergent path from the prior decades had emerged from the difference in *power* between companies and workers and was inherently flawed. On that path, every productivity improvement yielded more production with lower wages and aggregate demand. On the new path, both the company and the workforce were getting the *value* from the productivity. Value creation was in the driver's seat where it needs to be for sustained economic growth.

And, here's the simple answer. It wasn't about labor, it was about people.

People matter in this world. Their dignity and well-being shape, indeed *define*, the value of our society. The depression had delivered a devastating blow to the country's sense of worth and identity. It hit every one of us, changing how we felt about ourselves, our families, our communities, and our country. What all those new programs did was breathe confidence, life, and pride back into every one of those dimensions.

When the men and women who fought the war returned they had a new freedom to decide exactly where to go and what to do. The GI Bill helped immensely by supporting their education needs and home mortgage financing. They also returned with accumulated savings from the World War II period. Consumer goods and spending had been severely constrained, and the pent-up demand was substantial.

We now had an updated national infrastructure thanks to the WPA and CCC programs, a completely retooled industrial base, built to scale, with productivity-enhancing processes and capital, paid for by the government, and a motivated, trained workforce with built up savings who were earning good wages all of whom were inspired by our country's victories over our enemies and our own self-doubts. The better question would be, how *couldn't* we grow?

Let's close this with a few observations. The boom that was to come did not arise out of tax cuts. It did not arise out of protectionism. It did not rely on wage cuts or declining working conditions. It was not based on deregulation. It did not entail a collectivization of agriculture, nor a public seizure of private assets. It was not based on a return to excess speculative capital. It was not based on denying people access to health care. It did not require we leave the elderly to survive on cat food. It did not require us to tear down things that were "evil" by dint of government money like the Triborough Bridge or the grand lodges in our National Parks. We did not have to shut off the government-built electrical grid in Appalachia or the western states. It happened because we as a society had decided that farmers needed to survive; and that, if manufacturing was to provide the jobs of the future, they needed to be good jobs with good wages and good working conditions; and because we collectively, through our government, had just footed half the capital costs to retool a newly proud and inspired America.

Some of the most important lessons for the twenty-first century come from this period. We've forgotten just how amazing the difference is between a government locked in ideology and one that takes bold, pragmatic actions to fix deep socioeconomic problems; a government that delivers on its responsibilities for the national infrastructure and social well-being. The deep underlying current of people, as people, revealed one of its crucial dimensions in this period. People don't "flow freely," they are not economic "production factors," and the forces that fuel them include pride, dignity, and the values of family, community, and country. There is substantial economic might that flows when the true value of people is fully engaged, and when their true economic value is reflected in their wages. We used our democratic government to intervene on the behalf of people to redesign the economy by altering the power dynamics enabling them to achieve those wage gains, to reduce fear, and to enable respect and dignity.

These were not government guarantees, nor was this a government takeover. This was a redesign of the core rules that shaped how our complex society and economy behaved. Those new rules reflected the real-world needs of our maturing agricultural sector and our rapidly growing industrial sector. Not only were they not based on any particular ideology, they flew in the face of the prevailing ideologies. In fact, they were fought by ferocious ideologues at every stage. What they did reflect was a deep commitment to ensure our new economy really worked, and that meant that it worked for everybody, not just a few.

In an unexpected way this was a reaffirmation of the socioeconomic paradigm put in place by our Founding Fathers. That design balanced the power of our economy with the power of our government. When the markets failed our society, we were in position to turn to our government to exercise that corrective and balancing power. When we did so, we thrived.

As we look to our future we can and must do the same once again.

OTHER NATIONS, OTHER STRATEGIES: FROM FAMINE TO FASCISM

When seen in this light it's interesting to look around the globe at other examples of the struggle to absorb such a deep structural economic shift. After all, there is nothing uniquely American about the shift from agriculture to industry. That's happened everywhere.

At almost the same time as the American Depression, the Communists in the USSR were applying their approach to the problem. They used forced collectivization and relocation of the population. The result was the famine of 1932–33 which left somewhere from 2 to 5 million people dead. More would follow. The philosophy that explicitly used a government takeover and treated people as "workers," as economic production factors, was a horrific failure.

The Chinese warlords did no better. Their feudal system hadn't really changed yet, but the ineffectiveness of the government was pronounced. The famines of 1928–30 and 1936–37 lost an estimated 8 million lives. When the true communists eventually assumed full power, they were even worse. The Great Chinese Famine of 1958–62 was caused by the Great Leap Forward, their version of a forced agricultural collectivization and relocation program. That cost the lives of an estimated 15 million people. People aren't "workers" and using government power to force them to "flow" based on economic shifts is not an answer.

Turning to Japan, their feudal system was also slow to evolve. In the early 1900s they began creating local "cooperatives" that operated in many ways like the CBOT in the United States. They provided services to farmers as well as those both buying and selling to them. Just like in the United

States they had their own form of "speculative" exploitation. The cooperatives were implicated in the rice riots of 1918. Those riots arose when farmers saw steadily declining purchase prices from their cooperatives at the same time the consumer prices of rice skyrocketed. Rice farming has been protected in one form or another ever since. In addition to subsidies to reduce planting they have relied on steep tariffs against imports. For market purists this is anathema and can be "proven" to be economically suboptimal. Others simply note that small farmers were able to continue to eke out a living and there were no large-scale famines.

The European colonialists did not resort to the kind of "mass-relocation" strategies of the communists, but in the end their laissez-faire approach was no better. Their exploration of the continent of Africa had taken most of the nineteenth century. Northwestern Africa was mapped by 1835, followed by vast stretches of the interior during the 1850s and 1860s. The final charting of the Nile River would happen in the ensuing decades. At the Berlin Conference of 1884–85 the major European powers agreed on a set of rules to guide the colonization of Africa. These set out territories and claims for different European nations with a shared agenda to carve up the vast continent. In 1870, only 10 percent of Africa was under European rule. By 1914 it was 90 percent. Over 9 million square miles of territory were added to European control.

The Europeans found that gold, copper, tin, diamonds, ivory, cotton, rubber, cocoa, and tea were all available in abundance. The coastal regions offered stopover ports for the rapidly growing Asian trade. The colonies were managed to extract as much of this wealth as possible providing agricultural goods based on African labor and the raw materials needed to fuel the rapidly growing industrial sectors of Europe.

The locals were treated with thinly veiled contempt. One administrator commented that "the colonizer must never lose sight of the fact that the Negroes have the minds of children." Conditions and treatment were often harsh. In the Congo under Belgian control, 8 million of the total population of 16 million would die between 1885 and 1908. The citizens of Africa were left with a poorly managed and unproductive agricultural sector along with the raw material extraction infrastructure of the industrial sector. That's the lowest value component of any industrial economy and one that leaves enormous environmental destruction in its wake.

The British colony of India was handled a bit differently, though once again the outcomes were dire for the local population. The Indian climate is one of extremes. Much of the year can be unbearably hot. Then come the monsoons. Without the monsoons nothing can grow. In 1875 there were no monsoons throughout most of southern and central India. In 1876 they failed again. The prior three years had produced an enormous abundance of wheat and rice, but the vast majority of that had been shipped to Britain. The precolonial tradition of local village and regional stockpiles no longer existed. Famine began to set in followed by food riots. With the growing scarcity, prices began to skyrocket all over the subcontinent. Even in regions where famine had not set in, food costs escalated so high the average Indian could no longer feed themselves nor their family.

The central viceroy, Lord Lytton, was a devout worshiper of free markets. As his authority, he cited Adam Smith's passage from *The Wealth of Nations* that "famine has never arisen from any other cause but . . . government attempting . . . to remedy the inconvenience of dearth." Clearly the lack of rain had nothing to do with the failure of the harvest. He issued the order that "there is to be no interference of any kind on the part of the government with the object of reducing the price of food." His status report back to the home office denounced all the "humanitarian hysterics." He organized a grand pageant that included a weeklong festival for 68,000 top officials and princes that ranks to this day as perhaps the most colossal and expensive meal in the history of the world.

Over the next two years, British grain merchants would export a record 6.4 million tons of wheat from India to Europe. The viceroy was presented with a proposal to divert some of these shipments to feed the local populace. He declared it would be a mistake to "spend so much money to save a lot of black people."

From 1876 to 1878 over 10 million Indians would die of starvation. In many cases, the food was available, but simply priced too high for Indians to buy. It was truly an "inconvenience of dearth." None of them endured the kind of forced mass relocation of the Communists. They just died in place because the power imbalance between people and wealth was left unaddressed.

Europe itself was able to use its colonies to absorb some of the social and economic disruptions of the shift. They were, nonetheless, not immune and were also caught up in the complex dynamics unfolding after World War I. The Russian revolution had ignited large and growing communist movements all over Europe. For those seeing what was happening in Russia this was a scary prospect. Just as we saw in the United States, the disproportionate power of industry over labor led to poor working conditions and steadily shrinking real wages. These conditions triggered numerous large-scale industrial strikes in almost every European nation. Those strikes stoked fears of a violent Bolshevik revolution erupting almost anywhere. At the same time, the perceived early success of the Fascists under Mussolini in Italy led to widespread nationalist movements. The deep social stresses of the shift were pushing the continent toward polarized extremes.

The situation in Germany was further compounded by the actual outcome of World War I. Most Germans did not blame themselves for the failure of that war. The Germans felt their loss was because of feckless bureaucrats, bankers, Bolsheviks, and Jews. Being forced to disarm, surrender territories, and pay reparations was humiliating and deeply undermined the standing of the Weimar republic that had been put in place after Kaiser Wilhelm's abdication.

Hitler joined the German Workers Party, which was to become the Nazi party, as member number 55. His oratorical skills soon made him their top spokesman. He filled his speeches with what he himself would later describe as "colossal untruths." The lies were loud and relentless. His targets did include Jews, but he also railed against the French and British for their reparation demands and heavily against the communists.

The Nazis were very much in the minority until the Great Depression hit. After that, both the Nazi party and the Communist party began to grow steadily, with supporters from all walks of life. By the end of 1930 the Nazis had risen from ninth position to the second largest political party after the Social Democrats. The Communist party was right behind. After a narrow election victory over Hitler in 1932, Germany's president, Paul von Hindenburg, sought to form a coalition government with the Nazis. Hitler was adamant that he would only do so if he was personally in charge. The fear of an eventual communist success led Hindenburg to conclude by 1933 that he should accept Hitler's terms. Hitler took over legally, despite never having won a majority in a national election.

The existing political establishment felt confident they could manage Hitler. He seemed a far lesser evil than the communists. Hitler, obviously, had other ideas in mind. He told a colleague at the time that "Our great opportunity lies in acting before they do. We have no scruples. . . . They regard me as an uneducated barbarian. Yes, we are barbarians. We want to be barbarians. It is an honorable title."

It is startling to look at that 1933 quote from Hitler alongside a 2018 quote from Steve Bannon. He told an audience of the National Front in Lille, France, "Let them call you racist. Let them call you xenophobes. Let them call you nativists. Wear it as a badge of honor."

Then, as now, the enormous socioeconomic stresses created by the large-scale transition from one economic paradigm to another led inevitably to the rise of extremists of all political stripes. Markets on their own simply cannot make adjustments on that scale for the simple reason that people are people not economic production factors. They don't "flow" and when they and their communities get torn apart they look for political solutions that match the level of pain and stress they experience themselves and see all around them. In Germany of the 1930s that meant a choice between Hitler and the communists. The German people chose Hitler. In the United States at the time, we chose to redesign our economy, so it would once again work for all of us. It was a far better choice and one we face again today.

The exact details of what happened around the world varied based on local government, culture, and history. However, the deeper pattern was everywhere. Capital and goods may fluidly change, but the people involved are another matter. One can use the totalitarian method of coercive starvation, the capitalist method of price-based starvation, or the humane method of government subsidies and protection, but something must be done to deal with the reality that people don't "flow" the way capital does. Those ideologues who maintain that subsidies and protections are a form of communism need to be reminded of what real communism has actually involved. The United States may have allowed a level of distortion to the precious market, but we did not lose millions of people to mass starvation, nor did we forcibly relocate people from their homes and communities.

THIRTY YEARS OF SUSTAINED, BALANCED ECONOMICS

To understand just how incredible the economic boom of the late 1940s actually was we need to look at a few detailed numbers. The first point is that the period of 1870–1929 saw a fairly consistent improvement in overall productivity of 1.9 percent per year. This applied both to output per person as well as output per hour. It was a remarkably consistent trend.

During the early years of the Depression the output per hour of work took a brief dip, but then returned to its prior growth rate. The output per person dropped much more steeply, because of the severe drop in overall employment. In the late 1930s right up until the United States' entry into the war in 1941, employment was recovering, along with the total hours worked, though both numbers were still well below the long-term trend line. Then during the war, the productivity level jumped to well over 20 percent above the long-term trend of 1.9 percent per year. After the war with employment strong, the hours worked dropped below the long-term trend, reflecting shift from a 60-hour work week to the now standard 40 hours. However, overall productivity continued to grow strongly, well above the historic 1.9 percent.

One of the obvious contributors to that improved growth was all the deployed capital coming out of the WWII production investments. A second major driver came from the improved skills and education level of the workforce. The overall education level had been growing strongly since the beginning of the twentieth century. That had been a factor for decades. However, many people also returned from the war with new skills in things like logistics, supply chains, and planning. Many more would take advantage of the GI Bill, getting high school and/or college educations. In fact, almost 8 million

Americans would take advantage of this program. This produced a spike in the availability of more advanced skills. The new workforce was substantially better trained and educated.

For economists there is a metric known as total-factor productivity, or TFP, which includes all the other contributors to productivity above and beyond the basic skill and capital elements. This includes things like technological advancements, process improvements, organizational and management improvements, infrastructure improvements, etc. These are the "extra" contributors that add to the underlying drivers of education, skill, and capital.

In the early part of the twentieth century these "extras" added generally less than half a percentage point to the overall equation. Then in the 1920s they began adding just over one point. In the 1930s that grew to a bit over 1.5 points. In the 1940s that exploded to nearly 3.5 points. Remember, this is all against a long-term baseline of 1.9 points. The TFP accelerator slowed a bit in the 1950s and '60s, but only in comparison to the 1940s. In the 1950s it was just over 1.5 points and in the 1960s just under 1.5 points. The party came crashing to a halt in the 1970s which will be central to our later discussion. This enormous productivity bubble, beginning in the 1920s, accelerating through the 1930s, exploding in the 1940s, and then being sustained for another 20 years was the central economic driver of the growth in the US standard of living in the twentieth century.

Part of the key to that success was the corresponding growth in real wages. From the mid-1930s, when people were first empowered to fight for improved wages and reduced working hours, all the way up to 1973, real wage growth tracked almost exactly with productivity growth. Unlike the nineteenth century, the economic benefits of productivity growth were now flowing to both companies as well as the people working in them. Those individual earnings improvements flowed into consumer spending. People moved to the suburbs, bought new cars, radios, and appliances and began to take family vacations, the early harbinger of a leisure industry. That consumer spending provided the fuel for business growth as well. The growth in aggregate demand was now strong enough to sustain the growth in production. The socioeconomic equation was in balance, possibly for the first time since the beginning of the Industrial Revolution.

The new economic force that enabled that sustained balance was the collective bargaining power of unions. Like any complex system, changing the bargaining rules in the 1930s did not "dictate" a result. But it did reshape how the system behaved. In this case, using unions to address the power imbalance between people and wealth brought wages and productivity in line and yielded a far more sustainable economy. Unfortunately, this success came with a fatal flaw. The union movement, from its inception, was focused almost exclusively on power, not value. As always happens when power is the sole focus, the movement generated massive resistance and has struggled to maintain its vital role in our economic formula. That failure is one that haunts us to this day.

To close out this section let's note the astonishing economic vitality that emerges when infrastructure, capital, wages, people, and technology all align in a complete and balanced paradigm. Markets can "self-tune" this process, but only to a degree. When economic shifts deeply disrupt the core engine of the economy and its associated employment, markets reach their limits. Those limits arise from the inherent truth that people are people, not economic production factors. When the people and communities at the core of the economy get ripped asunder, the economy needs intervention to achieve the right new sustainable design point. Those interventions are a core responsibility of our national government.

The new design must deal with the realities of the old economy while being optimized to that of the new. It must balance the power of people versus business, and it must ensure that the new regulatory environment serves to make markets, not fracture them. It needs mechanisms to ensure that the balance between aggregate demand and production is maintained. It needs tax, fiscal, and monetary policies that ensure that adequate liquidity and capital flows are maintained. It must include government investments in science, research, and development as well as maintain our existing infrastructure and build the infrastructures needed by the new economic design point.

None of these are simple tasks. There are no textbooks that hold the answers. Academic experts can help identify and classify the problems, but few offer much in the way of practical advice. What's essential is to maintain a pragmatic perspective rather than an ideological one; to deal as much as possible with root causes centered on value, power, and people; and to recognize we're adjusting the rules that will shape the dynamics of our free and democratic society, not defining deterministic plans or outcomes.

Most of all, our leaders and government need to inspire confidence and hope in people. People need to know that their lives matter more to our society than any ideological purity around the "sanctity of markets" or any other drivel. Their inspiration must be rooted deeply in all the complex human hopes, dreams, fears, and limits that come when we address them as people, not "workers" and not "interest groups."

As we sit here in the early twenty-first century we need a new socioeconomic paradigm. Once that design is in place, then, and only then, will people and markets once again carry our nation forward on a sustainable basis.

3

THE DISASTROUS PIVOT TO THE TWENTY-FIRST CENTURY

THE INCREDIBLE ECONOMIC success resulting from FDR's redesigned economy came to an end in the early 1970s. All of the positive and well aligned trends around wages, productivity, growth, wealth generation, and living standards began to break down. The nation executed an economic pivot to our fourth paradigm that would eventually lead to the incredibly perilous state we're in today.

This was not some poorly conceived policy lever pulled by the Nixon administration at the time. It involved a wide variety of complex and interlocking shifts, most of which had nothing to do with the government. Both the composition of the workforce and the core, value creating engine of the economy were undergoing radical change. The socioeconomic impacts from those early trends were then kicked into high gear under Reagan. The spectrum of policies implemented and encouraged by his administration accelerated and expanded the process of hollowing out our value creating core and crippling the demand side of our economy. While it would be ferociously denied by its proponents, the fourth paradigm was and is focused on the extraction of value out of the economy, not the creation of new economic value.

These trends were amplified even further by technology shifts, corporate management and governance shifts, the rapid growth of the global economy, and an unprecedented breach of our national social contracts for health, education, retirement, and support for the poor. To understand what we need in our fifth paradigm we must examine each of these unfortunate trends. We've been on this problematic path for well over four decades and our redesign must correct all these broken shards.

THE PIVOT FROM GLORY TO PERIL

The 1970s and early 1980s were difficult times for our nation. We struggled to get ourselves out of the morass in Vietnam, faced the crisis of Watergate, endured the boycott of our essentially needed oil, and grossly mismanaged our national currency. All of these brought major disruptions economically, socially, and to our core confidence in government and our nation. As bad as these were, their impact for the most part has faded with time. The real pivot was much deeper, and those trends and impacts continue right up to today.

Probably the most important shift was the waning role of manufacturing as the core value generating engine of the economy. As we'll cover shortly, employment in that sector wouldn't peak until 1979, but even in the early 1970s its role was slowing. There was also an incredibly important shift as women began entering the workforce in steadily growing numbers and increasingly important roles. That structural employment growth substantially expanded the potential scale of the entire US economy. This happened at the same time the post-WWII productivity bubble began to slow, creating a shift in the core math behind GDP growth. What had been slow workforce expansion with strong productivity now became strong workforce expansion with slowing productivity growth.

Meanwhile the steady decline in union membership was reaching a point where it was increasingly unable to counter the economic power of business. From 1973 right up until today wages have been stagnant in real terms and have stopped tracking productivity growth. When you look at the specific details it's a dramatic and hard shift. It's not slow and it's not subtle. Thirty years of history suddenly changed direction. The result has been to undermine and erode the demand side of our economy, which at this point has reached the same stage we hit right before the Great Depression.

Just as we saw in the late 1920s, when the demand side weakens, capital flows into speculative opportunities. With a brief interruption caused by the Great Recession, speculative capital has exploded from the early 1970s up until today. It will come as no surprise that the math of all those statistics has resulted in inequality levels now actually exceeding that of 1929. As an aside, it's important to note that's a math comment not a merit comment.

Lurking behind the scenes for much of the 1970s were a pair of philosophies that would become the central pillars of the acceleration of these trends under Reagan and every subsequent administration. The first of these, neoliberalism, is one we've already met. That philosophy would be the rationale behind the massive privatization and market experiments that would create such enormous damage to our economy and our social contract. The second, equally destructive philosophy was a shift in the beliefs about corporate governance to favor shareholders above all other interests, including the core value-creating engines of the firm.

THE REAL PURPOSE OF BUSINESS: THE FALLACY OF OWNERSHIP

This philosophy of corporate governance has become one of the most insidious and destructive conceptual traps in the fourth paradigm. In addition to shareholders being the sole motivating purpose of the firm, the frame asserts those shareholders are the "owners" of those corporations. Versions of this belief have been around for a long time, but it really sunk its deep roots in the late 1970s. This frame enjoys near religious adherence down inside the rabbit hole so recognizing it for pure modern fiction is a big step out into the light.

Let's take this apart in a few layers starting with the word "owner." It's a big and slippery word. It carries all kinds of tacit beliefs about rights and powers. I "own" the coffee cup I'm currently sipping from and that means I can throw it across the room, leave it dirty in the sink, or use it to drink coffee as I am. I could even theoretically sell it to someone in a garage sale, but if I assumed that sale would yield anything like my original purchase price I'd be sadly mistaken. In that sense, my ownership of the cup has limits. Specifically, I own the cup but not its value. When we use the word "own" it brings many assertions about rights, but often omits the reality of those limits. It's also a word that basically ignores the notion of responsibility. I have rights with respect to my coffee cup, but no responsibilities. In fact, in some ways the notion of "ownership" frees me from any obligations or responsibilities. As I said, it's a slippery word and all those tacit interpretations can be extremely problematic when it comes to the socioeconomic construct we know of as a "business."

Now let's look at a modern company and track its evolution from a venture-capital funded startup through a series of growth stages. In the first stage, I as the founder may have reserved 60 percent of the equity in the firm for myself, my partner, and my expected management team. I may have split that as 30 percent for me, 20 percent for my partner, and 10 percent for the rest of the management team. The other 40 percent I provide to my investors in return for the financing I need to get the business launched. That financing may be used for some amount of capital investment, but it also includes the initial payroll for everybody working in the company until we begin to get revenues. At this point the ownership is clear, we all have a stake in the success of the company, the investors are risking their capital, and my team and I are risking our time and talents. We agree to a series of quarterly checkpoints to track our progress on development and sales. When I find myself struggling to find the right person for a critical hire, my investors help make connections with talented recruits. Everyone is contributing in their own way to our efforts to create value. It's also important to note in that example that the ownership share of the capital providers is less than 50 percent. That's actually the norm. Nobody in the venture world would assume the mere provision of initial capital was worth more than half the full value of the company.

At a subsequent stage I may decide I need to raise more capital. However, I've already allocated 100 percent of the equity in the firm. To raise more, somebody, if not everybody, from the first stage has to agree to dilute their holdings, even though they've done nothing "wrong" nor has the amount of risk they put forth been diminished. All the investment may have been spent and my team and I have been hard at work, but that's all "sunk." Hopefully, the projected value of the firm has grown so that the reduced ownership share still has value appreciation otherwise I've got a tough sell. My team and I all want the added investment, in some cases to grow the company and in others just to continue getting paid. The initial investors are being asked to reduce their stake in the company to make room for others. At this point the share of ownership allocated to the providers of capital may well exceed 50 percent and the longer it takes to reach a stable operational business the more that stake is likely to grow. That's *not* because capital is contributing more to the value creation process. In fact, its real share of value creation is almost certainly diminishing. The growth in equity participation by capital is an artifact of the process, not a reflection of increased contribution to value creation.

Now roll forward several years after many ups and downs to the point where the business is successful, and my team and I have decided to "go public." I bring in a Wall Street firm who agrees to underwrite the process and they set about determining an initial share price and associated valuation. The Wall Street firm contacts their best customers (and internal buyers) and offers them a chance to be the first in line to acquire the stock at that initial share price. On the big day the shares are sold, my company, my team, and our early investors all finally capture the value we've worked so hard to create. And then, by the end of the day, the value of the stock has doubled. My team and I may or may not have converted some of our initial sales back into the stock, but regardless of what we've done all those "best customers" of the Wall Street firm have just cashed in a value capture equal in total to everything we had worked so hard to build. They did literally nothing to contribute to that process. The doubling of the value of the stock was not a fluke. The Wall Street underwriter was careful to set the initial offer price to ensure they could appropriate a value in a single day equivalent to what my team and I had labored on for years. We struggled, sweated the hard times, and took tons of risk. For all of that we did get our payoff. However, this new set of shareholders just got the same payoff with no struggles, no expended time and little to no risk.

Now roll forward again, to where I've issued a few more rounds of shares, and all the original investors have long since departed. My partner and I along with our management team hold lots of shares, but they're worth only a few points of equity. We issue quarterly reports on earnings and have occasional stockholder meetings attended by various financial institutions and possibly a few actual investors. The sales of our stock are primarily controlled through those institutions and rolled up into mutual funds and literally none of that investment flows to the company. Lots of people get excited when we launch new products or announce competitive wins, but none have any involvement in that value creation process. Their decisions about when to hold or sell the stock are based on their own financial considerations. Their focus is on their ability to capture some piece of the value my team and I are creating. They have zero involvement in the actual value creation process. By this point, my capital is now being raised through my own cash flow, loans, and maybe a few occasional new stock issues, though those are mainly associated with executive compensation plans.

The fiction of ownership definitely has reality in the first stage of that corporate evolution. However, it dilutes quickly and by the last two stages calling shareholders "owners" is an utterly inaccurate description of their role. They are holders of stock, not "owners." Frankly, most of them aren't even really stakeholders. In many ways they have become a version of the "looters" abhorred by Ayn Rand. They're capturing value they've done absolutely nothing to create.

The real purpose of business is to create value in the marketplace. It's *not* to enable massive value capture for outsiders with no involvement in that value creating process. That's a conceptual frame introduced and accentuated by the finance industry to enable them to siphon off the value created by every other part of the economy. They built that frame by arguing that maximizing the market capitalization of the firm was the best way of ensuring the firm truly was creating value. However, that subtle shift introduced countless conceptual diversions, many of which have reached the stage where they actually jeopardize the core value-creating engines of the economy.

To understand how this happens we need to dive into a little bit of finance. A firm's market capitalization is equal to the number of shares in the market times the price per share. The price per share is equal to the earnings per share times a number known as the price-earnings ratio or P/E. There are many factors that go into a company's P/E, but one of the primary drivers is growth. From that pair of formulas, we can see that companies have three major ways to increase their stock price. They can increase their growth, which should drive up their P/E; they can increase their earnings with the same number of shares; or they can reduce the number of shares in the market at the same earnings level. Mathematically, any of those, alone or in combination, will increase their earnings per share.

Let's look at the ways each of those three strategies can go wrong. First, growth is generally considered a good thing but not all growth is the same. When a company's growth comes from real, sustained success in the market that's great. However, companies will often strike short-term contracts that provide immediate results but at the sacrifice of the long term. They can also sacrifice profitability and in many circumstances jeopardize long-term customer relationships. The growth focus can also cause companies to pull forward deals from subsequent quarters introducing volatility that can damage the long-term financial health of the company. Furthermore, in many cases the focus is on profit growth, not revenue growth and that introduces all kinds of additional and problematic financial shenanigans. So, growth *can* be good, but we can't take that for granted.

How about earnings, surely that's a universally good thing, right? Well, let's think about our three main pillars of economic value creation. For firms focused on operational efficiency value, the earnings focus can be healthy, at least when there aren't big changes happening in the market. The big mistakes tend to come from issues around timing. A company may need to make operational investments that create a short-term reduction in earnings in order to achieve a much more substantial long-term sustained value. This is a very common trap and frequent cause of failure. Firms focused on innovation face even bigger problems from an earnings agenda. The market is littered with companies who did great in venture mode, but once faced with the quarterly earnings crunch did not sustain their investments in ongoing innovation activities and soon found themselves by the wayside. Firms focused on customer intimacy face similar deep challenges. Customer engagements are situations that frequently need investment, customization, service, and flexibility in timing, all of which can be anathema to a quarterly earnings agenda. Far from being a reliable tool to ensure long-term economic value creation, the earnings focus is actually fraught with strategic risks to the core engines of value creation.

The third ingredient in the formula is the number of shares in the market. Stock buybacks are the tool of choice to manipulate this piece of the equation. This seemingly creates no operational penalty to the firm, other than the demands it places on cash utilization. But that's actually pretty important. After all that's what sustains a company's ability to create value. This has become an enormous factor in the market and a substantial vehicle for the transfer of value away from the real value creators in the market. In many of my earlier examples the "looters" were catching an "unearned ride" but in this case they're actually draining the cash lifeblood of the value creators. They've become leeches on the economy.

The neoliberal faith relies on many stories, many fictional accounts about the world. One of those stories is that the best way to ensure that businesses create value is to allow the finance industry to siphon that value away. It's pure fiction. This successful story line has drained an enormous amount of the economic lifeblood of the nation away from our crucial value creators. It's also one of the primary reasons for the breakdown in wages that's such a deep issue in the nation.

How Modern Corporations Work

Corporate governance is not the only misleading and inaccurate aspect of understanding modern businesses. When most people think about a "business" they have a fairly clear and simple concept in mind. They might envision a retail shop where goods arrive in a storeroom, get brought out and put on display, and then get sold to customers. Or, they may envision a factory with a large, nondescript building, a receiving dock where raw materials arrive, and some sort of workflow with machines and people working to transform those raw materials into finished goods that then go to a shipping area for transport to their customers. In both cases the assumed management structure is hierarchi-cal and fairly simple. There's a store manager or a plant manager in charge of the whole operation, engaged in ensuring the work gets done on time and with acceptable quality.

There was a time when that model was reasonably accurate. It was about 50–100 years ago. These days all of that activity is little more than a surface-level manifestation of what's really going on. This is particularly true for any larger organization, but even fairly simple operations have layers of complexity that would surprise most people. Way back in 1946, Peter Drucker published his study of the inner workings of General Motors in his book, *Concept of the Corporation*. To this day that book remains on the reading lists of MBA pro-grams all over the world. Instead of having a monolithic hierarchy with clear command and control from a single leader, Drucker observed, even medium size corporations often have multiple divisions with their own structures. They also break down and manage every work process and activity. Much of that work is actually performed by the plethora of specialty groups like customer service, marketing, and finance, all of which work together in a loosely choreo-graphed dance. There certainly are clear leaders, and the very top still has ulti-mate authority, but the actual operational mechanics are highly decentralized. Command and control exists in a balance with debate and consensus. There are "line" organizations with clear profit and loss responsibilities who work in coordination with "staff" functions that specialize in various disciplines. These different groups often work in "matrix" structures with multiple management chains, measurements, and incentives.

From the mid-1940s until today all those diverse activities have also been evolving globally. The earliest form of "multinational" was often the simple practice of selling one's wares to markets in other countries. What might have been done originally through some sort of intermediary, or export firm, companies began doing themselves, placing their own people and resources in overseas offices. Those early sales functions evolved over time to include ser-vices and marketing. Soon after, companies began looking at putting different manufacturing operations in place to serve those markets directly. Whole divi-sions began to be built in these overseas locations. Before long companies were acquiring other companies in other countries based on their local knowledge, contacts, and resources. These were the early seeds of what would grow into entities that now span the globe.

By the early 1970s, multinational corporations would account for 70–80 percent of all global trade. These firms have enormous flexibility in deciding where to place jobs and operational centers, giving them substantial negotiating leverage with national governments. Furthermore, intracompany trade normally operates on the basis of internally defined "transfer prices" that may or may not have any connection to external prices. This makes it possible for companies to manipulate exactly how and where they report profits. Since taxes are based on profits, not revenues, multinational firms can "place" profits in countries with low tax rates. One of the most common ways to do this without impacting any real physical activity is through internal royalty payments for intellectual property. In fact, there are estimates that 80 percent of global technology royalty payments are actually intracompany, most of which is driven by tax avoidance.

As multinationals develop it is more than just the scope and complexity of the operation that changes. Organizational and management structures begin having a distinct multinational diversity. What might begin by having US executives stationed abroad evolves to promoting and hiring senior executives from the local population. The entire organizational culture begins to operate and "think" differently. The original "country of origin" can easily evolve to a quaint artifact of history, something that becomes essentially irrelevant to actual operations.

This kind of organizational specialization and "de-structuring" has been under way for probably a century. It accelerated dramatically over the last several decades, changing the very nature and fabric of the corporation. The story of how this came about begins in the early 1980s with the rising economic importance of Japan.

Japan had been a factor in the global economy for decades, but for most of that period they were synonymous with poorly made cheap "junk." That would begin changing in the latter half of the 1970s until by the early 1980s people feared they would economically take over the world. Countless articles were written predicting the demise of one US industry after another. For any-one with a clear grasp of economics those fears were wildly overblown. As we discussed earlier, any country's GDP can be equated to the size of their workforce multiplied by the productivity of that workforce. As nations reach comparable stages of development with associated education, infrastructure, and capital deployment, their average productivity tends to converge with each other. That means their relative size ends up being driven by the size of their workforce. The Japanese workforce was a quarter of the US workforce, mean-ing it could never seriously rival the United States in overall scale. This simple equation will completely flip when we get to the discussions about China and India in the twenty-first century.

The fears of Japanese dominance were fueled by the powerful rise of their auto industry and the seeming inability of US auto manufacturers to respond effectively. There were many reasons for this, most of which are out of the scope of this book. One of the primary answers was hidden in plain sight. The Japanese were maniacal followers of the quality principles articulated by W. Edwards Deming. As businesses all over the world began realizing how crucial this was to the seemingly unstoppable Japanese they all went back to school on quality. Literally. In that period the number of management education classes on the topic of quality absolutely exploded. The management teams of every major company on the planet began learning a whole new set of management principles. This rippled from the most senior levels right down to the shop floor.

Much of that learning is also out of our scope, but there were two prin-ciples every manager and executive learned that have changed our business and economic structure in ways that very few understand. The first, and simplest of these is the notion of *continuous improvement*. We tend to think of change in big steps that are highly visible. What Deming taught was that slow, steady, almost invisible change can be far more powerful and transformative if it is managed in a way that it steadily accumulates. It's the difference between an earthquake leaving a crack in the ground and the creation of the Grand Canyon through millennia of slow erosion. It is precisely this sort of slow, steady, invisible change that has been occurring inside businesses for decades that has changed how they function in deeply profound ways.

The second, and equally impactful principle is *benchmarking*. This simple practice has had far more impact and significance to the twenty-first century than most people realize. What Deming taught, and the Japanese had embraced, was the notion of learning *best practices* from other companies. A team of managers from company A would pay a visit to company B and discuss the tools and techniques they had tried and found to be most useful for some specific business process. Company A would then adopt some subset of these for their own use and share it with Company C, when they came for their benchmarking visit. These types of discussions were easiest when they involved companies that were not competitors or were from other industries. However, Deming taught that even between competitors there could be opportunities for constructive exchanges. Companies all over the world have now been doing this systematically for decades. When we begin assessing the US socioeconomic system we will use benchmarks with other nations as a primary diagnostic tool, just as is done every day by modern business leaders.

Then in the mid to late 1990s an unexpected thing happened. Software companies began writing application packages that embodied those very same best practices. The practices themselves began to converge, making it even more fruitful for those software companies to include in their offerings. The world of business practice is enormous, with all kinds of complexity and variation. No one would have expected it to begin "standardizing," and yet that is exactly what's been happening. As larger and larger chunks of business process began converging and those best practices were captured in application software that any business could buy, their adoption spread. This technology trend would intersect with a set of management trends to set the stage for a radical transformation of corporate structures.

The key management trend centered on out-tasking and outsourcing. Drucker's studies on the inner workings of corporations led him to be an early advocate of this trend. His observations on the internal specialization of different tasks and processes led him to believe many could be candidates for external sourcing. The practice had been around for ages, but on a relatively small scale. That began changing in the late twentieth century and accelerated dramatically over the last 30–40 years.

The final piece of the acceleration puzzle is something known as the Coase Theorem. This was originally articulated in Ronald Coase's 1937 paper, "The Nature of the Firm." It was further refined over the years and codified in 1960. It took a long while for his ideas to start appearing in reality, leading eventually to his being granted the Nobel Prize in Economics in 1991. His theory asserts that the primary determinant of which functions should be done within a firm versus which should be done by an external source are *transaction costs*. Transaction costs include all aspects of securing, managing, and controlling a business function. It's important to note that his theory is not based on there being wage disparities nor differential operating efficiencies. Those add to the equation, but even in their absence, once management transaction costs drop, processes can and will be outsourced.

The slow convergence and relative standardization of processes driven by global benchmarking has included all of the metrics and management activities associated with those processes. Those have also been embedded in software packages that are widely shared across industries around the world. Transaction costs have been plummeting as a result. This means almost every business process is beginning to feel the economic pressure of Coase's theorem. It's a new *invisible hand* that is subtly, but inexorably, pulling apart the fabric of traditional businesses. This is the real culprit behind outsourcing. It isn't evil Western managers nor inscrutable Chinese schemers. It's one of the many new "invisible forces" driving contemporary economics.

One of the key strategy questions for modern businesses is figuring out which processes are at the core of the company. The answer to that question takes us back to the concept of value creation. Every company needs strategic clarity about where and how it creates value, and needs to retain ownership and control of the assets, people, and processes that make that happen on a sustained basis. Everything else can be outsourced. Everything. When that happens, the bulk of the sheer activity associated with a business actually begins to happen outside of its "borders." It changes what a business is. Modern companies are not defined by the people and activities inside their boundaries, they are defined and operate through the networks of their associations.

This subtle economic force was strongly accentuated by the labor arbitrage arising from the differential workforce costs around the world. China's contract manufacturing was and is a part of that, but in truth it's been much, much wider than that. India, Costa Rica, the Philippines, Eastern Europe, and many other regions have been frequent destinations for work that is increasingly "free flowing." Standardized management of converging processes operating on a digital infrastructure is now allowing *work* to move instead of *people*. And that's exactly what has happened.

Hand in hand with these fragmentation trends have been orders-of-magnitude increases in the amount of collaboration that goes on between firms. There are certainly relationships that operate in a command and control structure, but the vast majority are far more collaborative than that nineteenth-century vestige. This is true across the spectrum, but particularly acute at the frontier of innovation. Today's innovations are not simple things. They really no longer spring from an inventor in his garret. They are incredibly complex, drawing on skills, resources, and creativity across multiple disciplines, companies, and nations.

This reality has turned the management of intellectual property (IP) assets on its head. The largest patent holder in the world is IBM. That's been true for a very long time and by a very large amount. The way IBM manages its patent portfolio provides a useful illustration of the new reality that emerged in the technology industry but is now a growing practice in many other industries. One of the things IBM realized as early as the 1960s was just how much IP was needed to build computer systems. IBM was large and an early leader, but there were still countless pieces of IP that were held by others. Consequently, they began a practice of "cross-licensing," in which IBM would approach some other large patent holder, like AT&T, and cut a deal in which each party granted the other free and unlimited use of their patents. This enabled both parties to operate "freely." If those deals weren't in place neither party would be able to make anything.

IBM refers to these as "freedom of action" deals and they were essential not just to IBM but for the whole industry to develop. As vice president of corporate strategy, I did a review of our entire patent portfolio. We found that we were using less than 5 percent of our patents in the traditional mode of excluding competitors from using our IP. We had another 5–10 percent we licensed to somebody else, so they could use the patent in that traditional mode. The remaining 85–90 percent of our portfolio was being used for freedom of action. In other words, the vast majority of the patents owned by the largest patent holder in the world are being used for the *exact opposite purpose* of the patent system. It was truly eye opening. Retaining our exclusive rights to the 5–15 percent where we wanted that exclusion was certainly important, but we realized what mattered most about our IP was using it to enable the *collaborative creation of value* across the industry.

This profound shift in the corporate management of IP is not reflected in any existing national or global trade regulations or policies. Not only can work now flow between firms and around the world, but innovation processes and the assets they create can as well. Once again, this trend offers substantial new threats and opportunities that our strategies need to address.

Unions Fail the Power-versus-Value Game

The shifts in corporate structure and the emphasis on shareholders over the core value-creating interests of business have unfolded at the same time as the decline in unions. Their power to bargain for work and wages waned just when it was needed most to balance these powerful and somewhat invisible forces. The trends were not related. They each had their own underlying drivers. However, the combination has been deadly for American jobs and wages.

The early union movements had been a necessary counter to the power of corporations. They achieved many valuable things that helped both workers as people and, through improved wages, had restore the balance needed for a healthy economy. Without their contributions the whole incredible post-WWII economic trajectory simply would not have happened.

However, they were also causing a great deal of problems. I had my own firsthand exposure to the craziness created by union work rules in the early 1980s when I was a young IBM systems engineer working with a customer who had a heavily unionized shop. One of my jobs was to oversee the deployment of new computer terminals. I would wait at the loading dock for the truck to arrive, with my clipboard in hand. When the truck got there a few men would come forward, take the boxes off the truck, unpack them, place the terminals on the floor and then remove the packing material. Nothing more. Then another group would arrive and pick up the terminals and load them on a cart. Nothing more. Then another guy would come and wheel the cart to wherever I told him the terminals needed to go. And nothing more. Then another individual would arrive, take the terminal off the cart, and place it on the desk where it was to be used. And nothing more. Then another person would arrive to plug it into the power socket. And nothing more. Finally, the last individual would arrive and plug it into the communications network. It was only then that I would be allowed to touch the terminal, set it up and test it. How many union workers does it take to install a terminal?

Aside from the obvious humor the example illustrates a few key points. This was a substantial and complex factory. Among other things they built the turbine engines that go in the M1A1 battle tanks. The people I'm describing didn't spend most of their time installing computer terminals. They were usually handling shipments that could range from large rolls of steel or aluminum to complex machine tools that were literally two stories tall. The forklifts and automated carts weren't all that complex to drive, but some amount of training was essential and safely navigating the shop floors with speed was a real skill. My terminal only needed a simple wall plug, but some of the machine tools had far more complex power needs. The trades associated with all those tasks were real and did have a true and valuable element of specialization.

It is possible to imagine a union that worked with management to figure out how to best use the workforce to most efficiently and safely accomplish all the tasks at hand. Indeed, there are many such examples. Both the hotel and airline industries in the 1960s struggled to match available workers with unpredictable and fluctuating demand. Their respective unions worked out solutions that met both that business need and the individual challenges of people who needed some level of predicable work and wages. But, that was not the usual focus for most unions. Unfortunately, the primary focus was using union power to demand work rules that ensured as many people as possible could play a role. They had little to no direct interest in the value the business was trying to create so they used their power to extract value for their members, not maximize the shared value of the enterprise.

That focus on power over value wasn't a superficial point, it was an existential flaw. Right after the end of World War II the unions, particularly the CIO, began a series of strikes. This was a naked exercise of power at a time when the country had no patience with its blatant self-interest. The nation responded with its own demonstration of power. Congress passed the Taft-Hartley act which established a series of "unfair labor practices." It was fought intensely, but the statute exists to this day. It was an entirely predictable outcome. The exercise of power always generates resistance.

The political forces against unions ramped up their aggressive campaigns by tying the union movement to communism. It was certainly easy for them to make that claim. In the postwar period the AFL and the CIO were separate, and competing, organizations. The AFL had been vocal opponents of the presence of actual communists in the labor movement. The CIO, in contrast, welcomed them at least for a time. That support eventually changed and by the late 1940s or early '50s essentially all the real communist party members had been driven out of the union movement. Despite this fact, the accusations of external communist influence continued to be effective as propaganda tools well into the 1960s and 1970s.

Beginning in the early 1970s the union movement began to lose their collective battle over wages. Much of this can be attributed to the growth of jobs in industries with weak or nonexistent unions. Some is also due to companies, and the courts, finding ways to limit the effectiveness of union organizing efforts. In the wake of the civil rights movement, affirmative action, demands for equality by women, and the slowly growing importance of health care and other benefits, the unions also had their plates filled with numerous issues above and beyond wages and work rules.

Then, on August 3, 1981, the air traffic controllers union went on strike. Reagan ordered them to return. Less than 10 percent of them complied. After two days, on August 5, 1981, Reagan fired all those who had not obeyed his orders and banned them from any federal jobs for life. It would take three years before enough replacements had been hired and trained for full nationwide flight schedules to be restored. The act emboldened employers all over the country to use the same "mass firing" tactic against union-ordered slowdowns or strikes. The union movement, which had been in steady decline since the mid-1950s, would never recover.

The combined effect of all these factors has been the return to the situation that created so many problems in the 1920s. Wages are no longer keeping pace with productivity gains and once again the economy is on an unsustainable path. That path continues to this day, along with all the problems it creates, and is a major contributor to our current crisis.

This combination of factors is critical to understanding our modern economy. From the earliest chapters of this book we've highlighted how the dynamics of markets can be destructive to people. For nearly 40 years this was balanced by the power of unions. Now that we have lost that balancing power and now that much of the *work* done by business can flow with the same independence as capital and goods, we've entered a new territory with new complexities. The potential destructive impact to people and communities has increased enormously.

However, there are equally enormous possibilities to bring work to people wherever they are. Our economic strategies need to be designed to maximize the upside of this new reality and minimize the damage done to our communities. The challenge is to find a "balancing power" or other economic driver to make this a sustained reality.

THE ECONOMY SKITTERS TOWARD THE BRINK

These business and labor structural trends unfolded invisibly as the economy went through a series of growth periods interspersed with slowdowns and recessions. The 1980s recovery began in 1983 and lasted about six years. Growth was fairly consistent, averaging 4.4 percent per year. This was followed by the weak and recessionary years of 1990 and 1991. Growth returned in 1992 and ran right up until the year 2000. Much of that is credited to the technology and internet boom. Once again, the growth was fairly consistent, but averaged only 3.8 percent instead of 4.4 percent. Then the internet stock bubble burst and 9/11 hit. Those shocks brought another two years of weak or recessionary results. The next growth period ran from 2003 through 2006 and averaged 3.1 percent, another step down. 2007 was weak and culminated in the crash of 2008 and 2009. The Obama recovery began in 2010 and was still going strong as of 2017. However, while growth has been fairly consistent it has ratcheted down once again to only 2.2 percent.

This trend, where each successive growth period is lower than the past, is almost completely due to the waning of the long-term productivity trend that began in the 1920s, peaked in the 1940s, and continued to propel the economy right up until the 1970s. Since then we have been steadily falling back to the long-term 1.7–1.9 percent level we saw in the latter part of the nineteenth century. Our simple little equation for GDP tells the rest of the story. GDP growth is equal to the growth in the workforce added to the growth in productivity. With the workforce relatively flat and productivity falling back to its long-term base line, GDP growth is mathematically doing the same. The only things that would cause a change in that trajectory would be either workforce expansion or improvements to productivity.

While the overall productivity of the economy has slowed, manufacturing productivity has exploded. The resulting decline in manufacturing jobs is eerily parallel to the loss of agricultural jobs in the 1920s and 1930s. Also like then, wage growth and the entire aggregate-demand side of the economy are no longer aligned with the supply side and unions are fading into the background. Wealth concentration and inequality are now at the same level they were in the gilded age. The complete economic parallel to 1929 is scary.

When the Great Recession of 2008 hit we were as structurally weak as we were on the eve of the Great Depression in 1929. It's well known that this was the worst financial crisis since the 1930s. What's less understood is how close we came to a repeat of that horrific event. Our story begins with the 1999 repeal of the Glass-Steagall Act, the depression-era regulation that mandated a separation between investment banks and commercial banks. While both speculative and productive capital exists in both of those banking systems, investment banks operate with much higher levels of speculative risk. The regulation was over 65 years old and the global banking and financial worlds had evolved considerably over that period. The assertion that it was in need of an overhaul to reflect contemporary reality had validity. However, the modern dangers inherent in mixing those two modes of capital were no different than they were in the 1920s and 1930s. By repealing the act, we were once again vulnerable to those dangers.

The repeal was followed by a period in which steady encouragement for increased homeownership, low interest rates, and a decline in underwriting standards led to an equally steady increase in risky real estate loans. Real estate seemed like an investment category that could only go up. Average US home prices increased by over 400 percent from 1979 until its peak in 2007. Banks felt certain those assets were secure even if the loans themselves carried risk. At its worst, banks began issuing so called NINJA loans which stood for No Income, No Job or Assets. These highly risky, subprime, loans carried high interest premiums. The world of global speculative capital was hungry for those premiums.

In 2004 the finance industry introduced a new set of financial instruments known as collateralized debt obligations or CDOs. These offerings took various different loans, with various risk levels, and blended them together. The core idea was that even if the riskier pieces of the offering were to fail, the overall value would still hold up. There were many of these ideas including hedges, swaps, and other tools all used to "manage" the risk. One company, AIG, used these same tools to offer "insurance" to those who were buying them. It was a circular house of cards. If all these new instruments worked, everything was fine. If they started to fail, then everything would fail because the whole system was built on a common set of assumptions about risk mitigation.

Once these instruments were in place the subprime mortgage industry exploded from 5–7 percent of all new issuances to 20 percent. The whole field of "residential mortgage-backed securities," or RMBS, grew overnight. These were now supposedly "low risk" and "high yield" investments, exactly what the speculative capital market wanted. This type of financial behavior was also exactly what the original Glass-Steagall Act was intended to prevent, and that the new regulatory environment welcomed as "innovation."

When home prices began to fall and the bubble burst, all these "innovations" also began to fail. Lehman Brothers, holders of over $600 billion in mostly real estate assets, declared bankruptcy in September 2008. It was the largest bankruptcy filing in US history and it triggered a series of dominos, rippling through the overleveraged banking industry. The blended CDOs and swaps all began collapsing in value. The entire risk mitigation strategy proved to be wrong. The failing loans were not confined to any single entity, they had been spread to literally every corner of the global financial and banking industry. AIG's insurance policies never actually had sufficient assets to adequately back all these instruments and they began plunging into the same dire condition. With assets collapsing the banks all called in obligations from other banks, all of whom were facing the same calamity. It was a run on the banks, not from consumers, but from the banks themselves. One entity halted all withdrawals from its hedge funds because of "a complete evaporation of liquidity."

On the third day of the collapse the Secretary of the US Treasury and the Chairman of the Federal Reserve warned congress that over $5 trillion in wealth would disappear by that afternoon and to stem the tide they needed $700 billion in bailout money for the banks within three days. Despite everyone trying to minimize panic and the constant public reassurances from industry CEOs, those in the know realized we were literally only days or at most weeks from a complete collapse of the entire global finance industry. It was not only possible, but in fact probable, that absent government intervention over 50 percent of the wealth of the planet would be destroyed. Some estimates were much, much higher.

This led to the Troubled Asset Relief Program (TARP), whose original purpose was for the government to buy "bad" assets from the banks. Within days of its passage that plan was converted to one in which the government simply issued loans to the banks, infusing them with cash and allowing them to decide how to best use the funds. The full extent of these direct loans was later reduced from $700 billion to $456 billion. Almost all of the banking industry loans were eventually paid back, with the AIG bailout being a notable exception. Out of the $339 billion the government put into the banks, the country would make a small positive gain of just over $12 billion. When the loans to the auto industry, described below, and assistance to homeowners are added into the picture, the overall cost to taxpayers was $12–40 billion.

In addition to this highly public program the government put in place a semisecret liquidity pool that would only come to public light many years later. This pool made funds available to selected banks at rates below those from the official federal reserve. Those banks would avail themselves of approximately $7.8 trillion dollars from this "special" reserve. It was an absolutely massive infusion of liquidity at rates that enabled those banks to basically print money. Many of them used those funds to pay off the TARP loans that had many more strings attached to them.

One of the visible TARP strings was a requirement that any recipient of TARP loans not use that funding for executive compensation. Unfortunately, that string only applied to cash compensation which is normally a very small component of most packages. A later study looked at the stock options granted in that period to the top five execs of the top 18 TARP recipients and found they had made over $450 million from those grants. They may have been primary culprits in this disaster, but, thanks to taxpayer intervention, they bore none of the cost.

In 1929 it was the market that triggered a banking collapse. In 2008 the same connection worked in reverse, with the banking collapse triggering a collapse in stock values. By the end of 2008 Americas real estate equity would drop by $4 trillion, retirement accounts would drop by $2 trillion, and pensions would drop another $2 trillion. Over $8 trillion in total wealth would be lost in just over a year. The GDP of the entire economy at the time was $14.7 trillion. And, it could have been much, much worse.

All of that wealth destruction led to massive drops in consumer spending, triggering the Great Recession and loss of jobs. One of the worst hit was the US auto industry. GM and Chrysler were both facing bankruptcy and Ford was teetering on the brink. Over 1 million direct jobs were at stake. The entire Midwest economy would be ravaged if they failed. As happened in the 1930s many argued they should just be allowed to fail. What was eventually engineered was a government takeover of GM and Chrysler, an infusion of immediate funds, followed by a formal bankruptcy process and an eventual government exit from its ownership position. The initial cash infusion amounted to just under $81 billion, which was subsequently sold for a bit over $70 billion. The net cost of about $10 billion was a lot of money but compared to the potential economic consequences of a Midwest regional collapse was a bargain.

All of these direct, active interventions drew lessons from what happened in the Great Depression. There were many conservatives who wanted, even demanded, we take the same sort of austere actions that had transformed the crash of 1929 into the depression of the early 1930s. The "Tea Party" movement made that their centerpiece. They strenuously argued that any action by the government to help the nation would only accomplish the opposite. Fortunately, there were enough leaders who had learned the lessons from history that we avoided that path. Even though we dodged the worst depths it would take almost a decade for the overall economy to recover. We're still carrying all the debt associated with the government tax shortfalls. There are many who believe we'd be better off if we had allowed another, even deeper, Great Depression to happen. They think the debt would be lower and their relative financial position not much worse. It's an incredibly narrow and naïve set of thinking, but it's widely held. Many of the regulatory changes put in place in 2010 to prevent the recurrence of this sort of crisis have already been repealed.

As hard as it may be to believe, the finance industry and their conservative regulatory friends are well on their way to creating the next crash with almost the exact same characteristics as the last one. This time around, instead of dealing with unqualified mortgages to risky consumers, the focus is on unqualified loans to risky businesses. Once again, they're creating financial instruments that blend thousands of different loans with different risk profiles. Last time they called them "collateralized debt obligations." This time they're calling them "collateralized loan obligations," or CLOs. I guess they hope nobody notices that "debt" and "loan" mean essentially the same thing. Once again issuance of these instruments is rising rapidly and enabling rapid growth in bad loans to risky businesses. They're even moving toward the business equivalent of NINJA loans, by eliminating the normal covenant protections traditionally associated with high risk commercial loans. One of the specific protections put in place after the 2008 collapse was a requirement that any institution that issued these kinds of instruments needed to retain ownership of at least 5 percent of the risk. Several firms have already been granted exemptions from this requirement. That means they can avoid holding any of the toxic time bombs they're concocting and placing throughout the global economy. When the next downturn hits, it's a near certainty these time bombs will go off and once again wreak havoc on the world. One observer has remarked that its "possible" these CLOs and their associated debts (sorry, loans) will only trigger another massive recession instead of the more likely repeat of the Great Depression. If this crisis hits too soon, we could well lack both the financial resources and political acumen to prevent the complete economic destruction of the nation. This is a far greater existential threat to the US way of life than all the Islamic terrorists in the world combined.

THE SLOW-MOVING TRAIN WRECK OF EMPLOYMENT

When national news media provide regular reports on the overall level of unemployment in the country they're broadcasting what may be one of the least meaningful data points in the economic portfolio. It's in the dynamics underneath that number that all the promise and peril for society are hidden. I'll be unpacking this in layers, first to understand our history and then to understand our twenty-first-century roadmap.

We need to begin with the deeper story behind manufacturing. The evolution of manufacturing is directly analogous to what we saw in the transition from agriculture in the late nineteenth and early twentieth century. Just as was the case in that shift, total output from the manufacturing sector has *not* declined. The pattern in the case of agriculture was that employment first reached a peak percentage of the total workforce, then later reached an absolute peak in jobs, which was followed by an absolute decline. That's exactly what has happened in manufacturing, where the peak percentage of the workforce was around 37 percent right before World War II. The absolute peak was 19.6 million manufacturing jobs in 1979. Manufacturing employment then declined by over 7 million jobs between 1979 and 2015. That's an employment drop of over 35 percent even while overall output has continued to rise. The pattern and percentages have followed the agricultural path to a "tee."

One of the key points in that progression is that manufacturing employment began declining right after 1979, long before the Chinese had any impact on the market. If there was any real global competitive factor at work in that period, it would have been the Japanese. The decline did begin to accelerate after 2001, so there has certainly been an impact from China, it's just not the underlying cause. In fact, of those 7 million lost jobs, China is estimated to account for only 1 million. The major employment drops occurred during the recessions in 2001 and 2008 and did not recover. There's no question the first of those was accentuated by the entry of China on the world stage, but the deeper cause is automation and technology. Just as improved seeds, fertilizers, tractors, combines, and all the other agricultural technology enabled vastly more crop production with fewer people, the same thing has happened in manufacturing. It's not just robotic machinery. It's also processes, techniques, training, and the whole panoply of continuous improvement factors arising from the quality movement. The reason all these productivity improvements haven't lifted the aggregate economic numbers is the relative decline in manufacturing's contribution to overall GDP. Both the number of workers and total GDP contribution have dropped to around 10 percent.

Those jobs are not coming back any more than the agricultural jobs of the nineteenth century. In the years between 1979 and 2015 the US economy added a total of just over 52 million jobs. That's a substantial number. In fact, in represents just over half of the total new jobs created since World War II. The growth is usually attributed to the broad category of "services," but what does that mean? We'll examine this shift in much more detail in later chapters. For now, let's just look at the three largest categories.

Education and health care added over 15 million jobs, most of them in health care. Unfortunately, approximately 70–80 percent of those new health care jobs had nothing to do with actual care. They were centered instead in the administrative overhead associated with our dysfunctional health care system. So, probably 10–12 million of those new jobs were economically unproductive overhead.

The second biggest category is professional services which added over 12 million new jobs. Some of those are whole new job categories. Computer services and web design didn't even really exist as industries in 1979. Many others have arisen out of the deconstruction of businesses described earlier. That hyper-fragmentation was not solely an "offshoring" phenomenon. It also drove growth in a wide range of business processes that are now consumed as services. Those activities had always existed, so they weren't really "growth," but based on the Coase Theorem, the new structures are economically more efficient. All of those business service categories are solid, productive, valuable trends for the economy.

The third largest category is leisure and hospitality which added over 8.6 million new jobs. Over 90 percent of those jobs were in bars and restaurants. When you hear people say "we're shifting from manufacturing to burger flipping" that's what they mean. While that pejorative sentence may not be wholly fair, there's no question this economic restructuring has an unsettling mix of outcomes.

What's even more troubling is how much of this growth comes in the form of temporary, part-time, or contingent work. These "contract" jobs have no permanence and force people into situations with highly uncertain income. The majority also bring no benefits. It's a deeply stressful way to live or try and raise a family. This is the same type of employment structure that was common in the 1930s and that placed so much of the economic burden on people instead of businesses. It's returning in spades. The most recent estimates claim that 94 percent of all the jobs created since the Great Recession fall into this employment category.

These shifts are all still under way and are just the beginning of the story. As we've seen throughout, the economic blessings from steadily improving productivity bring their own curses on jobs. This double-edged sword is poised for another slice through our society. This time we have an amazing combination of wireless communications, sensors, data, mobile, artificial intelligence, electric propulsion, and battery technologies that are creating capabilities few would have dreamed possible. Both McKinsey and Deloitte have done studies on the impact of all these new technologies on jobs over the next 10–15 years. Their conclusions are sobering. The McKinsey study concluded that 60 percent of the jobs in both agriculture and manufacturing will be impacted by this next wave of automation. Not only are the jobs we've already lost in those sectors not coming back, there are probably many more losses to come. They also concluded 57 percent of the jobs in transportation and warehousing will be impacted. Those are jobs that have seen some impact already but much more is coming. Just go out to YouTube and look up "Amazon warehouse robots" if you want to see the future. But here's the real news. Over 50 percent of retail jobs and over 70 percent of hotel and restaurant jobs also have the potential to be impacted by the new technologies hitting the market. Since those have been two of the biggest sources of job growth in the overall economy you can begin to see a disturbing set of questions.

The bottom line of the McKinsey study was that roughly 60 million US jobs have the potential to be eliminated through all the new and emerging technologies. The Deloitte study used a different methodology, but also came to roughly the same number. Sixty million jobs lost. McKinsey cheerfully asserts that when this has happened in the past, something has always come along to create new jobs, though they acknowledge they have no idea what that might be this time. Following their rosy assumption, they conclude these improvements could add up to a 1.4 percent productivity improvement for the overall economy. Deloitte estimates there could be 20 million new jobs arising out of sheer economic growth. However, they observe the same wage gap disparity I've been highlighting and conclude that growth isn't likely unless we deal with the demand side of the equation. Both studies conclude we're looking at the displacement of 40–60 million jobs in the early twenty-first century. That's a lot. Its more than all the new jobs created since 1980. Its 6–8 times the total number of jobs lost in manufacturing. We need a strategy other than hope or rosy assumptions to deal with it.

4

WHERE MARKETS FAIL

O UR ATTEMPTS TO use markets in health care and education are two more hidden root causes of much of what is broken today. Current efforts to exercise a similarly flawed faith in markets to our national retirement is an enormous threat to most of the nation. To understand where we are we need to review a bit of how we got here and why market experiments in these sectors have been such devastating failures.

The origins of these mistakes can be traced to the early 1980s. Both Thatcher and Reagan responded to the many 1970s-era governmental failures with programs aimed at minimizing or eliminating the role of government in society. Reagan's famous line, "government *is* the problem" became the core governing philosophy. Regulations, all regulations, any type of regulation, were regarded not as "market making" but as crippling factors destroying both nations.

The companion piece to the "government is the problem" was "privatization and markets are the answer." A drive began to examine literally every aspect of government for its potential to be handed to the private sector. Health care, education, prisons, retirement, and infrastructure were all declared to be inappropriate for government involvement or at least areas where private enterprises and markets should take the lead. In each case, concerted efforts began to package up assets and responsibilities and hand them to new profit-driven owners and investors. This has been a consistent pillar of the neoliberal paradigm.

All of these efforts were deeply flawed and would prove disastrous. The entire movement was based more on neoliberal beliefs than any real understanding of fundamentals. Millions of smart and well-intentioned people would eagerly follow those beliefs and ride the trend. Most of them are still on that ride. They would be joined by a frightening number of shysters, speculators, and downright crooks. Many of them would walk off with millions while only a few would be caught in their frauds and sent to jail. The entire neoliberal mess continues to this day.

While the specifics of each story are different there is a clear and common pattern across all of them. In each case the *market demand* for the service in question is highly *price inelastic*. That means there is essentially no change in demand as a function of price. The number of people having a heart attack each year does not change based on hospital costs. The factors driving people to education, including higher education, are so powerful the volume does not change based on price. The cost of a prison bed does not change how many people commit crimes. Therefore, there is *no market mechanism to set prices, nor any market-wide incentive to lower them.* There can be competitive dynamics, but as we will see in the detailed examples, in the absence of a market price mechanism those have severe limits. The incentives on all parties to raise prices are simply too high.

The second problem in each case is they are all heavily dependent on government subsidies which are viewed by the market as essentially unlimited. When you insert a number of profit driven market entities between consumers with zero price elasticity and government funding that is unlimited, only one thing can happen. Prices and costs will skyrocket. That's what has happened with both health care and education.

If that market dynamic isn't bad enough, this formula is also incredibly ripe for fraud. The true believers in the paradigm feel that any regulatory oversight is a defect and have been careful to set up these privatization programs with as little oversight as possible. For fraudsters, the combination of inelastic and poorly informed demand with no oversight and a large stream of guaranteed government funding is a gold mine. They jumped in with both feet and began using their profits to fund campaigns that ensured they remained unregulated and amply supplied with tax dollars to line their pockets.

The root cause of the problem is trying to use a market system in situations where the fundamental necessities of elastic demand, along with cost and price transparency, are impossible. In those situations, markets will always increase costs and that's what has happened. When you look at the underlying data, in each case the point where American cost trends separate from per capita growth and from comparisons to other nations can be found in the early 1980s. The neoliberal faith in the infallibility of markets has been a proven failure.

HEALTH CARE BECOMES AN ECONOMIC CANCER

Far and away the most important failed market is in health care. The roots of this problem go all the way back to our emergence from World War II. The 1942 government freeze on wages and "no strikes" agreement by unions during the war put businesses in an interesting position. On the one hand it meant the substantial wage pressures they had faced before the war, and that would resume afterward, were off the table. On the other hand, they were competing with each other in a drastically reduced wartime labor pool and needed some way to attract workers. The answer came in the form of generous benefits, specifically health care. In 1943 the IRS was convinced to make this a tax deduction for business which further cemented its popularity. After the war, in 1945, Truman proposed moving to the kind of national health care system that was emerging across Europe. By this point businesses, unions, and the health care industry had negotiated working agreements among themselves and didn't want to make the change. It was an unplanned artifact of the war and has been with us ever since.

Health care costs grew modestly, pretty much in line with inflation, for much of the next couple decades. Blue Cross Blue Shield was the largest benefit provider and they operated as a nonprofit. That all began to change in the late 1960s and early 1970s as costs began growing a bit more rapidly, though still roughly in line with what was happening in other nations. For-profit insurance companies began entering the market and, with the passing of the 1973 Health Maintenance Organization Act, HMOs did as well. The HMO Act was specifically aimed at reining in the cost escalation. The hope was their managed care approach would reduce absolute costs and the introduction of increased competition would begin bringing more market driven cost reductions as well.

That didn't work quite as anticipated. Costs continued to grow and were beginning to rise faster than elsewhere in the world. By the early 1980s the gap to the rest of the world was becoming measurable. Amid the "markets are the answer" religion of the time, the answer was to increase choice, bring more payers into the market, and push to privatize everything possible.

Unfortunately, costs continued rising, pulling even farther away from every other nation. By the 1990s that gap was becoming alarming, particularly because our quality of care actually seemed to be declining compared to the rest of the world. Most neoliberal observers thought the answer was clear. We needed even more choices, more market forces, more competition.

What nobody understood was that *markets weren't the cure to rising costs, they were the cause.* We were caught in a deep conceptual trap associated with the fourth paradigm. This trap was the belief that competitive forces always drive costs down. That's a false belief. In markets with zero price elasticity, like health care, the dynamics are more complex than that. I'll unpack all those details in a bit, but at the time we just kept trying to apply more and more market solutions. And the more we did, the faster costs accelerated.

Which brings us to 2010 and the passing of the Affordable Care Act. This was Obama's long overdue effort to begin fixing the now completely broken health care system. The program brought a deep flaw from its very beginning. The focus of the plan was aimed at improving coverage for the over 45 million Americans who lived without any insurance. It was a coverage strategy not a cost strategy. Unfortunately, in the case of health care, we really have to fix the cost problem first. Once we do, the coverage issue will be vastly easier to solve.

The plan was modeled on a 2006 Massachusetts plan that had its origins in a set of concepts laid out in 1989 by the Heritage Foundation. It combined an individual mandate with a health insurance "exchange" that would create an open market for insurance. It also legislated a set of "market making" standards for those insurance policies that included coverage for women's reproductive needs and preexisting conditions. The core ideas behind the plan had been major pillars of several Republican proposals and bills since the original Heritage Foundation work. It fit perfectly in the "markets are the answer" belief system as well as the "personal responsibility" values of most conservatives.

It seemed like a strategy that should lead to strong bipartisan support. It was not. Senator Mitch McConnell led a Republican revolt against their own basic ideas. They chose the individual mandate as their specific target. Republican senators who had long supported, even demanded, that feature suddenly flipped and began declaring it unconstitutional. Clearly this had nothing to do with the actual content of the bill. It was a strictly political ploy, but one that was playing with the health care and lives of millions of Americans.

The bill eventually passed with no Republican support and went into law. The early experiences were quite shaky. The exchanges themselves had scaling problems and there were issues and confusion all over the country. Accompanying these real start-up problems was a ceaseless chorus proclaiming the evil this was perpetrating on the nation. It was labeled a "socialist takeover" of the entire medical establishment. Republican-led states began mounting legal challenges in an attempt to undermine the entire system. Many of those states engaged in active sabotage with the deliberate intent of denying health care to their citizens.

The overall results definitely achieved many key goals. Coverage has dramatically improved with 12 million people getting insurance through the exchanges and another 11 million through Medicaid expansion. The cost picture is a bit more complex. Those states that implemented the full plan have almost all seen premium reductions, but only after factoring in subsidies. The Republican-controlled states that sabotaged different aspects of the plans have seen substantial premium increases which they blame on the plan, not their acts of sabotage. The true core costs of health care haven't improved at all. Those weren't the target and until they're fixed the entire system remains broken.

The level of "bad faith" throughout this process has been jaw dropping. Major political leaders have openly and defiantly declared they do not want their citizens to have access to health care insurance. Sean Hannity at one point justified their acts of sabotage, explaining it was within their rights to intentionally break the system just because they didn't want it to work, not because they didn't think it could. The opposition is even more fascinating because the actual nature of the program is one of the most "market oriented" that anyone has ever come up with. This reality became exceedingly awkward once the Republican party found themselves in power and therefore responsible. They were committed to eliminating the Affordable Care Act, but nobody had any ideas that were workable, fit their ideology, and were different. This had been the main line of Republican thinking for almost two decades and the rest of the cupboard was bare. Their ongoing political ploys continue to endanger the health and lives of millions of Americans.

HOW EDUCATION BECAME A DEBT TRAP

The other public good that many conservatives do not support is education, specifically the post-secondary segment. That system has been under attack by the anti-democracy movement for decades. Between those persistent efforts and the severe retrenchment during the 2008 recession, the economics of higher education have been utterly transformed. The primary victims have been the students and their families. An entire generation of Americans are suffering as a result. The damage continues with a monstrous lurking iceberg of student debt and new victims every day.

Let's start with a few basic data points. If we examine the costs of tuition and fees compared to inflation we find that real costs were basically flat throughout the 1970s. Inflation levels were frequently high during that period and costs did go up, but only in line with inflation. Then, in a now familiar pattern, beginning in the early to mid-1980s something changed. Costs began going up much faster than inflation and have done so consistently ever since. Adjusting for inflation, the cost of a higher education in 2017 is four times what it was in 1982–83. Meanwhile enrollment has also grown consistently throughout the period as well. Every year. Year after year. Prices go up and enrollment goes up. The combination has resulted in over $1.3 trillion dollars in government-backed student debt as of early 2017.

To understand what is causing all this we need to dive into the details. The first observation direct from the data is that the demand for higher education is highly price inelastic. The number of people seeking these credentials is essentially independent of price. Enrollment goes up and up and up even as prices go up and up and up. The only thing that seems to change the enrollment trajectory are recessions and they cause enrollment to go up, not down. The lack of income and employment in a recession is taken as a reason to go back to school, not to avoid those costs. From the data, this appears to be true basically regardless of what those costs are. Our society is well aware that improving education and skills leads to greater job and income opportunities and these factors simply outweigh all others. This inelasticity is not new. It shows up in the data going back to the early 1960s. So, what changed in the early 1980s that caused prices to begin detaching from inflation?

Here we need to look at four different parts of the higher education system. There are publicly supported for-profit institutions, state-funded institutions, private institutions with substantial endowments, and private institutions with limited endowments. There are other complexities as well, but we can illustrate the core issues by focusing on these four. Part of the key to this topic is to recognize that while the dynamics in each of these categories are different, the things that happen within each have an impact on the others. This would be true in any market, but it is particularly important in a market with zero price elasticity. With essentially no demand force on price, the only restraining market force comes from the competitive dynamics both within and across these categories.

Let's look at each of these categories to see what's been happening, beginning with the publicly supported for-profits. There had been versions of these institutions since the end of World War II when for-profit trade schools popped up to address the opportunities growing out of the GI Bill. Those ended up having a dubious track record with a 1965 Government Accountability Office (GAO) investigation concluding that 65 percent had committed some form of fraud. It was a harbinger of what was to come. They grew more popular after 1972 when Congress began allowing them to participate in the Guaranteed Student Loan Program. This accelerated strongly in the early 1980s under the impetus of the privatization movement and the regulatory changes that allowed those loans to be given to students who had never completed high school. By the end of the 1980s these schools had accounted for almost half of the enrollment growth during the decade.

Something else also came to light at that point. Student loan fraud and defaults were skyrocketing, and these schools accounted for 74 percent of the fraud and 77 percent of the defaults. Further investigation found that when controlling for all other factors, these institutions were charging fees that were 78 percent higher than comparable nonprofit institutions and that literally all of this increase could be attributed to the government-provided aid. They were sending recruiters to drive around unemployment offices promising people great jobs and basing those claims on falsified data about graduation and job placement rates. In a few cases, 80 percent of their expenses actually went to these recruitment efforts with little to no spending on actual education. They were fraud mills, pumping money out of the government while saddling unsuspecting students with debts they could not repay and providing little to no actual education.

When this was all discovered several of the worst offenders were put out of business and various oversight reforms were put in place. Under heavy lobbying pressure many of these regulations were then rolled back in the mid-1990s and the industry once again began to grow. These institutions get 90 percent of their income through the manipulation of government programs. They set their prices based on the terms of those programs, not any market or student considerations. A GAO sting operation in 2011 found fully one quarter of the institutions in the sting were coaching students to commit fraud on their government loan and grant applications. Literally 100 percent of those in the investigation made fraudulent claims to the government about costs to be recovered and about graduation, employment, and income results. A later study found that 72 percent of the graduates from these higher education firms were earning less than high school dropouts with otherwise similar backgrounds.

This is exactly what you would expect if you stick a for-profit institution into a market like this. Students on the low end of the income scale depend almost entirely on government assistance. Despite their lack of income, they themselves have zero price elasticity, just like every other student. Therefore, the price is 100 percent determined by the terms of the government program. The institution's revenue is therefore almost 100 percent determined by enrollment rates and that can best be increased through fraudulent claims. The same is true for all of the institutions so they all raise the stakes on each other, escalating the level of fraud. There's no oversight and these students have no discernable voice in the process. Every time the sector has been investigated it's been found to be rampant with fraud and clearly designed around extracting government dollars, not educating students. Attempts at oversight and reform are consistently resisted by lobbyists and rolled back by the true believers in the neoliberal paradigm.

This sets the first stake in the ground. Poor education results with fees that are determined by government spending which in turn is driven by an ideological preference for profits based on fraud over results based on education.

Next up are the state-funded colleges and universities. In many ways, these are the real lynchpin both of this industry and what's gone wrong. These colleges and universities have generally been quite well managed, both financially and as providers of quality education. On a per student basis their costs have stayed low, rarely growing faster than inflation. In many of the worst tuition escalation periods they've actually kept costs flat. The tuition culprit here is the amount of state subsidy being provided, not their costs.

Those subsidies have been under sustained attack. From its earliest days state education funding has been one of the top targets of the anti-democracy movement. One of their primary objectives is the complete removal of all public support for education. The campaign has been fought at the state and local level since that's where most of those funding decisions originate. Adding to this steady political pressure is a second challenge. Most state budgets must be kept in balance and consist of only four major categories—education, prisons, roads, and Medicaid. Whenever tax receipts fall, as they do in a recession or due to tax cuts, one of those segments must be cut. The national mass incarceration strategy takes cutting prisons off the table and Medicaid spending is growing, not shrinking, because of the broken health care system. Education cuts are therefore almost unavoidable in any budgetary downturn.

When state-funded educational institutions get their subsidies cut the only place to turn to make up the shortfall are tuition fees. In almost every state and period over the past few decades the increases in fees above simple inflation can be attributed almost completely to cuts in subsidies. The clear and unambiguous cause of spiraling tuition at state colleges and universities are the steady drops in state subsidies magnified by the dramatic cuts during the 2008 recession.

This second stake in the ground is a bit more complex than our first. These institutions have always provided excellent education for their students. They have also provided two distinct price tiers that served to define the market more broadly for this caliber of education. Students from within the state paid very low fees, as low as zero in many states in the 1970s. Out-of-state students paid a higher fee. Those higher fees were set somewhere above the in-state fee and equal to or below the fees charged by private institutions. Their education standards were high, so they established a crucial market-competitive benchmark that helped restrain the pricing tendencies of those private institutions. What's happened since the mid-1980s is the subsidized gap between in-state and out-of-state fees has dropped dramatically, even to zero in many places. The fees themselves have increased above inflation, even though costs have not, because of the steady decline in subsidies. That combination has taken the competitive market pricing floor up, enabling, even driving, the rest of the market up as well.

We next jump to the high end of the market, the private institutions with substantial endowments. In total there are about 850 institutions with private endowments, but there is a substantial spread between them. Harvard is always at the top with an endowment in the $35 billion range. They're followed by Yale and Princeton. The top 50 schools have a median endowment of $3.5 billion. The overall median is much smaller, only $113 million. This gap is also steadily widening. The top 40 schools in the nation receive over 60 percent of all private donations. Similarly, the top 60 schools get an average annual yield from their endowments of approximately 9–10 percent while the bottom half of the entire distribution gets closer to 5–6 percent.

The funding picture for this high-end tier is quite different from the rest of the post-secondary market. In addition to those large donations and invest- ment yields these institutions compete heavily for federal research grants and they get profits from patent licensing and, in many cases, hospital operations. In the top 20 schools, tuition only accounts for 15 percent of annual income. When the recession hit, their endowment investment yields came down but there were ample ways to deal with that impact.

These schools have been spending heavily and growing. For those who have them, hospital operations have been riding the health care spending rocket ship. Patent licenses, beginning in the early 1980s after the passage of the Bayh-Dole Act, have become lucrative profit centers. Having personally negotiated licens- ing deals with several of them, I can attest that the schools range from great collaborators just looking for a slice of the pie to absolute rabid extortionists, and everything in between. With all their other sources of money, they have the option to keep tuition increases down. However, the zero price elasticity of the overall market is particularly pronounced in this category. In many ways their primary competitive strategy is not tuition costs, it's actually driving up spending, which demonstrates an apparent market dynamism that's far more important to applicants than costs.

This is our third stake in the ground. The high end is flush with resources, rapidly outgrowing everyone else and happily exploiting their essentially unlimited pricing power to drive tuition fees ever higher.

This takes us to our final grouping, those institutions that receive little to no state subsidies and have modest to zero endowments. These organiza- tions are not totally reliant on tuition, but they are heavily so. On average they get 75 percent of their funding from student enrollments with the other 25 percent coming from research grants and other sources. This category is heav- ily influenced by the competitive dynamics above and below them. Both of those dynamics are pushing them higher. To compete with the larger, wealth- ier universities for grants and other funding sources they must drive spending up. They can't begin to match the big guys dollar for dollar, but they can't afford to fall too far behind either. Fortunately for them, and unfortunately for American students, the state subsidized schools they compete with for students are rapidly raising tuition fees for the reasons noted above. That gives them the leeway to drive up their own tuition fees to fund their competitive efforts with the richer schools which is exactly what they have done.

So that's the overall picture. The for-profit publicly funded schools are rampant fraud machines pumping dollars out of the government and stranding students and the government with bad debts. The state schools have steadily lost their subsidies, driving up tuition costs and altering the competitive dynamics in the mid-tier of the market. This has allowed the broad base of private institutions to raise their own prices, giving them funding to pursue their competitors at the high end. The top of the market is flush with cash and happy to continue pulling away from everyone else using all their resources, including unlimited pricing power with students.

RETIREMENT: INSURANCE VERSUS SAVINGS

The third public good under sustained assault by misguided believers in markets are the resources to support the retirement needs of the nation. The Social Security Act of 1935 was an important milestone in our development. It is viewed by many as a form of "welfare" or "safety net" and indeed it did grow in response to the countless human tragedies that were so widespread at the time. However, its nature and structure are quite different from any true welfare program. The obvious and often misunderstood difference is that it is a "contributory" program. What's more, it is actually structured as an *insurance* program. The notion of a form of insurance against the various unknown risks to one's social and financial well-being had been developed in Europe in the late nineteenth century. The first nation to actually create such a program was Germany in 1889. By the time the United States began serious consideration of our own insurance program in the 1930s there were 34 nations around the world who had done so.

Like any insurance program, the financial logic is that a group of people can put money into a pool to provide insurance against some shared risk. While the needs of each individual in that pool are highly uncertain, the aggregate total can be statistically estimated with a reasonably high degree of accuracy. By ensuring that the total pool is large enough to cover their aggregate needs, every participant can be confident their specific withdrawals will be covered.

This is the most economically efficient way to manage shared risks. If every participant is forced to retain enough assets to cover their worst outcome the total assets consumed will be far too high. If every participant only covers their minimum, most will suffer the ill consequences of the risk. If everyone covers only the average, then half will end up holding too much and half will suffer. Risk pooling is the economically most efficient and correct answer.

In this case, the primary defined risk is one's needs for funds once one is no longer able to work. The original act was actually separated into two major elements. The first included a set of grants to the states in support of existing state welfare programs for the aged. The second, which was the primary focus, was the creation of this new insurance program with associated mandatory payroll deductions. That's what we now know as Social Security. In fact, the name is a direct reference to the insurance structure of the program. There are some people who think about social security payroll deductions as a form of "forced savings," but in reality, it's not a savings program, it's an insurance program. This basic conceptual misunderstanding has been the cause of countless political debates. The mandatory nature also causes many people to think of it as a "tax," but it isn't structured in some sort of progressive tax scheme. It is structured around contributions to our individual insurance programs based on our individual earnings, and our eventual insurance withdrawals are based on our contributions and our longevity.

This is not some sort of government provided entitlement safety net. That's exactly how it is described today, but it's a false characterization. That mischaracterization enables some politicians to suggest this is some sort of "government benefit" that they might or might not choose to continue providing under the guise of "entitlement reform." In reality it represents a specific financial asset, an insurance policy, that each of us has purchased under a specific set of financial terms. Anyone questioning our right to own and exercise our policies is seizing private assets, not reducing government entitlement benefits.

One of the less visible side effects of the decline in wage growth since the 1970s was to Social Security. In the history of the program, roughly $2.5 trillion dollars have been paid in premiums by all of us in excess of our withdrawals. That amount is known as the Social Security Trust Fund. Beginning in the mid-1980s and growing in urgency through the 1990s was an alarm that the fund would be insufficient to meet all its obligations somewhere in the coming decades. Most blamed this on the demographics of the baby boom. However, those factors were known to the actuaries in the Social Security administration and were built into their models. What was not in the models was the failure of wages to track GDP growth which had never occurred in the history of the program.

Equally problematic is the unfortunate reality of the composition of that fund. Some probably envision a giant $2.5 trillion dollar mutual fund making various prudent investments like other insurance operations. That's not what has happened. What has actually happened is the federal government has been steadily withdrawing those funds to cover various budget shortfalls and replacing the funds with noncommercial promissory notes. That $2.5 trillion dollar "asset" pool is now really just $2.5 trillion dollars of government debt. Adding to the problem, the interest rates being earned on all that debt are probably one half to two thirds of what they would be if they were actually invested commercially. All of us who have purchased these insurance policies have had our assets stolen by the very government officials we hired as the stewards of our resources.

Some of those officials have argued those promissory notes are backed by the full faith and credit of the United States. Those exact same officials then claim our assets are actually entitlement benefits they think should be reduced or eliminated. There are other factions who want to privatize the entire program and convert it into a savings program managed by large financial institutions. This is similar to the shift that occurred in the private sector from company provided pension funds to individual 401(k) savings. Once again, the core problem is hidden. When we rely on individual savings instead of pooled insurance we're using an economic model that is ill suited to the purpose and structurally guaranteed to produce poor results.

Retirement experts often refer to a "three-legged stool" which includes Social Security, pensions, and personal savings. Both Social Security and pension funds are structured as insurance programs. Unfortunately, pensions have become quite rare, and most experts believe Social Security will run out of funds by the mid-2030s. Almost every discussion on the growing crisis assumes some sort of improved savings plan is the only answer, which ignores the structural financial problems of variance and risk. There are financial assets like certain annuities that factor uncertain life expectancy into their yields but most of these offer poor returns. They also do not provide the asset pooling and shared risk variance that is such an integral aspect of a true insurance model. Compounding the problem is the fact that as a direct result of wage stagnation the overall savings rate in America has been gradually eroding since the early 1970s. Any strategy that relies too heavily on individual savings is simply the wrong financial model with the wrong funding source.

The only viable financial strategy is to repair the damage done to Social Security. Probably the easiest plan would be to remove or increase the earnings cap that currently exists on Social Security contributions. That approach isn't quite as simple as it sounds. One of the essential aspects of the program is that it serves to set a minimum baseline for the nation. Most people will want more than that minimum which is where their individual savings do come into play. If you raise the earnings cap without ensuring that those larger contributors get a larger return that "fairness" logic can be put at risk. Tackling this may seem like a political impossibility at this point, but the politics are likely to change as the crisis becomes more acute. There are some projections that as many as 30 million people who currently enjoy solid middle-class lifestyles will find themselves living in abject poverty by the time they reach their 70s. That's a lot of people who will be very unhappy with the poor stewardship of the insurance policies they've paid into for a lifetime.

5

OUR BROKEN SOCIAL CONTRACT

To get the full extent of the failure of the neoliberal paradigm our economic challenges must be paired with insights on our current social cohesion. To examine that dimension, we need a brief conceptual interlude on the underlying nature of our sense of identity within society, our moral beliefs, and the paths and tools we use to understand the world, to understand "truth." Each of these play a critical role in how we see the world and react to events.

For much of human history and for many in today's America, all three of these belief systems were and are defined by religion. Religious affiliations are core to many people's identity and serve to define their communities. Religion has also been the source of ethical guidance and held the final say on "truth." While religion has offered a path for many, these philosophical components are actually universal. They propel the thinking and behavior of all of us, regardless of any religious context.

As such, shaping individual and social perceptions along these three dimensions are among the most important and powerful cultural framing tools used by leaders. Before we can set any strategy along those lines we first need to understand the current lay of the land in twenty-first-century America.

IDENTITY: FIXED VERSUS CREATED

One of the central, even defining, beliefs about America is that every citizen has the opportunity to pursue whatever they seek in life. In fact, the "pursuit of happiness" is right there in the Declaration of Independence as an "inalienable" right. We each have the power to follow our own journey, to find our own sense of purpose, to create our own identity. We are defined by our character and what we do, not where or to whom we were born. This belief sits at the very core of our national identity. It's what enables us to welcome immigrants to our "melting pot" from which we all emerge as Americans. It reflects our founding ideals.

This sits in stark contrast to the widespread custom at the time of our founding where identity was defined by genetics, skin color, birthplace, and family heredity. Under that tradition our identities are immutably defined and fixed by nature. Escaping from this life-stifling custom was a central driver for our earliest settlers and remains a primary attraction for people from all over the world.

There is, however, an enormous challenge arising from the collision of our ideal beliefs and the real world. After all, from our earliest days we have treated skin color as an inescapable identifier of different classes of people for whom opportunities have been radically different. We withheld the rights of women to vote or even hold credit cards for a shameful length of time. We also know that those born into wealth have far more life options than those born into poverty. We have asserted the belief in our ideal even as we lived our lives to the contrary.

The tensions and struggles driven by this conflict have been central drivers of our society throughout history. The battles over racism and women's rights have been long, protracted, and fraught with violence. These days the questions of sexual identity, ethnicity, and nativism have become equally prominent conflicts to which every participant brings a complicated and sometimes contradictory set of beliefs and assumptions.

Most members of our various ethnic and LGBTQ communities share a commitment to our original founding ideal. They see identity as something that is theirs to explore, discover, and create. They reject anyone else asserting they have the right to define who they are or how they should live. Their personal heritage may define their starting point and may shape their journeys, but that's only one element in their identity. As they grow it is those personal journeys of discovery that really define who they are and who they become. These are true believers in the original American ideal.

In contrast, contemporary nativists have basically abandoned this core founding principle of our nation. They do believe in opportunity, but only for those who were born in the United States to parents who were US citizens. For many, the only acceptable skin color is white. In their minds everyone else should be excluded. For them, identity is no longer something we discover or become. We are defined by where we begin our journey, by our birthright and skin color, not by who we are or what we do.

As described below, this isolationist mind-set has been further sharpened by our divides over ethics and truth. Instead of our original open ideal, the contemporary nativists now demand conformity to a particular ethical belief system and an equally particular set of shared stories, many of which are based on "alternative facts." Unfortunately, this tribal identity system has grown from the small fringe groups where it began to the point where it now dominates many contemporary conservative communities.

ETHICS: POWER VERSUS VALUE

An equally challenging social divide comes from our very understanding of morality. It is often associated with religious belief, but its roots are deeper. George Lakoff refers to one side of this as the "strict father" belief system. This belief system starts with an assumption that we live in a dangerous and competitive world. There will always be winners and losers in this world. The winners will be those with the discipline and strength to do what is "right" and "just" rather than what is "easy" or "comfortable." We are all born with a tendency to do the opposite, so we must be raised with strong discipline by strict fathers who will punish us when we fall short. Those fathers will also protect and support us and must be obeyed at all times. We will know those who are right and moral, by seeing who wins. For it is they that have learned the real ways of the world from their fathers and have developed the inner strength and disciplines needed to win at all times. Those who adhere to this collection of moral beliefs are also the ones who are the most adamant and aggressive in seeking explicit punishment for any transgressions.

Lakoff contrasts this with what he calls the "nurturing parent" belief system. He describes this as having three key elements. These are empathy for others, taking responsibility for oneself and those under one's care, and doing one's best to aid and support one's family, community, nation, and the world. These values translate directly into support for the freedom to seek one's purpose in life, as well as the principles of fairness and opportunity for all. The values of community building lead to an emphasis on cooperation, trust, and honesty.

Others who have studied the subject have confirmed Lakoff's basic characterizations. Various large-scale studies have found these two distinct ethical orientations all over the world in every culture and across all religions. These appear to be human traits, not cultural ones. Specifically, those studies found that one orientation places its moral emphasis on avoiding harm, caring for others, fair treatment for all, and a principle of reciprocity. This is Lakoff's "nurturing parent" which I describe as an ethical focus on *value*.

The second group recognizes all those value attributes, though it gives them much lower importance. This group focuses instead on respect and obedience to authority, conformance and loyalty to community, and maintaining a purity or sanctity to whatever norms are commanded by accepted authorities. In the United States this sanctity is often rooted in sexuality but elsewhere around the world it can include diet, forms of attire, or many other customs. This is Lakoff's "strict father" which I describe as an ethical focus on *power*.

The value believers recognize the human reality of all these power attributes but regard them as at most tangentially relevant to morality or ethics. In fact, believers in value assert it is our moral duty to challenge and resist authority if that authority is actively creating damage or harm to individuals or the community.

The conflicts between these alternate moral systems have always existed. They began to rip our nation apart in the 1960s and early 1970s. The entire value-driven spectrum of civil rights, women's rights, and sexual freedom movements from the period triggered strong resistance from the believers of the power ethic. They viewed those movements as disobedient to authority, fracturing the conformance of the community and in direct violation of what they viewed as morally correct sexual purity. Some of those believers were undoubtedly also racists and/or sexists, but even those who were more tolerant on the identity politics found all those new movement's actions as morally questionable if not reprehensible.

They were equally repulsed by the protests against the war in Vietnam. "My country, right or wrong" embodies the belief that moral behavior requires obedience to authority and conformity to community expectations. In their minds it is the very definition, literally, of patriotism. Challenging that authority undermines the core strength of the nation. Furthermore, those challenges appeared to be based on looking for the "easy" and "comfortable" path instead of the "right" and "just" path. Protestors were seen as cowards, lacking the moral courage and discipline to do what was patriotic, right, and necessary.

For those on the "ethic of value" side who felt the war had questionable purpose and was unwinnable, and who were morally horrified by the destruction and loss of life on all sides, those beliefs seemed bizarre and misguided. In their minds it took great moral courage to resist the demands of authority, and that in so doing it was they who were the true patriots.

The power ethic also sits at the core of those who believe husbands should be able to "discipline" (beat) their wives, those who believe policing is "war" not "protection," those who view poverty as a moral failing, and those who advocate torture. Most recently it's been the "moral" basis for supporting policies of imprisoning law-abiding asylum seekers and forcibly separating mothers from their babies under the guise of "tough love." This is the ugly side of the ethic of power.

The "ethic of power" belief system is correct in noting that power is not just a major factor in the world, it's omnipresent. Even in the economic exchanges that some want to believe are free from its influence, we've been clear it plays a substantial role. Power and value are deeply intertwined in human society. The alternate morality, which I advocate throughout this book, is not ignorant about power; it just places value on top. Ironically, the Bible itself is split in this regard. The Old Testament tends to put power on top, while the New Testament puts value on top.

This is not a new social schism and it should surprise nobody that there are plenty of people who fall on both sides. Those who believe power dominates see the world that way and believe anyone who does not is naïve. Those who believe value is more important see the world through that lens and believe value eventually prevails. The very qualification criteria between the two views—"dominates" versus "more important"—reveal how deep the schism can be.

Those who follow the power ethic often create specific hazards for other members of society. Many of these people are simply unable to refrain from being highly judgmental. This tendency is not unique to the power sect, but it is a central feature of that set of beliefs. Those who base their ethical system on the unyielding imposition of discipline have trouble refraining from doing exactly that if they see someone engaged in what they regard as "misbehavior."

Those who reject the ethic of power also reject the power adherents' assumption that they have the right to pass moral judgment on those following the value path. Their attempts to place legal intrusions on other's rights has been a struggle since our nation's founding. Laws against alcohol, marijuana, and sexuality continue to challenge what should be inalienable freedoms for American adults. We are not "children" in need of someone else's "discipline."

One of the crucial targets of this judgmental power belief system is anybody who is less fortunate or less successful than those doing the judging. Power always exists in a hierarchy and holders of this belief system are constantly looking down to apply judgment. The weakest members of society receive the greatest approbation from the full hierarchy. Because weakness is equated with, even defines, immorality for these believers, the most vulnerable members of society become targets of an almost vengeful, righteous wrath.

Finally, this belief system can be problematic because of the explicit role it places on leaders. Even adherents of the belief realize how vulnerable the system is to exploitation by power-wielding "strict fathers" who may themselves lack any value elements in their moral compass. In deciding to place power in the driver's seat, instead of value, that just goes with the territory. There are those who will assert they only allow God in the ultimate seat, but power always brings a hierarchy and the seats occupied below God have a lot more say in most people's lives. This is simply inherent to any system that puts respect and worship of power over the creation and joy of value.

As noted at the beginning of this section, both of these orientations exist in societies from all over the planet. This is part of what it means to be human. The conflicts between these two orientations won't ever go away. The key to our national strategy must be ensuring that tolerance works for everybody. Part of this must include ensuring that the power-driven "strict fathers" do not inflict their harmful judgments on those oriented toward value, nor on the more vulnerable in our society.

REALITY: TRUTH VERSUS STORIES

For many people, if not most, "reality" doesn't seem all that mysterious. We see and experience things in the world and those observations define what's real. However, our understanding of reality is far more complex than that simple empiricism. Our ability to observe is always limited and often narrow in scope, depth, and time. We rely on countless clues to help us focus and "fill in the blanks." Most of that is quite unconscious. All of it is inescapable. Without those conceptual tools we would simply be overwhelmed with minute by minute minutia. Some of those clues are strictly perceptual, but many, if not most, come from our social and educational context. Our understanding of basic reality, of "truth," is far more dependent on those contextual forces than most realize. This is true across all forms of knowledge, but it's particularly acute in the social, political, and economic domains.

Our insistence on the importance of "truth" has its own complex history. We often attribute the Western origins of scientific thinking to the ancient Greeks. The famous Greek historian Thucydides once asserted the duty of historians was not to describe what "actually" happened, but rather what "should" have happened. After all, he reasoned, everyone knows what "actually" happened. He was not abandoning the existence of a core "truth," merely reflecting on how different perspectives cast events in different lights and those lead to different stories.

An important example of this phenomenon is the "Lost Cause" narrative. The culture and identity of southern white society had been dealt a devastating blow by the results of the Civil War. There was a natural tendency to portray the outcome in the most favorable light possible. That began with the assertion that the antebellum South had achieved a near ideal society. It was peaceful and noble, with a deep and devout dedication to family, religion, chivalry, and honor. They had simply attempted to exercise their right to secede, an expression of inviolable "state rights." Their generals and soldiers had fought with gallantry and heroism against an overwhelmingly larger foe who resorted to dishonorable conduct throughout the war. Slavery was merely an incidental aspect of the conflict, exaggerated by the north to justify their heinous aggression. Furthermore, the story asserted, the slaves themselves did not want freedom and their lives would become incomparably poorer afterward. The noble, honorable society of the South had been subject to the unjustified, violent intervention by unscrupulous and immoral elites from the North. To this day, this remains a central teaching across great swaths of the southern education system. Whole generations have grown up not only believing its veracity through the schools, but also through its centrality in the shared belief system of everyone they encounter.

It might seem this is just a harmlessly different story told about the same underlying events. However, the story does not really include a rejection of slavery, nor any sort of deep acceptance of an integrated society. In fact, it rejects that outright. Its widespread belief means there are different groups in this country with deeply divergent understandings of history, of reality itself. Those beliefs are propagated and reinforced through our shared stories.

This is a common pattern for many of the topics in this book. Perceptions of reality are shaped by the contextual stories that surround each of us. In ways that can be completely invisible to our conscious minds, we see certain things and miss others. We become curious about some gaps in our knowledge and blind to others. In the process of filling in those gaps we are guided by others who share our context and echo our stories. Our shared reality becomes ever more complete, but also ever more specific to those who share our stories—our tribe. We descend deeper and deeper into the rabbit hole.

This tribal specific reality is particularly acute in the realm of social change. The nineteenth and early twentieth century included many social struggles each of which met fierce resistance. In each case the different tribal stories of events left little in the way of common ground on facts, on reality itself. Freeing slaves, emancipating women, teaching science and evolution were all milestones of progress for some and inexplicable losses for others. Most of the population regards these as old conflicts, long since settled. But, for probably 20–30 percent of the US population these are "injustices" or "indignities" that continue to burn to this day. The tribal stories around these "losses" rely on a toxic mix of partial truths blended with deep distortions, willful blindness, and a profound disconnect from reality.

For many, the very concept of truth versus falsehood has been slowly replaced by the struggles over which story wins versus which loses. The seductive power of stories becomes a substitute for the more intractable notion of "truth." These shared stories create and define culture and become social realities. Social realities become absolute realities when endorsed by figures of authority. For those who substitute stories for truth as well as believers in the power ethic, that most certainly does *not* include anybody from the world of science or academia. It includes leaders with *social power*, specifically including religious power and wealth.

"Truth" thereby becomes an exercise in power and for those on this particular philosophical path the ethic of power expands to encompass reality itself. This subtle, but deeply profound, shift now pervades much of the contemporary conservative dynamic. The three core philosophical dimensions of *identity*, *ethics*, and *truth* have been linked to a common worship of power in a way that makes them extremely difficult to disentangle.

For contemporary conservatives, the steadfast adherence and loyalty to a false narrative endorsed by figures of authority has become a moral and identity issue more than a factual issue.

As a result, no amount of fact checking can dislodge any of these beliefs. This deep shift poses a substantial risk to our republic. The entire edifice of truth and value defining our society has been replaced for some by stories endorsed by those with power. It's a pre-enlightenment culture akin to when priests held the power to define good and evil and dictated the very nature of truth. Proving a priest to be wrong was often fatal and that exercise of deadly church power was the "winning" that *defined* what was right and what was "true."

The original vision for America emerged from the philosophical movement of the enlightenment and was rooted in the elevation of facts, reason, science, and humanism over superstition, magic, religion, and authority. Without a shared understanding of facts, truth, and reality, we have no basis for a shared compass, shared values, or a shared vision for society. We cannot debate and make decisions based on logic and beliefs. Our Founding Fathers' deep belief in our ability as a society to govern ourselves is wholly dependent on there being an underlying edifice of truth.

Unfortunately, that edifice is under direct assault and is currently crumbling.

THE NEW STORYTELLERS

The assault on truth is not new to our society. We've fought over the findings of science for as long as the nation has existed. Those fights continue to this day. Most of us have celebrated our expanding sphere of knowledge, but for some that expansion is a threat, an invasion. For them the battles over evolution and creationism, among others, continue to blaze brightly. Most of these fights have centered on the threats to religious dogma, but we've also allowed ourselves to be blind to the realities of racism, sexism, and sexuality.

Over the last few decades this has escalated dramatically. We now have large, pervasive institutions dedicated to constructing an entire alternate world down inside the rabbit hole. They do this through stories many of which depend on "alternative facts," on lies. Just as we saw in Vietnam, this is inevitable when deeply flawed conceptual frames reach their limits in the real world. In fact, the depth, pervasiveness, and magnitude of the lies is a testament to how badly suited the frames of the rabbit hole actually are for our modern world. This modern world of propaganda is a desperate attempt to hide the deep flaws of our broken ideological paradigm.

The evolution of our various "truths defined by stories" into outright demagoguery and propaganda is an important part of what defines our modern landscape. The seeds of that process were planted in the post-Reagan 1980s. Conservative radio commentary had been around for a long time but turned into a completely different phenomenon beginning in the latter half of the 1980s. There had been a category of on the air "hijinks" referred to as the "shock jocks" since the early 1980s. Howard Stern, Don Imus, and others would engage in deliberately provocative behavior. Some of that was scatological, some sexual, and some simply politically incorrect. In 1984 they were joined by Rush Limbaugh who took the politically incorrect dimension and made it his own specialty. When the Fairness Doctrine moderating broadcast behavior was dropped in 1987 he was able to spread his program far more broadly. By 1991 he had the single leading program on radio nationwide and held that position for almost a decade.

Rush Limbaugh is the literal embodiment of Yeats's "the worst are filled with passionate intensity." One of the core story techniques of him and his compatriots is to lump people into categories and call them names. One of his favorites was to call feminists "feminazis." He has several variations on the following quote about women seeking equal rights, "Feminism was established to allow unattractive women access to mainstream society." He perfectly embodies the "strict father" power ethic. Consider the following quote: "In a country of children where the option is Santa Claus or work, what wins?" He deeply believes in individual responsibility, but makes no room for individual exploration, discovery, and decisions about ethical matters. Here's a representative quote: "Morality is not defined and cannot be defined by individual choice." He firmly subscribes to the "harsh discipline by stern fathers" ideology. Here's a classic in that vein: "If you feed the children three square meals a day during the school year, how can you expect them to feed themselves in the summer?" He leaves no room for finding common ground nor understanding. Here's a final quote: "Liberalism is a scourge. It destroys the human spirit." The scourge he is referring to are the human spiritual qualities of empathy, kindness, and compassion. "Passionate intensity" indeed.

Rush has been joined by a whole host of conservative commentators who can be described as modern "storytellers." The stories they tell define a reality believed by millions of Americans. The original stories, like the Southern Lost Cause, took substantial time and energy to develop into credible alternate realities. Today the entire process can unfold in a matter of days or weeks. Someone like Sean Hannity can make up a story, using a phrase like, "folks, I don't know whether this is true or not, but it seems possible to me that . . ." xyz. Then someone like Alex Jones will pick up the thread saying something like, "I've started hearing about xyz and I tell you . . ." A Rush Limbaugh figure will then jump in with, "it seems to me there's a consensus emerging that" xyz. Which will allow Sean to respond with "Xyz has now been clearly established as fact." At which point "xyz," which was made up from whole cloth, is now added to the shared reality of millions. These commentators have become self-anointed modern priests with the ability to define both morality and reality.

Much of the country relies on these sources along with Fox News and Sinclair Broadcast Group for all their news. In fact, there was a recent study comparing the primary news sources used by Americans. The study found a large segment of the population relied almost completely on Fox News, Breitbart, and a handful of commentators like Rush Limbaugh. For that segment, Fox was far and away their primary and often sole source. It's interesting to note that all these sources keep their stories consistent with each other, rather than with regard to specific real-world facts. They live in a socially defined and socially consistent reality, not a factual one.

The study also found another, equally large segment that relied on CNN, MSNBC, *The New York Times*, and *The Washington Post*. All those sources rely on independent confirmation for their stories, rather than mutual consistency. They strive, however imperfectly, to define a factual reality. The segment that used these sources was pretty evenly spread across them and people tended to use many or most of them. Neither of these two groups ever really used sources from the other segment. If you compare the stories over a few months between the two categories, you will find they live in different worlds. It's not just opinions and discussion points, either. Entire subjects, themes, and facts are different.

Fox News now defines an entire alternate world. Their stories often contain a few tendrils of truth woven with enormous omissions and distortions. There are times when they enter the world of pure fiction. These have evolved over the years into an entire epistemology. As a result, close to half the country now lives in an alternate reality filled with occurrences that simply never happened. There was a massacre at Bowling Green; there's a secret child sex ring run by the Clintons out of a pizza shop; the US government hired actors and staged a shooting in Connecticut, etc. The shared facts are not true. The shared reasoning defies logic. The followers are described by social scientists as members of a tribe but could more accurately be considered members of a cult.

MYTHS ABOUT CRIME IN AMERICA

One of the many pillars of this alternate world has to do with crime in America. In some ways this is not new. Crime has been an enormous feature of the social-conflict landscape since the early 1960s when it began a steep and steady rise. There was a peak in 1980, followed by a short drop and then another steady rise up until the early to mid-1990s. Violent crime rates more than doubled between 1960 and 1970. They then almost doubled again by 1980. The rise was steady and uninterrupted. The years of heavy riots in the 1960s did not change the curve, they simply fell right on the line. Political candidates of both parties would run on the promise of getting "tough on crime" and the rate would go up again, right on the curve. Nothing seemed to get to the core of the problem. All the promises and programs from the left and the right were utterly ineffective. Government was failing in one of its most basic roles, keeping citizens safe.

Under Reagan there were several changes introduced. One of these was the "war on drugs," a repeat of a campaign from the Nixon era, but with even less tolerance. This was combined with increasingly strict and lengthy sentencing guidelines for all types of criminal activities. The total number of Americans incarcerated in state and federal prisons skyrocketed. This trend was further exacerbated by the 1994 Omnibus Crime bill, passed by Bill

Clinton. The absolute imprisonment level, which had hovered around 200,000 people, would grow to over 1.3 million by the early 2000s. The steep increase would slow somewhat after that point but would not begin leveling out until after 2010.

It remains at an incredibly high number compared to any other nation on earth. To give a sense of just how high, consider the following. On a per capita basis, US prisons hold between four and eight times the number of people as the major European countries, almost 15 times as many as Japan, and 20 times the number in India. Even those countries with far less democratic norms than the United States cannot match our prison populations. We hold at least 50 percent more prisoners per capita than Russia and 5–6 times as many as China. And, that includes all the political prisoners in those nations as well. The only nation that might exceed our per capita level is the Seychelles, where the imprisonment of Somalian pirates distorts the relatively small native population.

This Reagan era mass incarceration program has been studied in considerable depth. There were no changes to the growing crime rates until 1990. None. Any attempt to claim the post-1990 reductions were due to a "delayed" effect from the mass incarceration program begun in the early 1980s needs some careful analysis. Such a study was conducted by the Brennan Center for Justice, which found mass incarceration had zero effect on violent crime and somewhere between 0–12 percent of the measured decline in property crime from 1990 to 1999. They also found that even this relatively small and isolated reduction dropped to essentially zero after 1999 even though incarceration rates continued to rise. In that same period, they concluded increased police presence could explain 0–10 percent of the decline, growth in income could explain 5–10 percent of the decline, and decreased alcohol consumption could explain another 5–10 percent. Other detailed studies have confirmed this pattern of findings with most concluding that improved police methods and social conditions are probably the dominant drivers of the post-1990 decline in crime. None of these studies is definitive in fully explaining the decline, but one thing is clear from all of them—it's not mass incarceration.

One of the perverse elements contributing to this sorry state was the decision to begin expanding the use of private, for-profit prisons. The US prison system has always used private companies as subcontractors for things like food services, laundry, and other specific services. The new idea was to privatize entire prisons and their full operations. This strategy was rooted in the belief that any profit driven organization is inherently superior to any government organization. The specific expectation was that these operations would reduce costs. Given the huge increases in planned incarcerations under Reagan that seemed like a great neoliberal strategy.

The promised cost savings never really materialized. Some organizations would carefully cherry pick prisoners who could be incarcerated with lower levels of security and therefore costs. Essentially every major study that controls for these effects has concluded there are no cost savings for the government. However, they are profitable and the way they do that is by severely cutting staffing and training levels. The results have produced the worst prisons in the nation in terms of violence, unrest, breakouts, and treatment. For example, assaults on guards are 49 percent more likely in private prisons and assaults on other prisoners are 65 percent more likely. And, these results are with populations that are far less prone to these sorts of incidents than the overall prison population in the United States. The neoliberal belief in infallible markets has been proven wrong yet again.

It's also important to note that private prisons are a failed answer to a problem that we need to put in our rearview mirror. The decline in crime rates since the early 1990s has been enormous. All forms of crime, but particularly violent crime, have dropped to levels not seen since the late 1950s or early 1960s. The criminal epidemic is over. This reality is never found in opinion polls which continue to show the overall population remains deeply concerned about crime. Part of this gap in understanding comes simply from perceptions shaped by current news events. No local reporter ever comes on the air to announce that 5 murders *didn't* happen in the last month. But the other reason is the deliberate vilification and fearmongering by those whose agenda is supported by perceptions of high levels of crime. The facts may have changed, but the stories endure and, for many, those stories, not the facts, are reality.

TRAGEDY OF POVERTY

A second social pillar of this alternate reality also comes from the Reagan era and was intensified by Rush Limbaugh and his ilk. These stories focus on the social programs aimed at helping the poor. One of Reagan's favorite stump speeches was his story of a fictional "welfare queen" who was able to gain enough income from a variety of social programs to drive around in a Cadillac while being completely and forever unemployed. Rush and his millions of followers continue to this day talking endlessly about the legalized theft of their private property through the horrible tax burdens created by the "hordes" of lazy, undisciplined poor. Their ethic of power doctrine provides all the proof they need of their own virtue and the lack thereof in the poor. They view compassion toward those folks as misguided, stupid, a "scourge." They believe only by withholding assistance will those lazy "children" choose to work instead of getting gifts from "Santa Claus." If the resulting desperate poor fail to find work and resort to crime they will happily add them to the ranks of the incarcerated. If they have the discipline to avoid crime and simply die, that's fine by Rush and company. In their minds, it will improve the breed. If they just struggle and endure, who cares? They don't matter. Some of them are probably "illegals" anyway and therefore not even a part of America. These are stories told by bullies who prey on the vulnerable.

This was the backdrop for the welfare reform program enacted in 1996. The program was signed into law by Bill Clinton, though its origins were in the Republican caucus and the hordes of Rush followers. There were good intentions in that bill, and indeed many felt it was working in its early years. Unfortunately, time has proven that those early success stories were due to the improving economy, not the program, and, once the economy faltered, the program's deep flaws were revealed. It stands today as an utter sham and should be regarded as a national disgrace.

To chart our way through this topic we need to start with a few important data points. It begins with a recognition that poverty, and any government program associated with poverty, is inextricably linked with the low end of the working wage scale. In 2016 the median income in the United States was $69,000 per year. In that section of the curve most people get their earnings as a salary, and there are all kinds of differences in vacation days, actual hours worked, etc. However, for simplicity's sake we'll ignore those complications for now and just translate that as roughly $34.50 per hour. Dropping down to the next decile, 40 percent of Americans earn under $50,000 per year, or $25 an hour. At the next level we have 30 percent of Americans earning under $35,000 per year, or $17.50 an hour. In 2017, the average wage paid to manufacturing workers was $20.94 per hour, which is squarely in the middle of these two deciles. Somewhere in those two deciles one could draw the line on "low income" America. The exact line would be arbitrary so let's just assert we have 10–15 percent of the population living at a "low income" level.

Moving down to the next level we have 20 percent of America living under $25,000 per year, or $12.50 an hour. The "official" poverty line varies by size of household. For a family of four, that line is right around $25,000 per year. Dropping to the next level we have 10 percent of America living under $15,000 per year or $7.50 an hour. For a single individual the "official" poverty line is roughly $13,000 per year. The federal minimum wage is $7.25 per hour which translates to $14,000 per year. Getting a full-time minimum-wage job basically puts you at the poverty line. That's true for individuals, and, if both parents work full time and have two kids, its true for those households as well. Full time minimum wage work *is* living in poverty. It is not an escape.

The official statistics on the total number of Americans living below the poverty line has hovered fairly consistently in the 12–15 percent range. There's lots of debate about the exact definition of "poverty" so let's just take all those below $25,000 and call them "poor." So, 20 percent of the country is poor, with slightly more than half of those living in poverty, and 30–40 percent of the population is either poor or low income. Whichever line you decide you want to care about, that's a lot of people. As in 40–50 million in poverty, and 70 million who are undeniably poor. At the very extreme end we have over 600,000 families and over 1 million children living on less than $2 a day.

These statistics are not all that different in other parts of the developed world. As noted, the "official" definition of poverty varies around the world, but most developed nations report somewhere between 10–20 percent of their populations living in poverty. As India and China have climbed out of their stunted development status they have made steady improvements across their vast populations. A recent report on India asserted they now had less than 25 percent of their population below the poverty line. There are no magic solutions that will cause these numbers to dramatically drop. There are and probably always will be somewhere in the 15 percent range of people living in poor conditions. That seems inescapable. Whether you care about them as people or not, they reflect a substantial amount of potential demand for goods and services. They matter to both the potential workforce and to the potential strength of the overall economy. For those of us who care, they also matter just because they are people.

One of the centerpieces of the 1996 reform act was the replacement of the Aid to Families with Dependent Children (AFDC) program with the Temporary Assistance for Needy Families (TANF). The AFDC had been put in place in 1962 and was itself a replacement for the original Aid to Dependent Children (ADC) act from the 1930s. The ADC program, as its name implies, was focused on women with children and did not assume they had ever nor would ever be part of the working population. It did, however, have a strong set of requirements about who "deserved" to be part of the program. It specifically excluded men as well as women who had never married or who had gotten divorced. It also excluded anyone who was not white.

The concept of "deserving" is one of the underlying issues throughout this book. It's obviously a central, almost defining, aspect of the ethic of power belief system. It's fraught with problems, magnified by its own entanglement with a wide range of ideologies. The very concept itself implies a judgment by one group of people over others. Those doing the judging hold assumptions about their own moral superiority. They assert their own morality on others, often in complete and utter ignorance about the real conditions and backgrounds of those others.

Over time, the country realized that white women were not the only ones who could be *deserving* of aid for their dependent children. We also realized that children of widows were not the only ones in need. By 1960, the original program had reached a point where 40 percent of recipients were black and almost two thirds were unwed. The AFDC program was intended to bring the official laws more in line with how they had evolved in practice. It was also buttressed by court rulings that made it clear any racial exclusions were illegal. However, it did not do anything about the original assumption that the recipients had never and would never be employed.

The rules around the program actually created a set of disincentives for finding work. Every dollar earned was subtracted from the benefits one received. Unless you could find a job that paid more than your benefit and that you were confident would not go away it did not make a lot of sense to leave the program. As a result, once people got on the program they tended not to leave. Ironically, Reagan, who hated the whole program, made matters worse by changing the rules so you lost more than a dollar in benefits for every dollar you earned. This structural flaw became the center of deep, ongoing policy debates right up until 1996 and was the primary focus of the reform program.

The TANF program had work and work-related assistance right at its core. The program required one to find a job within two years of getting assistance and capped individuals to five years of lifetime participation. It was also set up as a "block grant" program providing money to the states and allowing the states wide leeway in deciding how best to use those funds. There is essentially no oversight on how the money is actually used and the only guidelines are its four intended purposes which are:

1. Provide cash assistance to the needy. (Most of this was intended for those earning less than 50 percent of the poverty level.)
2. End dependence on government assistance through helping people get jobs and by promoting marriage.
3. Reduce out-of-wedlock pregnancies
4. Promote two-parent families

It's an interesting list of guidelines. It would prove fateful to the program's evolution. The cash assistance was obviously the primary purpose of the entire program. Helping people find jobs, get training, and secure childcare were exactly in line with entire focus on linking the program with work. The marriage and pregnancy points came from the intrusion of the Power ethic. For those of the "strict father" mind-set, poverty has nothing to do with economics; it's the result of a moral deficiency. Addressing the lack of marriage and pregnancy were in their minds central to improving the moral posture of the recipients, making them more "deserving." Others might reject that "moral" intrusion but would not argue that single mothers had much more difficulty getting out of poverty than those with a partner.

In practice the program has been a mess. Under the prior AFDC program over 80 percent of qualified individuals living below the poverty line participated to some degree in the program. Today, under TANF, that number hovers just above 20 percent. In Texas it sits at 5 percent. Prior to TANF, 50 percent of those below the poverty line did not work. In 2012, after TANF and after the great recession, 59 percent of those below the poverty line do not work. Studies have concluded the work incentive aspects of the program have been ineffective because the number of unskilled jobs, particularly for men, continues to decline. This is not a "moral" deficiency on their part, nor a lack of effort. It is an economic issue. Equally problematic has been the impact on actual earnings, particularly for those who did get jobs as the program intended. A full-time job at minimum wage is right at the poverty line. For those who got part-time or temporary jobs their actual job-based income is well below that line. Unfortunately, the combination of low TANF benefits and poor wages has actually produced total incomes on average that are lower than they were under AFDC.

Even worse, of the money provided to the states only about 25 percent makes its way to those recipients as cash assistance. Another 8 percent is spent on training and finding jobs. Childcare, which is a necessity for many seeking work, particularly at this income level, takes up 16 percent. Program administration takes another 7 percent, roughly two to three times what most private charity programs spend. Over 45 percent is spent on other uses, mainly under the marriage and pregnancy guidelines. A great deal of that spending is focused on denying women access to abortions. Most of these other programs have no means testing and cover everyone. At least one state uses the money for college scholarships for families with up to $250,000 in income. What had been the primary source of cash assistance to the poor is now perversely becoming an anti-abortion program for the masses.

How did this evolve that way? Some of this can be chalked up to well-intentioned efforts to deal with all the different complexities of the topic. As an example, the breakdown of the family has been proven to be one of the major factors turning poverty from a "situation" to an inescapable "trap," ensnaring not only the parent but their children as well. These are complex dynamics that actually begin with the early neurobiology of children and then extend across generations. The parenting clauses may have originated in a set of simple moral beliefs, but there was real complexity to deal with as well and many people sincerely wanted to tackle those deep problems.

When most people think of welfare they have some sort of cash payment to the poor in their minds. From the perspective of the poor that actually is crucial and is the reason I have focused so much on the TANF program. When conservatives scream about the horrific burden placed on them by federal programs for the poor this is what they have in mind. But, here's the reality. The TANF program makes up about one half of one percent of the federal budget. And, only 25 percent of that is actually paid to people as cash. Which means we're talking about one tenth of one percent of the budget. It is, quite literally and mathematically, a rounding error. There are other programs like SNAP (food stamps), housing assistance, child nutrition assistance, and the Earned Income Tax Credit, many of which are aimed at what we referred to earlier as "low income" and "poor" Americans. When all of those are added together, the total is still less than 5 percent of the federal budget. All of these programs are dwarfed by Medicaid which we will cover as part of the health care story rather than the poverty story.

What's more, essentially all of these benefits get spent by recipients in their local community. It may be given to them, but they then spend it with others. Money in this part of our world is never static. It flows. That flow fuels the demand side of our economy which generates economic growth, opportunities, and jobs. With the right balance, helping those in need is not a drain on our economy. It's actually an economic stimulus precisely targeted at those communities in greatest need. This crucial observation sits squarely in one of the many blind spots of the neoliberal paradigm. That paradigm simply has no place for market demand as a form of economic stimulus. For anyone with any business experience whatsoever it's a monumental disconnect from reality.

6

China: The Billion-Headed Dragon in the Room

C HINA IS NOT the cause of all these national failures. They actually may contain important parts of the solution. They are almost certain to be as important to the twenty-first-century global landscape as the United States was to the twentieth. That will bring challenges, but it will also bring opportunities. We need to shed all of our preconceptions and stereotypes and begin to learn more about this incredibly complex society. They are culturally more like the United States than many people realize, though they also have their own profoundly different stories and history. They are also increasingly prominent on the global leadership stage, a trend which will only deepen and accelerate in the years to come.

It may take 50+ years for everyone to agree, but eventually history will conclude the most important event of 2001 was China's reengagement with the world, its opening of markets, and its sprint toward world economic leadership. That last statement is not an ideological claim, it's a mathematical one. Indeed, it was China's acceptance of the pragmatic necessity of private property, open markets, and a semi-capitalist economic system that dropped ideology out of the equation and put mathematics in the driver's seat. Let's recall our basic formula describing the size of a nation's economy—GDP equals the size of the workforce multiplied by the productivity of the workforce. In fact, the way the productivity number in that equation is determined is by dividing GDP by the size of the workforce. This is all pretty simple math.

Right now, China's productivity is much lower than any Western nation. However, that's because they are still climbing the development curve. Their productivity is growing much, much faster than any Western nation. Again, that's not because they're working harder, it's just a reflection of where they are on the evolution of their market. Over time their productivity level will converge with that of the more developed nations. That's exactly what has been happening. Once they do, it's the size of the workforce that will dictate the relative size of the various markets. And, the Chinese workforce is literally five times larger than the United States'. That's right, five times. They're also more than three times larger than the EU's and 60 percent larger than India's. Some will argue their demographics will cause those factors to decline a bit. But, in even the most extreme cases, its only by a bit. The relative positions are not going to change.

There are two different methods for comparing economies around the world. One simply uses currency conversion. The other uses a method called purchasing power parity (PPP) to adjust the converted currency for the vastly different prices and costs found in different nations. On a PPP basis, China's GDP has already passed the United States', as has the EU's. On a currency conversion basis, they rank number three after the United States and the EU. On at least one major economic measure they're already the largest economy in the world and over the next 5–10 years there is little doubt they will surpass the United States and EU on every major metric.

America is in the process of ceding economic leadership to another nation for the first time in our history. There are very few who seem to have fully acknowledged that reality. That does not necessarily imply we are ceding over-all global leadership, but it does mean we will be sharing the stage in a way we have never done. It won't be a comfortable evolution.

The Chinese are often accused of IP theft and of being unable to innovate. Having personally been involved in numerous complex business deals with the Chinese over the years I can sympathize with that point of view. However, a little perspective is needed on this matter. In the nineteenth century, IP theft between the United States and Europe, in both directions, was pretty common. That dropped dramatically going into the twentieth century, particularly after World War II. The Japanese were accused of being copycats and IP thieves well into the 1960s. Then their own internal innovation began growing and IP enforcement quickly rose to Western norms. The same pattern unfolded in Taiwan and South Korea. And it is now happening in China. In fact, we may well have reached the point where their internal innovation strength will cause them to evolve the same way the United States, Europe, Japan, Taiwan, and South Korea all have. Their "copycat" stage is coming to a close.

There's an annual list of the top supercomputers in the world that the United States has dominated since its inception. In 2015, China took that leadership, including the top spot. Even more impressive, while many of the machines on that list rely on Intel microprocessors, the number one spot uses all Chinese technology. They expect to unveil the first commercial jet that can be a real global rival to Boeing and Airbus in 2019. Eric Schmidt, the former CEO of Google, has warned repeatedly that he fully expects what he calls a "Sputnik moment" in the field of artificial intelligence (AI), sometime in the next 5+ years. He foresees the Chinese unveiling an AI system that will leapfrog the best from the West. In the arena of modern high speed trains, China has already caught up with the best from Germany. The days of characterizing China simply as the land of low cost assembly are over. They still do much of that, though in actuality they themselves often farm the lowest value work to places like Vietnam.

China is also reaching outward. In some ways this is the biggest cultural shift for this ancient land. They have always seen themselves as global leaders, but they now see that role as encompassing more than just their own territories. Their largest program is called the Belt and Road Initiative (BRI), which is an economic development initiative that reaches from the westernmost regions of China across Asia and all the way to Europe. The closest parallel would be the post-WWII Marshall Plan, which eventually funneled approximately $13 billion in aid all over Europe and beyond. That was a massively complex endeavor. Many of the "investments" were actually nothing more than loan guarantees. The projects themselves were highly diverse including organizing educational tours for European manufacturing executives to US plants to learn best practices. Probably as important as the direct capital infusion was the knitting together of US and European business interests, relationships, and beliefs.

China's BRI along with their related economic development efforts throughout Africa have similar objectives. Both of these are extensions of the programs they have used inside China to drive their own development. They are massive displays of economic power. The BRI alone is *budgeted* at $900 billion. It will dwarf the Marshall Plan. It has been estimated to impact 65–70 percent of the world's population and GDP. Their development programs in Africa similarly dwarf the activities from any other nation or region. There is no doubt many of these will suffer from corruption, there will be several boondoggles along the way, and the overall program will be uneven in its success and impact. But amid all of that there will be successes and, just as the United States experienced through the Marshall Plan, deep relationships and enduring partnerships will certainly emerge. They are laying the foundations for an economic empire that has high odds of leading the globe.

Those plans, like most economic plans, can seem benign. After all, when the United States set out to help rebuild Europe and develop multinational business relationships, the results were pretty good for most of the world. However, China in the twenty-first century is not the United States in the post-WWII period. For all its economic flowering, it remains a tightly managed and controlled society. There are estimates that somewhere around 800,000 Muslims are currently interred in Chinese prison camps. Chinese citizens are monitored and "scored" on a "social index" that essentially measures a form of conformity and loyalty to the party. That score can impact a wide variety of rights that we would put in the "inalienable" category. Repression can be swift, seemingly arbitrary, and brutal. The reality that we will soon be sharing the global leadership stage with such a regime should give us pause.

That's an unsettling reality and it brings into question just what role we're playing in the world. It may be mathematically impossible for us to match the eventual economic scale China is likely to achieve, but that doesn't mean we need to cede complete leadership. Unfortunately, the contrast in global strategies with the United States is striking. Our errors have clear parallels to what happened when nations around the world began throwing off colonialism. As we noted, in the lead-up to the Vietnam war, the United States and the West offered no vision for the future to the countries seeking a path of escape. We gave some encouraging lip service, but no more. The communist regimes in Russia and China offered both visions and real, active, assistance. Those were all tainted offerings, but in the absence of real alternatives they were frequently embraced. Similarly, the United States looks at all the poor and developing nations in our modern world with either pity or disdain. Neither of those leads to growth and development. We send food and medical assistance, which may be appreciated, but does little to put any sub-Saharan or Central American nation on a productive path. The Chinese send planners and investors to build railroads, ports, roads, and public buildings. Some of this is obviously a result of our reliance on the private sector. And there certainly are investments flowing in from the more enlightened global corporations. However, our collective impact is tiny compared to China's.

To highlight this, imagine if you will a completely different strategic approach for the United States to take with Mexico. Today we view that nation as a member of NAFTA—to buy things from us; as a source of low-cost labor, to make things for us; and as a consistently irritating source of immigrants we don't want. We focus on our power and wealth, not on the value creation potential latent in the Mexican population. What if instead we decided to work with the Mexican government on a joint investment program to build up their economy and infrastructure. The biggest problem with such a strategy, frankly, would be the deep and widespread corruption of the current Mexican government. Simply sending money would be a disaster. To make this strategy work we need a direct "hands-on" engagement. We could approach it in ways that were similar to the Marshall Plan or how we built the US rail infrastructure in the nineteenth century. Joint government programs could provide vision, planning, right-of-way access, and loan guarantees. Private investment and organizations from both the United States and Mexico could build. We could team up to control the criminal cartels. Despite those who believe the contrary, the cartels do not represent Mexico. If we did it at the scale the Chinese have been doing it in Africa we'd probably have Americans wanting to move down to Mexico to participate in all the construction. Would the whole endeavor be expensive? Sure. Should we do the same for ourselves first? Absolutely. That's actually what China did. We'll come back to that priority discussion later; for now the point is the choice between a strategy focused on value creation versus a strategy focused on power and value capture. Ironically, and possibly dangerously, on today's world stage, it is China embarking on value creation strategies around the world, not the United States.

The other misleading trope about China is that all of their economic growth came as a result of US outsourcing, specifically contract manufacturing. Like many of these beliefs there's a kernel of truth that's been turned into a highly misleading caricature. This is not to say they haven't been a major global supplier of contract manufacturing. They certainly have. However, that's not the main economic force driving them forward today and much of the manufacturing work they do these days is for local consumption. Just as Toyota and BMW use plants in the US to build cars for the US market, GM and others use plants in China to build cars for China. The main difference is that China was able to force most of that activity to be done in partnerships with local companies. Those local companies are well on their way to becoming future global competitors. That's the actual form used for most of the IP transfer that has happened over the past two decades. It wasn't outright "theft," it was mutually beneficial partnerships.

Clearly, the Chinese used market access as the "club" to force those deals. It's a great example of how important power is in economic transactions. The Chinese market is simply too large to ignore for any global business. Doing so would not only forgo direct business benefit from that market, but also jeopardize any business strategy that relied on global economies of scale or scope. The Chinese have also been quite adroit at ensuring that their market has pursued the innovation frontiers in sophisticated manufacturing, high tech, clean energy, and electric vehicles. Western firms were able to find terms they could live with even though in every case they did so under duress.

7

SUMMARIZING WHERE WE STAND

IT's EASY TO lose sight of just how much progress has been made over the last 150–200 years. Famine deaths which were major factors of the human experience well into the twentieth century have dropped dramatically and now occur only in small, though tragic, pockets. Overall life expectancy has risen substantially. Extreme poverty is still a problem but has dropped enormously around the world. To our great shame, one of the worst places in the developed world is the United States. The large-scale wars between great powers and in fact the total number of deaths in battles have all dropped substantially.

All major developed countries around the world have established programs and institutions to ensure that basic social needs are in place for their populations. Those programs include retirement insurance, health care, education, and other social services. Around the developed world spending on these services as a percent of GDP appears to have reached a stable plateau. The world has found a sustainable balance between assistance and moral hazard. We'll examine the problems the United States has on this metric a bit later, but overall the planet is converging on a healthy and globally consistent balance.

Crime rates in the United States have dropped to levels not seen since the 1950s. Like our examples of famine and extreme poverty, crime is still a problem in certain pockets, but overall, it's no longer a national issue. And, while we do have a critical growing problem with wages and inequality, most of us now spend only 30 percent of our disposable income on necessities instead of the 60 percent we spent in the late 1920s. We're making steady progress climbing an economic version of Maslow's hierarchy.

We've also made progress on increasing our tolerance for the diversity in America. Both our real demographic diversity as well as our awareness of the range and depth of humanity have grown dramatically in recent decades. We have begun the process of embracing each other and healing. For the majority of us, this is a source of national pride and delight and our laws are steadily shifting to reflect those truths.

I'm confident our glass is more than half full.

However, the minority who find these changes threatening has been digging in their heels, becoming steadily more nativist, and allowing their fears to be turned into anger and hate. Their racism and sexism are more direct and overt than in the recent past. And, like a cornered animal, they have become far more dangerous. According to FBI statistics, in 2016 hate crime incidents rose by 4.6 percent. In 2017 that jumped by 17 percent. And it's actually worse than even those dismal statistics indicate. Independent audits of the FBI data have identified dozens of well-known hate crimes that are not included in the FBI statistics. The Anti-Defamation League has also calculated that 71 percent of all extremist related killings over the past decade were committed by white supremacists, 26 percent by Muslims, and 3 percent by a variety of left wing anarchists and black extremists. The violence of our home-grown white supremacists has become a real problem for America.

None of this resistance will halt our progress, but that very progress is putting substantial stress on our social cohesion. That in no way implies we should slow the ship, but we do need to set out some lifeboats for those who are struggling to stay on board.

This brings us to the darker sides of our current reality. Despite all our enormous progress we need a candid assessment of the damages we've collectively inflicted on each other and our world. One of the largest and most important issues is the reality of climate change. This is a vitally important topic that would easily fill an entire book. Most of it is therefore out of scope, but the policy recommendations to follow will include both key infrastructure investments and international accounting and trade agreements. The environment is only one of the many long neglected issues with global trade. Our utter failure to deal with working conditions, wages, and employment terms as integral components of the global economy is a disgrace that has brought enormous damage throughout the country. Most of the social ills we associate with "globalization" stem from this irresponsible neglect.

It's no surprise we've ignored all those topics in the global arena since we've also provided little more than lip service to those issues at home. The neoliberal paradigm simply doesn't see any of this as important. As a direct result, the demand side of our economy is a train wreck. Our economy no longer works for the nation and must be overhauled so that it works for all. In the process we need to reorient our businesses to once again focus on real and sustained value creation, not Wall Street–oriented quarterly shareholder shenanigans.

Just as a set of misguided neoliberal beliefs have caused our businesses to lose their compass headings, our government is suffering from similarly massive mismanagement. Our government has lost all understanding of the role it plays in creating value for our nation. It has allowed the voices who fear its power to rob it completely of its core purpose. We've allowed our social contracts for health, education, and retirement to be hijacked and turned into malignant cancers that prey on our citizens instead of serving them. We've sat idly while trillions of dollars of national infrastructure were left to decay and rot. We've engaged in tax schemes that literally suck trillions of dollars of value out of our economy and redistribute what remains into a casino of wild speculative capital.

These economic mistakes are compounded by government losing sight of its very reason for existence—the protection of our citizens from the predators of society. The core values of a democratic society have been subverted by the movement dedicated to the destruction of democracy. Our laws have been hijacked, and, with domestic political bribery now legal, so too has our election process.

Meanwhile the tectonic shifts from free-flowing global capital and goods are wrenching families and communities apart. Those impacts have raged like a tornado through major regions of the country. All of these stresses are quite deep and real. They are magnified by the simple fact that people do not understand what's driving all this change. Demagogues play on those uncertainties, whipping up fears about "others." Whether those are people of other colors, other religions, or other nations, they are "others" and can be blamed for everything.

Even when "others" are not being blamed, they are viewed with suspicion and distaste by probably a third of the country. That resistance has deep roots. The various "story-based realities" we've described beginning after the civil war and growing right up to the latest denials of climate change are now all interwoven into a complete worldview. Every thread of that worldview carries a few strands of truth blended with deep distortions, omissions, and hidden resentments. It's a toxic mix.

The demagogues have taken that to new levels with grand conspiracy theories and ever wilder departures from reality. Immigration is at all-time lows, yet they have convinced their followers there are hordes of violent, slobbering rapists streaming into the country. People are convinced whole US communities have been forced into Sharia legal systems and that abortion clinics routinely yank nine-month-old fetuses from their mother's wombs and slaughter them. Out of this incredible collection of fictions comes an enthusiastic embrace of Russian kleptocrats, European Nazis, and US white supremacists. Irrational nationalism is on the rise for the first time since the Fascist movements in Europe that led to World War II.

When that breakdown in social cohesion is combined with the economic instabilities described earlier, along with the inexorable rise of China to challenge our global leadership, we have reached a critical juncture. The path of history points toward economic collapse, the rise of internal authoritarianism, and the potential for devastating global military conflict. We need a better option and its time we figured out what we want that to be.

It's time for a fifth paradigm.

PART 3

THE FIFTH PARADIGM: A WAY FORWARD

1

A Twenty-First-Century
Political Philosophy

To chart that better path, to find a new paradigm, we need to start by getting centered on our core values and philosophy. When we extract ourselves from the left-right rabbit hole where do we land? The whole world understands the basic principle that private property and open markets are crucial to any real prosperity. It also knows that certain basic social services need to be provided by any civilized government. There are loud and insistent voices down in the rabbit hole that hate these truths, but they're truths nonetheless and widely understood.

The real world includes activities managed by the private sector, the public sector, publicly funded private sector, privately funded public sector, public-private partnerships, and probably many more blended constructs. In fact, I'm not sure there's anything that isn't some sort of blend. Certainly, every aspect of the private sector includes some sort of public sector role. The very fact that we can put trust in contracts and currency, let alone use the roads and breathe the air, is all you need to confirm that simple truth.

Even down in the rabbit hole only the most radical voices would attempt to argue for a pure form of communism, capitalism, fascism, libertarianism, or colonialism. As for "socialism," I'm not even sure what that is supposed to mean anymore. For our storytellers at Fox News it means Venezuela, even though most of that story is really about rampant theft, corruption, and currency mismanagement. For others it could be interchangeable with "European" even though none of those governments are even remotely similar to Venezuela.

For the most part all those terms have just become expletives used to sneer at or demean people, ideas, or proposals. Great tirades and campaigns are routinely raised against every one of those words, but those attacks are aimed at the people linked to the words, not the concepts they embody. In the early part of the twenty-first century all those concepts have lost both relevance and credibility. None of that is at all useful.

Our philosophical approach needs to be drawn instead from the strategic insights and lessons we've explored, and that new philosophy needs to be the basis for our roadmap for the future. Those lessons alone are probably insufficient for the full task, but they're more than enough to stake out some fairly interesting boundaries, starting points, and compass headings.

So, what is that "out of the rabbit hole" conceptual frame?

WHAT'S IMPORTANT TO OUR SOCIETY

We begin our work on this key topic with a discussion about what's important to our society. This needs to become a major part of our democratic social dialogue. Many in today's society have become ungrounded on these basics and serious discussion about what we each see as important will be essential to our healing. Consider this my opening contribution to that endeavor. And, to be clear, none of these are guarantees. All of these come with responsibilities. But, these are values I believe we share and hold important. They are compass headings, not edicts or promises.

It begins with people.

People are what matter. There are other things that matter as well, but this philosophy places people in the primary position of value. People need to be safe. They need to be safe from war, from crime, and from bigotry, misogyny, and harassment. People need to be healthy. That doesn't mean bad things don't happen, nor that health is some sort of guarantee or divine right. It simply means we recognize that health is an integral element of the well-being of our society and something we value highly. People also need lives of dignity, satisfaction, and purpose. Nobody can define what that means for any other human being, but for every human being it's essential.

The bedrock of all of this is freedom. People need to be free. They need to be able to explore and find what gives them satisfaction and purpose. They need to be able to hold and express their beliefs. They need to be able to associate and assemble with others. They need to be able to love, cherish, and be intimate with whomever wants to reciprocate. And, they need the freedom to be private whenever, or about whatever, they choose.

Our economic and political systems must recognize that people are people, not economic production factors nor political interest groups. We need to "rehumanize" our thinking and in the process, we will also revitalize those systems. The successes and failures described in this book are filled with the lesson that philosophical abstractions that ignore the complex realities of people are stepping stones on a path to failure.

To make any of the above possible we need sustainable economics. Without that, everything else is just fantasy. The wellspring of economics is value creation. It's not propertyor capital or wealth. Those are all manifestations or tools. The core is value creation, specifically *economic value creation.* In order to make economic value creation sustainable, our objective is to align value capture with its creators. Markets do not always do that on their own. As we've seen through our various lessons, sustainability requires the alignment of wages with productivity, which we have observed will not happen without intervention. We also know that sustainability requires economic behavior that neither destroys people nor our environment. This is *not* to say there will not be "creative destruction" as defined by economists. There will be. In fact, that too is essential for sustainability. In order for that to happen, we need free flowing capital, money, goods, and services. We also need to avoid the dangers and harness the potential of free-flowing work, not people.

Our society also needs a rich vein of value creation that is *not* strictly tied to economic value. The lives of satisfaction and purpose asserted in our opening paragraphs include far more than just our economic activities. This includes science, discovery, culture, arts, wisdom, and insight. Those may seem "highbrow," but they're important sources of value creation. It also includes music, entertainment, stories, sports, and competition. Those too are important sources of value creation for real people. The value we create when we nurture and affirm the value of people as people is important to our moral heart. Whether that's done through churches, charitable activities, or simply welcoming strangers, it's vital to who we are. The authenticity of local farms and craftsmanship is also a distinct form of value creation. Many of the things I've cited have their own economic value creation dimensions, but it's important to keep that distinct from the recognition of the direct value embodied in all of these aspects of our lives. These are things that are important to people as people and a society of real value is rich in all of these.

The next core value is our planet. Our society cannot be healthy if our lands, water, and air are contaminated. This is also something of direct value in and of itself. Its value is not dependent on economic exploitation either through resource extraction or tourism. It has value on its own. Again, this is not to say its economic role is unimportant. We're simply asserting that the planet is something we value independent from the needs of our sustainable economics. This bedrock set of human values is magnified enormously by the challenge of climate change. Simply put, we're on a path that will render much of the planet uninhabitable for much of the year. Since markets alone cannot address this issue its very existence is denied by those whose conceptual frames don't allow for the reality of any such problem.

Finally, we also value our social cohesion. We value being a part of a family, a community, and a nation, not just a group of unaffiliated individuals. This does not mean we agree on everything. Nor does it mean we have the same cultural background or racial history. It does mean we share some substantial subset of the values described above. It also means we agree on some meaningful shared understanding of reality, of truth itself. In fact, we unfortunately do need to be clear that reality and truth itself are crucial values of a healthy society.

To maintain cohesion amid all the freedom and diversity I've outlined we need a certain level of civility and tolerance for others. This obviously does not include rape, murder, theft, or any other behavior that is directly harmful to others. It does mean we cannot expect to simply impose our beliefs and desires on others, nor can we expect them to behave the way we think they should. We need to see each other as free adults, not children to be disciplined, and we need laws and customs that reflect the challenges that will naturally arise.

So, what we value are people, freedom, sustainable economics, diverse sources of human value creation, our planet and its climate, our families, communities, and nations, as well as the truth, civility, and laws to live together as free adults. These are our proposed compass headings.

MARKETS MAKE EVERYTHING POSSIBLE

Sustainable economics are only possible with free and open markets. That long running debate is over. This too is a core part of our philosophy. As we will cover below, these are not perfect instruments. They need more than just an invisible hand. However, they are far and away the best mechanism ever used to deliver the prosperity we need. With the exceptions noted below, this is in large part because they provide enough of a dynamic balance between value and power to align value creation with value capture. This is in no way a claim that every exchange happens in the absence of the power dimension. Power is *always* a factor and the differential power among participants consistently introduces distortions into the value equation.

Markets require capital to function. This means respecting private property rights are essential. There will always be a mix of productive and speculative capital. We recognize both have important roles to play in our sustainable economy. However, we also recognize they operate with very different risk profiles and that speculative excesses can be extremely harmful. When the private pensions and retirement savings of our society are used to fund reckless gamblers that is not sustainable economics. It is the opposite and is not something we need to tolerate as a society.

We also recognize there are a large and growing number of things that markets are either ineffective or unable to manage. In some cases that can be addressed through introducing certain regulatory functions, but in many cases, markets simply are not the right tool. The neoliberal desire to ignore this reality is not only not realistic, it's not even faintly desirable. We are more than economic creatures with a dollar amount stamped on our forehead. We'll describe our answers for these crucial dimensions of society in later sections, but for now let's run through the major lessons we've covered so far.

The nineteenth-century commodity exchanges demonstrated how essential it was to put controls on speculative capital to avoid market distortions. We also saw from that period the damage caused by monopolies, particularly those engaged in vital roles in other industries. Allowing railroad monopolies to destroy 95 percent of the oil industry just for the benefit of Standard Oil is not what we want from our sustainable economics. Replicating that mistake as we are with today's internet service providers is sheer lunacy. We've also seen that the power differential between people and businesses means markets fail to align wages with real economic value. The historic solution of unions probably created as many problems as it solved so we'll propose a series of different strategies, but there can be no doubt something is needed. Externalities like environmental impacts and things like product safety can be managed to some degree through markets, but only through the imposition of effective standards and full external cost allocations. The nation's infrastructure and basic schools are simply not suited to markets. Publicly supported higher education in particular is simply essential for a well-functioning democracy. The absence of any price elasticity makes the idea of markets in health care not just silly, but economically reckless. Having profits drive our justice system ranks among the many immoral things we as a nation have done at the behest of the neoliberal priesthood over the past few decades.

All of these will need strategies other than simple markets. The power of free markets is absolutely essential for our society, but they have limits and need regulation. Those regulations are needed for them to work as they are intended; they are needed to avoid abuse, particularly by speculators; and they are needed to ensure the economics they deliver are sustainable for society. Most of all, regulations are needed to ensure people are valued appropriately, both as economic participants and as people, and that the results keep the demand side of our economy in balance with supply.

If our values are our compass headings, markets are our vehicles. They aren't our only ones, but they will carry most of us, most of the time, so it's important they are well tuned machines.

GOVERNMENT HAS A VITAL ROLE

We will spell out specific strategies and policies in later chapters. This section is intended to be clear about the overall philosophy. It starts with the central phrase from our founding document, "to secure these rights, governments are instituted among men." It's a crystal-clear statement that the entire purpose of government is to be the guarantor of our rights, our freedoms. That foundation includes the formation and enforcement of laws that protect those rights. Society is filled with predators of all stripes, from common criminals to wealthy barons and petty princes. Government must specifically shield the vulnerable from all those who would prey on them, would deny them their rights. The efforts by the anti-democracy movement to turn this upside down must be resisted and reversed.

In addition to our internal protections, government must provide basic defense of the nation and must lead in the management of our relationships with other governments. There's an entire range of responsibilities associated with this topic, most of which are out of scope for this book. However, trade and immigration policies are integral elements of our twenty-first-century strategy and are vitally important government roles.

As we spelled out earlier, government has a crucial role in ensuring that our markets and economy function properly and sustainably. To reiterate, our government must ensure our markets have adequate liquidity, our currency remains stable, and that we take pragmatic action if and when there are serious economic disruptions. Government owns responsibility for our infrastructure. The shirking of that responsibility over the past several decades has undoubtedly played a role in our slowing productivity growth. Government also drives most of the basic scientific research of the nation. That is vital to maintain. On the technology side, government has tended to focus primarily on defense needs, but there's ample evidence in history that it is capable of creating far more value than that. Government also plays an important role in funding many of the noneconomic sources of value creation that are desirable for our society. That particular formula probably needs to be reworked for the era we're entering, as we will suggest below, but the role remains.

Government must also define the rules and regulations that determine how our markets function. Those rules must enable the market to thrive *and* must enable people and the environment to thrive as well. We need to seek strong, steady productivity growth while ensuring the aggregate demand side of the economy keeps pace with those supply side improvements. We need to define standards that ensure major externalities are properly accounted for in business expenses and liabilities. Finally, we need to define hard boundaries on morally unacceptable practices like slavery, discrimination, and wanton environmental destruction.

There are an important set of social functions that markets simply cannot address. This includes health care, education, retirement, and assisting the needs of those at the bottom of the economic pyramid. Markets do play a major role in handling retirement assets, but we know that needs oversight to ensure risks are transparent and it needs to be augmented with an insurance based financial model that pools our shared risks and a portion of our assets. There are many who want to debate these truths, but every developed society in the world has come to the same conclusions on every one of these points. In our later discussion on health care we'll discuss how our misalignment on that important social need is a major hindrance to the global competitiveness of the US workforce and has actually put our entire economy in jeopardy.

The resources to support all these activities must be secured through government-imposed taxes. This is one of the major exercises of government power. Our internal checks and balances provide some control over this, however, it is a power abused by both sides in the left-right rabbit hole. Many, if not most, of the debates about government's role in society are really poorly framed debates about taxation. Most of those debates end up being driven by various parties attempting to exercise power rather than any discussion of shared value. This is an important area where we need a new formula to put power back in balance so that the value of government can once again have relevance.

The entire social governance strategy chosen by our Founding Fathers was based on keeping different forms of power in balance. The strict separation of church and state limited the church to exercising its power only in the spiritual realm and then only for its freely chosen adherents. The military was placed under strict civilian/political control, neutralizing its internal power while ensuring that the value of its external power remained strong. Our democratic institutions are intended to protect people from predation by the wealthy but are themselves strictly limited in their scope and power to do so. Those limits are intended to ensure wealth can retain its ability to generate value. Finally, our democratic power is fragmented between national, state, and local levels, and within those between executive, legislative, and judicial branches. The value of people is paramount, but the power from that dimension must also be neutralized. The purpose of every element in that complex design is to neutralize power within and across its various dimensions. Democratic institutions are central to its design and people are of primary value, but it is far from a simple democracy.

All of these internal checks and balances are good, but government still holds the ultimate power in the nation. That power should be used to intervene in situations where power is badly out of balance and should be used to the extent necessary to put power back in balance. The government thumb on the scale should simply put other market and social forces back in play. There are many places where we've identified dynamics in the market where power is not in balance and therefore where a government role is needed. The trick in each case is to define policies that correct those imbalances, and no more. That will be the objective in the discussions to follow. And, like our discussion on values, those objectives are not guarantees, they are compass headings

REVISITING OUR NORTH STAR

Once you're out of the rabbit hole, none of the above is particularly radical. In many ways it simply reflects the pragmatic conclusions embodied in our history. In fact, the key elements could be derived from the central paragraph of the Declaration of Independence.

Let's revisit that for a moment and reflect on what it says in the context of the philosophy outlined above.

"We hold these truths to be self-evident, that all men are created equal . . ."

Just as we have asserted, the declaration puts *people* first. A modern version would probably replace the word "men" with "people," but we can set that aside as an artifact of history. Note that it does not say, "all property owners." Nor does it say, "all white people." Nor "all Christians." Nor "all businesses." It doesn't even say "all Americans." It says everybody.

". . . that they are endowed by their creator with certain unalienable rights . . ."

I personally have no need for the "by their creator" part of that phrase but have no objection to those who do. Since it makes no mention of *which* creator, it can include genetics along with the specific god of whatever religion someone might care about. More to the point, these are "unalienable rights." They are not rights that must first be earned or deserved. They are not reserved for the wealthy, nor those who hew to some specific moral or religious code. They are not given to us by the government, by our boss, nor any other authority. They apply equally to the poorest among us. They are innately human.

". . . that among these are life, liberty, and the pursuit of happiness."

As many have noted, "life" and "liberty" are viewed as rights in themselves, while in the case of "happiness," the right is its pursuit, not its realization. But, its pursuit *is* listed as a right and what is being pursued is happiness, not endless work. Those who feel they have the right to enslave others and deprive them of that pursuit are violating this precept. Those who feel even the pursuit of happiness must first be earned, need to look up "inalienable" in the dictionary.

"That to secure these rights, governments are instituted among men . . ."

As we noted above, the purpose of government is to secure those rights. That's its raison d'etre. When we use the power of government to correct imbalances in the market that's not an overreach. In fact, the declaration does *not* say "*markets* are instituted among men." It is for precisely the purpose of securing the rights of people over markets that governments exist. (As an aside, those caught up in the conservative trope that *The Federalist Papers* deny this role need to go back and read the actual documents much more carefully. While it is true that *Federalist* 10 spells out limits on this power the entirety of that document both assumes and acknowledges the vital importance of precisely this role. All of the government powers described in this book are, in fact, consistent with *Federalist* 10.) This is the central element the anti-democracy movement understands and rejects. This is what democracy itself is all about. Using government to secure the rights of *people* over the power of wealth, aristocracy, or heredity. Those who want to assert standing on the side of people is some form of communism have not heeded the lessons of history. Democracy is the political tool for the everyday man or woman and the current assault on this precious institution is a neoliberal knife being stabbed into the heart of our national soul.

". . . deriving their just powers from the consent of the governed . . ."

The consent is from all of us. Not just certain members of society. It is not just the consent of the wealthy, nor of property owners. The powers do not derive their just nature by being for sale to the highest bidder. They do not come from genetic heredity nor financial inheritance. For those powers to be "just" they require our democratic consent, meaning social cohesion is a necessity. Social cohesion and consent for the use of government power to secure our human rights is the heart of our formula.

The other elements of the philosophy we described above all build from that philosophical core using the lessons of history. At some deep level, we are not changing course in any fundamental way. We're just adjusting to the technical, economic, and social evolution of our society. We use cell phones instead of quill pens. Our agrarian economy has been joined by an incredible diversity of industries. We see all men and women of all races and denominations as members of the human race. Yet, at the core we're on the same course we've always been. Our true national compass settings haven't really changed, even though it often seems that many of us may have lost their sense of direction.

2

A New National Economic Strategy

Our philosophical compass heading may not have changed, but our strategy to get there definitely needs to do so. All of the strategies I will describe in this book are US strategies. They reflect our socioeconomic status, our history, our values, our social contract, and our priorities. However, these must all fit into a global context. One of the many lessons from the world of business strategy is the usefulness of benchmarking. Today's global landscape provides a rich and varied set of insights on many of the things we will seek to redesign.

Like any benchmarking examination we need to factor in the huge variations around the globe. Comparing ourselves to South Yemen or Hong Kong, to pick two extremes, isn't helpful. In general, the OECD averages are useful as are the specific major countries in Europe along with Japan and South Korea. For some exercises, we will toss out the "outliers" who represent extremes. When we look at taxes, for example, Sweden, Denmark, and to some degree Finland tend to distort the overall pattern. We will comment on them, but not use them as representative of the global norm we're examining. Similarly, China, India and to some degree Russia offer some useful insights, but our national systems are so different they too will be excluded from most of our comparisons. The same goes for countries like Saudi Arabia or Norway where state-controlled oil revenues make many comparisons meaningless.

REDESIGNING FOR THE TWIN TOWERS OF THE TWENTY-FIRST-CENTURY ECONOMY

We need to start our investigations right at home, looking at where we are today through the lens of the lessons from our review of history. We've highlighted a huge range of both economic and social parallels to the late 1920s that were all factors leading to the Great Depression and World War II. Having survived the Great Recession we may feel confident that we don't have an immediate financial crisis to deal with even if the economic structural instabilities of a weakened demand side and growing wealth inequality remain.

However, this predilection around finance has been blinding us to the full extent of the crisis. We've lost 7 million good jobs. The communities those jobs were concentrated in remain in serious distress. We've added over 50 million new jobs which is good. However, less than one-third of those are solid contributors to a healthy economy. Of the remainder, half are a wasteful side effect of our broken health care system and half are basically paid at the poverty level. And, "oh, by the way," none of those jobs are really viable replacement options given the skills of the 7 million people who lost their jobs. We can add to that our oft repeated point that across the whole national workforce wages have not grown with productivity and have barely kept pace with inflation. And that's been true for almost 50 years. Fifty years is almost two full careers, two generations of Americans with no real wage increases in their lifetimes. After two career lifetimes it's no surprise so many people struggle to find hope.

The unions that once helped with this have been under sustained neoliberal assault and are a mere whisper of their former power. They've collapsed. So too has much of small-town America. I've driven back and forth across this country almost a dozen times over the last few decades. With a few exceptions which we will discuss below, what you find are downtown Main Streets filled with boarded up buildings, graffiti, and broken windows. They are scenes of desolation and desperation. There's often a Walmart somewhere nearby, a fast food joint or two, a few national franchise outlets, including the ubiquitous dollar store, and that's it. These are no longer quiet hamlets with local character, dignity, and value.

Instead you find a growing opioid epidemic and the emergence of a phenomenon some refer to as "death from despair." People are killing themselves, either quickly through suicide or slowly through substance abuse and failing health. The crisis is here and now. People are the lifeblood of this country, not the New York Stock Exchange. They aren't just struggling, they're dying. Equally bad, those who don't succumb become fodder for demagogues fueling fears and anger toward "others."

The good news is our history shows us a formula to tackle this crisis. When our economy undergoes this sort of profound transition we know markets alone will not provide the answer. We need them, but the formula requires more. We need a modern infrastructure, productive capital, strong wages, and productivity driving technology that are all aligned around the new core of the economy. The key is ensuring that the new economy is a strong, sustaining, and rewarding economy for everyone. We also observed that capital will not be pulled out of speculative vehicles until labor costs rise to their full economic value. Only then will investments in the new technologies begin to fully penetrate and alter the productivity curves of the new core. Markets will not do this on their own. Some sort of intervention to ensure wages reflect economic value is essential. If that's not unions it will need to be the government. Those are really the only choices. Finally, and in many ways most important, people need to be engaged and inspired as people, not labor. They need hope, confidence, and dignity. They need a vision of a better future that is real, not based on fiction, and certainly not based on the hateful messages of demagogues.

To translate that formula for today we need to first understand the new core of the economy. What is it, really? What's the design point we need to align our infrastructure, capital, wages, technology, and people around? To answer this question, we need to look at four different segments of the economy. We'll keep an eye on GDP, but the main focus of this exercise is jobs. Where are they? Where are they growing? What's the new growth engine for jobs?

The first segment I will refer to as our basic foundation. This includes things like state and local government, our remaining agriculture and mining, administrative services, and wholesale and distribution. For this stage of our discussion we'll put construction in this category as well. We'll come back to that important sector a bit later when we discuss our infrastructure strategy. Collectively, all these sectors make up just over 50 percent of total employment. There's very little growth, in either GDP or employment, but it does represent more than half of us. It really is our foundation. Almost all of these jobs are not subject to global competition. The local fireman or trucker isn't competing with someone from Delhi. While immune from those particular dynamics many will be impacted by the coming generation of technology. We won't see a lot of new jobs in this segment and will probably see some amount of erosion.

The second segment is health care. This has been a huge driver of employment over the past several decades, but it has become a cancer devouring our economy from within. We will cover this in more detail in a following chapter. For the purposes of this section we need to expect this segment to become a major new driver of *unemployment*, reversing the role it has been playing. In other words, fixing this at the socioeconomic macro level is going to create a massive addition to our jobs problem which will probably be on the same scale as the loss in manufacturing jobs since 1979.

The third broad segment includes those sectors that *are* being heavily shaped by global markets and global competitive dynamics. The global market as a whole is vastly larger than the US market and it's exploding. A deep, active participation by US firms is essential to our economy and China is an absolutely critical part of that formula. During the 2008 recession, government intervention may have saved GM from bankruptcy, but it was the Chinese market that got them back on their feet. When IBM was experiencing strong growth in the 2000s, sales to China and the other emerging countries were a larger driver of growth than all other initiatives combined. It's not just manufactured items either. Agriculture exports grew for most of the 2000s peaking in 2014 at approximately $150 billion. The top three buyers of our farming products are China, Canada, and Mexico. The Chinese market alone grew by over 25 percent per year from 2002 to 2013 and was the primary driver of overall export growth. Ignoring China in the early part of the twenty-first century would be as economically foolish as somebody ignoring the United States in the twentieth century.

Global markets are equally important as sources of supply for our own production. When the global price of a component is lower than a domestic price, choosing the local source may feel good, but it will lead to offerings that are uncompetitive in the market. The same is equally true for critical capabilities. When China offers the best solar or battery technology we need to use those offerings. If IBM had not built up its services workforce in India it would have seriously jeopardized the entire company. All companies shaped by global competition must leverage the full global spectrum of suppliers and partners. To do otherwise is to head down the path of global irrelevance. Recognizing and enabling this global imperative will be essential for our economic health. There is no "magic door" that will change these realities. China will not suddenly decide it no longer wants to grow, nor will they accept some edict from us to abandon their plans for leadership.

Global demand and supply are both already important contributors to GDP growth and that will continue. There are also a lot of very good jobs in the sectors being driven by these dynamics. They often require high skills and reward those with generally high wages. However, the global realities also drive many high skilled and most low skilled jobs overseas and as a result the total number of jobs is currently projected to be basically flat to slightly down.

To understand our twenty-first-century strategy for this critical piece of the economy we need to turn to our simple heuristic around the three pillars of economic value creation. Operational efficiency in global production will have a US component, but that's our weakest leg. When all we do is bring foreign factories to our shores we're competing with places like Vietnam over the lowest value in the formula. Our real strengths come in the other two sources of value, innovation and understanding markets. Let's look at each of those.

GLOBAL MARKETS: THE INNOVATION OPPORTUNITY

Managing innovation to consistently deliver successful and valuable economic returns is one of America's great strengths. It's not a superficial feature of our nation. Our culture, values, skills, economics, and institutions have all been aligned over the last 100 years or more to enable this distinct capability. This strength will be a key element in our twenty-first-century strategy. There are, however, critical changes in the landscape we need to recognize.

The first of these deep shifts is the modern reality of diminishing returns. Diminishing returns simply means that adding more capability to an offering adds value, but only up to a certain point, after which the increased value slows and eventually halts. It forms a classic S-curve. This is a common economic reality and works in different ways for our different value creation dimensions. In the area of innovation value, it follows an interesting pattern. For any given "breakthrough" the curve follows its usual S shape, leveling out at some point. And then someone in the market comes up with a new "breakthrough" and the whole process starts again. This successive pattern is quite different from the diminishing returns that accompany economies of scale or scope.

That has led most to believe, implicitly or explicitly, that "there will always be something new" and indeed that does seem to be the case. However, like so many other points we've covered, it has reached a level where the realities no longer match our intuitions. Let's illustrate this with a few examples. First, consider the humble razor blade. When the first company came up with the innovation of stacking two blades instead of just one, that was a valuable innovation. When they went to three, it still had some value, but not nearly as much as the first step. When they went to four or five it became all about marketing. The "innovation" of adding yet another blade to the existing two or three didn't really add much value. That's a classic example of diminishing returns.

Now think about the cereal aisle in your grocery store. Back in the 1960s or 1970s you would find Cheerios, Corn Flakes, Wheaties, and a handful of other offerings. Today there could be hundreds. There could be half a dozen versions of Cheerios alone. That explosion of offerings enables even the oddest and most unusual tastes to find something they like. In aggregate the value being created has gone up. However, each additional offering is adding less and less value. At some point, the whole exercise begins to become so excessive that the added choices actually begin causing consumer stress and the aggregate value begins to decline. That's another variation on diminishing returns.

The third example is the auto industry. This one illustrates many different dimensions of the phenomenon, including how profound and subtle the impacts have become. The first point is that cars have been in "continuous improvement" mode for a long time; long enough that many basic assumptions have changed. Quality and reliability have improved to a degree that the expected economic life of an auto has increased dramatically. In the 1970s having a car last much over 100,000 miles was considered exceptional. These days that's one-half to one-third of the expected useful life. Tesla claims their latest model is designed to last 1 million miles with one or two battery pack replacements. Furthermore, the average family sedan today has acceleration and other performance characteristics that could only be found on a supercar from the 1970s. The average horsepower of new cars sold in the United States is expected to pass 300 horsepower in the very near future. When a performance vehicle that already has 500 horsepower gets to 600 horsepower it will certainly be a marketing point, but, like the shift from three razor blades to four, its real incremental value is questionable.

What has happened as a result of both of these points is that the market for used vehicles has gone from a sideline to a central feature of the entire industry. This trend is far more widespread than most realize. Various forms of "resale" have become major factors in one industry after another. Ironically, the initial high price and high quality of many luxury goods has made those markets some of the fastest growing. Whatever stigma may have been associated with "used" is rapidly vanishing.

However, this is not the end of innovation in autos. Quite the contrary. Over the next decade or so, electric vehicles are likely to explode from a tiny sliver of the market to *being* the market. Some of this will be due to worries about climate change, but that will not be the primary driver. Some of this will be due to the interests and desires of the Chinese market, which has now become the largest in the world. But, most of it will come from the enormous increase in design flexibility and sheer capability of electric vehicles. If you think about conventional cars there are inherent limits on their designs. The motor itself is large and heavy. The transmission is similarly substantial. There must be room set aside for a large gas tank that must be shielded in the event of a crash. Front and rear crumple zones are needed for safety. And then there are the aerodynamic realities. All of this changes in an electric vehicle. The engine is comparatively tiny, in fact there might be two, three, or even four of them. There usually is no transmission. Instead of a large bulky gas tank you have flat batteries spread across the base of the vehicle. The crumple zones and aerodynamic needs still exist, but without all the other large and bulky elements they can be addressed in substantially different ways. Future auto designs will be able to explore a huge range of new ideas, tailored for different buyers. It should provide an explosion of new innovation and new value creation.

Autos are but one example out of the numerous areas that are still vibrant with innovation potential. Other examples include technologies such as software, AI, aerospace, pharmaceuticals, genetics, electric vehicles, and many others. America can collaborate with the world, leading through our unparalleled ability to translate technical innovations into products and businesses. These may not generate the job growth they did in the past, but they will definitely continue to drive economic growth.

Innovation is also a major driver in the world of business services including technology services, legal services, marketing services, consulting services, as well as finance, banking, and accounting. Much of this work represents the "unbundling" of existing processes driven by the Coase Theorem. This whole segment is one that will be strongly shaped by the "free flowing work" paradigm. The large firms in this category are all adept at competing for work on a global basis and have spent the last decade or so restructuring their workforces around global skill pools. They move work around the world routinely. The big change coming here is for those technical and management trends to work their way into smaller firms all over the United States. As that happens, all these business service industries will find themselves being driven by the same kinds of global dynamics that have so dramatically impacted our manufacturing base. Some of that will displace local jobs and some will bring new work to our shores. We need to ensure our strategies move us up the value chain even if the total number of jobs edges down or remains flat.

GLOBAL MARKETS: BRINGING THE WORLD TO AMERICA

Our ability to innovate is not our only source of global economic leverage. We also have knowledge, relationships, and the ability to service all the customers in our own vast market. The rest of the globe needs access to all of that. This is one of the three central pillars of economic value creation so it's a substantial capability. In some cases, we may use highly flexible new production capabilities as well as embedded software and AI to mass customize or "tune" offerings for specific needs. In most cases, however, we can stay relatively low-tech and just rely on knowing exactly what a local customer needs. There's a lot of work done in this country by small businesses with clients they've served for decades or generations. Those businesses need to aggressively tap into global supply chains to remain competitive, adding their local familiarity and services as their piece of the value creation. The solar installation service industry is a great example of how effective this combination can be. Low cost and high efficiency solar panels from China have fueled enormous growth in installation service businesses all over the country. There will be more and more examples like that in the years to come and they will generate a sizable number of good jobs.

Many of these firms are small to mid-sized regional operations. They often struggle to get global traction or understand their potential role. They know their markets. They don't know the global sources of goods that could fuel their businesses. This is an area where a coordinated initiative among the chambers of commerce in cities and states around the country could truly help. Just as we did during the Marshall Plan, organizing trade fairs and exchanges between companies around the United States and their potential customers and suppliers in China or India could build important future relationships. The US Chamber of Commerce could take the lead, establishing "enablement" strategies that could include import regulatory assistance and Chinese partnership negotiation connections and assistance. These could then be propagated throughout the country. The more our companies of all sizes are able to effectively partner with these global growth engines the more value they will create for our society.

The overall strategy for the *Global Market Tower* is to fully embrace the global trends and bring our distinct value through our ability to innovate and our intimate knowledge and access to the enormous US market. That strategy will keep us at the forefront of the historic global value expansion and will drive strong economic growth for the nation.

Accepting, indeed embracing, global markets does not mean simply continuing on our current course. Countries around the world are at very different stages of economic development and have very different social contracts with their citizens. It's vitally important that we do not allow our economic engagement with them to drive us to a lowest common denominator that violates our own social contract. One of the biggest areas that hasn't yet sorted out are the global principles around labor laws and free flowing work. There are nations that have still not outlawed child labor and others that allow virtual, if not literal, slavery. We can and should advocate that those practices be changed. However, when they do not, that does not mean we allow ourselves to revert to those primitive social conditions. Even though we have not made any such direct changes to our laws, we *have* allowed the economics of those practices to impact our own and that must cease.

Once we address these issues we can be confident that the jobs associated with these higher value strategies in the global market will generally require high skills and/or local knowledge and will pay reasonably well. The total number of jobs is hard to judge, but we are likely to see modest growth at best. It's definitely core to our economy, but it won't be the new core of America.

All of which leads us to the last segment which is the second new *Tower* of the American economy. That's true for GDP contribution, but even more important it is core to both today's employment and the majority of employment growth. So, what is it? The short, if cryptic, answer is "personal experience services." Unfortunately, you won't find that category in any of the standard economic or labor reports. Not yet, at least.

A NEW VALUE CREATION OPPORTUNITY: PERSONAL EXPERIENCES

We noted earlier that innovation in many traditional segments isn't dead by any means. However, there are now large segments of the market where product innovation has reached deep into the realm of diminishing returns and where long-term reliability levels have dramatically increased economic life spans. For those segments as well as many others, the competitive dynamics are shifting in an extremely profound direction. That shift is also aligning with an equally profound set of attitudinal shifts in the market. In both cases the sources of new value are shifting from the product itself to the *experiences* people have using the product. In many cases that also implies people have less and less need or interest in *owning* the product.

> *Our interests and innovations are shifting from owning things to having experiences.*

Companies of all kinds are discovering this new reality. Every major consulting firm now has practices aimed at helping companies create new value in mature categories by transforming them through personal experiences. This is a massive and crucial shift and critical for our twenty-first-century economic strategies. To understand what this category is all about let's start by going back to all those drives across America. Not every small town has become a wasteland. There are many places with lively and colorful Main Streets filled with unique local businesses and nary a franchise chain in sight other than maybe the gas stations and motels. These are destination sites in the mountains, at the beach, in wine country, or in spots that are rich with some sort of cultural history or attraction. They're thriving with local innovation, crafts, dining, and other experiences. They're very much alive. So too are our National Parks. We may be loving them to death with excess crowds, but we're loving them. We hunger for the activities, discoveries, and joy we find in all these places.

The retail industry provides a further illustration of the dynamic that's under way. If you unpack the underlying business model elements, retailers have historically combined three layers of value creation. These included (1) a set of inventory and logistics capabilities, (2) the curation skills of their buyers, and (3) the experiences they create for customers in their store. All three layers have strong value creation potential. Traditionally that combined value creation has been captured through sales in the store. With the growth of "big box" stores like Walmart and the advent of Amazon the logistics layer of value vanished for most small stores. In fact, it became an uncompetitive aspect that penalized their business. Similarly, the curation value remained for some niches, but has been lessened substantially through the vast selection offered by Amazon. All that remains is the in-store experience. Those retailers that failed to deliver on that dimension have been falling by the wayside.

Now look at those small quirky shops in our mountain towns. They're playing "small ball" on logistics, finding local and unique sources. Their curation is narrow, distinctive, and an integral element of their instore experience. The shopping experience itself is highly personalized and probably includes recommendations for local restaurants and trails. It's a high value equation on a small, personal scale.

At the other end of the spectrum you find REI, one of the most successful retailers in the country. They're large enough that they can get within the realm of diminishing returns on the scale of their logistics. They're focused enough, with buyers who share their customers' passions and know how to curate an appealing selection of merchandise. Their stores are designed entirely around the experiences of their customers. Whether that's the photos on the walls, the displays designed to look like an outdoor setting, or a two-story climbing wall, the outdoor experience permeates the ambiance and mind of anyone walking through the store. They have recently introduced two new service families for their customers. The first are organized outings to various destinations and the second are training and education sessions to help people get familiar with their gear. Both sets of services are growing enormously and enthusiastically embraced by their best customers.

This trend, where the value frontier centers on enhancing customer experience, led a number of business consultants in the late 1990s and early 2000s to predict we were heading not to a "service" economy, but rather to an "experience" economy. Fifteen to twenty years later that appears to be coming true. The challenge has always been the need to create experiences that are both impactful and truly personal. There are several technologies that are finally enabling this shift. Mobile technology is central to our ability to both understand and deliver various types of value creating experiences to different customers at different moments. Insights from the holistic analysis of people as people, not segments, is also key. Those insights leverage big data and the emergence of powerful new theoretical frameworks many of which have emerged from social media analysis. Those working in the field are also predicting an enormous expansion through both the emergence of AI and through the still nascent fields of augmented reality (AR) and virtual reality (VR). Just look at the Pokémon Go game to see a hint of the some of the ideas under development. The new personal experience category will be propelled by these kinds of cutting-edge ideas. They will provide new sources of value creating experiences for companies seeking new differentiation in maturing product categories.

That futuristic vision is exciting but far and away the largest personal experience segments will be the well-established, low-tech, and traditional things we all know and enjoy. Those include shopping, travel, restaurants, bars, entertainment and sporting events. These are all things we consume in our "free" time, our "leisure" time, our time as "people." From that angle we can see it can also include things like religion, adult education, and charitable activities. These are all things we do as part of our "pursuit of happiness" which includes our "pursuit of meaning." It's also enlightening to see how the growth of the "slow food" movement, organic farming, craft beers, and fine craftsmanship in general are all aspects of this trend. Most of those aren't really "services" per se, but they all point to a desire, a hunger, for deeper value than pure economics. They feed our souls. They're designed around our passions as "people." Indeed, the whole economy can be seen as shifting up a sort of Maslow Hierarchy from the basic "life" subsistence provided by agriculture, to the "liberty" provided by appliances and tools, to the "happiness" from the style, comfort and prestige of ownership, and now to the "joy and meaning" that comes from personal experiences, both by ourselves and with companions. We can classify all of these as elements in a new "leisure" industry which allows us to make the following assertion:

The United States is in the midst of a historic transition to a personal experience economy, powered in part by a previously uncategorized leisure industry.

That's the major new economic design point. In total it represents over 60 per-cent of the new jobs being created over the next decade and will soon surpass 32 percent of total employment. All that "pursuit of happiness" is creating a lot of jobs.

There are obvious and simple layers to this trend, but it runs quite deep. Its full power is both subtle and profound. We find its roots when we realize we can, and should, live as people, not as "workers" nor as members of an "inter-est group." When we live our lives for the satisfactions that spring from our souls, from our friends, family, and loved ones, not our "boss." When we live that way businesses (and politicians) need to begin to serve us that way. We are no longer "cogs" in the value capturing machinery of markets. For the first time the market is literally there to serve our desires and to provide us with joy, delight, dignity, and to provide the experiences we use to find our own purposes in life.

TRANSFORMING PERSONAL EXPERIENCE INTO A NEW ECONOMIC TOWER

Before we develop our strategy for this emerging core there are number of questions and issues we need to address. First, setting aside the economics for a moment, is this something we want? Second, and closely related, what must we do for this to be good for society? To answer that we need to address two subsidiary questions. What does it imply socially, culturally, and ethically? And, what must change economically for it to be good?

At some level it seems the answer to the first question is obvious. After all, the pursuit of happiness is right there in the Declaration of Independence. Shouldn't we celebrate the fact that our society is actually reaching a point where that achievement is becoming real? On the other hand, the notion of a nation of leisure could easily be equated with a nation of laziness, or worse, indulgence. In fact, studies of how different segments of the population use their leisure time might seem disheartening. Among the younger male popula-tion, a substantial chunk of that time goes to video games and pornography. Some might feel a nation in perennial pursuit is more virtuous than one that actually achieves. It might also raise questions about global standings and leadership. Can a nation whose internal focus is on personal experiences and leisure be a role model for the world? Or, does it descend into the moral decay of ancient Rome?

These are fair questions, both to raise and to debate. To some degree the answers depend on the next two sections, which deal with social and economic aspects of the shift. However, I think we can begin to frame the answer by going back to the priorities we outlined in our philosophy. We put people first and sustained economics second. In other words, we work to live not live to work. All value is centered on people and our personal transformations come from our experiences, not what we own. We also put noneconomic value creation as an explicit source of value. A close look at that list shows a full spectrum of the things we do and consume when we are not focused solely on economic value. Some of those are leisure oriented, some merely focused on values that are not rooted in economic returns. They are all quite real and quite valuable. A nation rich in that diversity is a much more powerful and complete value creator. It's also true that the time we donate to charitable activity is time we take from our leisure bucket. A Habitat for Humanity home raising can be a fantastically rewarding use of one's leisure time. Last, but not least, we call "leisure time" "free time" for a reason. When we speak of a nation that is free, it must be a nation that has "time" that is free. In some ways our time is our most precious asset and our ability to spend it "freely" our most important realization of value.

A nation and an economy devoted to maximizing the value of our personal time is enhancing the greatest national asset of all.

This trend is real, probably unstoppable, and does indeed align with the values we outlined in our philosophy. How do we ensure it is good? How do we avoid the social and moral pitfalls we listed above? The first essential point is to distinguish between a "work ethic" and an "ethic of work." It's important we maintain a clear social value around work ethics. An erosion of that attribute would put the sustainability of our entire economics at risk. The potential to work less does not mean not working hard. Nor does it imply any diminution of focus on customers or innovation. In fact, both of those latter attributes will be defining characteristics of the most successful in the new economy. Creative experiences tailored for customers is where the value creation frontier is centered and should be a prime area of focus. Our own exploration of the things that bring us satisfaction has the potential to profoundly improve our ability to create that value for others.

Second, we need to rethink the trends around the blending of work and free time. I do not think that blend is bad. Not at all. In fact, I think it can become a central and important aspect of the emerging economy. However, I suggest we do need to flip our orientation about how we perceive and portray the trend. For many, the intrusion of a business call into a dinner at a restaurant is an opportunity for an ostentatious display of "how important I am." What about making that instead a demonstration that even though one has important business issues to handle, it does not mean you need to give up your leisure time. The phone call is the same. The difference is all in how we perceive and portray it. In fact, a full embrace of that insight allows us to dramatically increase our personal activities without sacrificing our critical work ethic. It's no longer an expression of "how important I am." It can become an expression of "how free I am."

Of equal concern is the tendency to allow those interruptions to take over every second. I see far too many couples and families sitting at restaurant tables and all staring into their phones. They've become consumed and no longer live in the moment. They have little awareness of where they are nor whom they are with. It's a sad way to live and hopefully one we can reclaim by putting more value on our time and more valuable personal and shared experiences into our world.

None of this means that there won't be many, even most, who end up spending their free time on activities that are less than noble. In my mind there are two perspectives on this. The first is to simply accept that none of us are in a place to judge what other adults do with their freedom. That's a big part of what it means to be free. If they waste their time, it is their loss. The second, however, is to consistently communicate as a culture the realization that time is our most precious asset. Some of my greatest regrets center on time that neither produced anything nor added to my store of experiences either on my own or in the company of family and friends. Most of us in the latter half of our lifetimes can count that kind of "wasted" time in years and that lesson is one we should share. It is not our place to judge, but there is wisdom in our experience. We need to have a culture that expresses the value of our time in at least equal measure with the value of our work. Hopefully once we do, some of the ravages of our current work obsessed culture can be brought to heel.

Turning to the economic side of the equation, how do we ensure this creates an economy we want? How do we make it sustainable? The first and most obvious issue is that too many of these jobs are simply not good jobs. They suffer from poor satisfaction and even poorer pay. Many are at minimum wage, which today means poverty. Many others basically depend entirely on tips. An economy where a third of the workforce and two thirds of the new jobs are at the poverty line will not have a healthy demand side. Hand in hand with the wage problem is the uncomfortable reality that today these folks need two jobs to survive. That means they do not have the time to be consumers of the very services being delivered by the growing part of the economy. And, as we saw in the McKinsey and Deloitte studies, there's the potential for 30–50 percent productivity improvements in these sectors over the next 10+ years.

Our proposed answer to this set of related problems comes from the lessons of the 1930s. We faced the same problem at that time. The jobs at the heart of the new economy were not good jobs. The formula back then was to reset the standard work week from 50–60 hours down to 40 hours and then allow unions to negotiate work rules and wages. That formula worked and brought the demand side back in balance for 25–30 years. Our recommendation has similarities but seeks to avoid some of the problems created by the original union structure.

There are three key components of the strategy:

1. Change the standard work week from 40 hours down to 32 and then 24.
2. Raise the minimum wage from $7.25 an hour to $18.75 an hour and then $25.00 an hour.
3. Index all wages to productivity growth by industry.

Let's go through each piece of that formula in turn.

The shift to a 32- and then 24-hour work week reflects the potential 40-percent productivity improvement estimated by McKinsey and Deloitte. It is a bit larger as a percent than the 1930s shift from a 60-hour work week to a 40-hour work week, but still within reason considering the looming automation potential. Eventually establishing 24 hours as the standard work week, along with the hike in minimum wage, will create the financial incentives to fuel investment in all that automation. Just like we saw in the 1930s, many of those investments are currently being held back because of the lack of business justification. The undervaluing of people distorts the capital investment incentives that would otherwise be happening if the true economic value of people was reflected in their wages. These steps will fix that.

The current minimum wage has not been reset for almost a decade. It's poverty. Tipped workers can generate better results, but it's a highly unreliable source of income and most of those jobs come without any benefits. Most cities that have looked closely at the issue have concluded $15 an hour is the absolute minimum level for a "living wage." However, that assumes a 40-hour work week. When converted to a 32- and then 24-hour work week it translates into $18.75 and $25 an hour, respectively. These minimums should apply to all hourly workers, both those who earn tips as well as those that do not. This combination of standard hours and minimum wage would generate a living wage AND ensure these workers have the available time to participate in consuming all these services. Remember, in this fifth paradigm we're seeking to put people's time on par with wages in its importance.

Part of the explicit intent of this strategy is to put upward pressure throughout the lower end of the wage scale. When some people find their jobs are no longer paying their old premium above the minimum, they'll begin demanding raises and companies will find they need to respond to those demands. We want that to happen. Our wage stagnation problem is much deeper than just those at the minimum tier.

The wage index would apply to all hourly workers and is basically a substitute for unions. It's admittedly a poor substitute. However, it should produce the vitally important alignment of wages with productivity to keep the economy in balance. It also provides a way of doing so that avoids the unproductive power-oriented struggles that are inherent in the union model. It does not address working conditions, work rules, benefits, nor any of the other myriad issues unions have traditionally dealt with. So, it's incomplete and will need to be augmented with other measures and laws.

It's also important to note that the index is to productivity, *not* inflation. Many, if not most, progressive labor indexing strategies have attempted to use the index to ensure people have a consistent standard of living. There's nothing wrong with that motivation per se, however, like unions it creates a power struggle between the interests of businesses and the interests of the people working in them. By indexing to productivity, all participants share a common interest in driving real economic improvements.

Let's now take a look at the economic consequences of this strategy. In addition to providing and aligning incentives for productivity improvements this strategy should also drive increases in both GDP growth and profits. There are several factors that contribute to this. The growth driver comes from the combination of providing a living wage to roughly 50 million people in the United States that will in turn be spent on the goods and services they and their families need. That money will flow throughout the economy. It's the economic fuel of the demand stimulus. Shifting to a four- and then three-day work week will double or triple the amount of time the entire 160 million working people in the country can spend on the personal leisure experiences at the heart of the new economy. That completes the alignment of our stimulus with the new pillar of the economy. A living wage combined with leisure time will drive demand for leisure services. Indexing wages to productivity will ensure that demand remains in balance with supply on a sustained basis. The changing workforce costs will then drive demand for all the cutting-edge automation and experience tools arising from the world of mobile, AI, and AR. All of these factors promise far greater GDP growth potential than any additional supply side liquidity through things like tax cuts.

The profit growth assertion is a bit more complex. It includes a couple reasonable, but ultimately unprovable, assumptions. There are three different factors to examine. The first of these are the automation investments and associated productivity. On the supply side of that process the providers of these new tools are far more profitable than most traditional industrial automation providers. Their growth will certainly drive increased overall profits. For the buyers of those devices and services, every single business case will be financially justified, but may well not fully offset the new workforce cost increases. If McKinsey and Deloitte are correct in their estimates it should fully offset the reduced work hours, but it may not recover the wage increases. On the other hand, a two to three-fold increase in demand could easily close that gap and drive real profit growth. This is one of those unprovable assumptions, but overall, I'd be quite surprised if the combination of automation profits and productivity coupled with demand growth didn't drive substantial profit growth.

The second relates to the development and use of a broader array of personal experience strategies and associated services. The expanded services offered by REI are a perfect example of this aspect of the strategy. When workforce costs go up good businesses will look at both value expansion as well as cost savings and the value expansion side of the equation is considerable. Those new services will be more valuable and enable increased pricing power as well as new revenue sources. These new sources of differentiation and revenue would be additive to the base growth and would definitely add profits and probably margins as well.

The third relates to a hidden pricing power I suspect is latent in the economy. With wages being depressed below their true economic value, current market prices are driven far more by competitive dynamics than real market value. Once that is normalized across all participants at a living wage there will be opportunities to recapture those costs through simple price increases. A recent survey by the National Restaurant Association found 70 percent of restaurant goers willing to pay more for their meals if it meant the people working there were being paid a living wage. If every restaurant was in the same situation I suspect there is far more pricing flexibility than most assume. And, again, if everybody in the country has two to three times more free time, and 50 million people move from poverty to living wage, I find it almost impossible to believe aggregate consumption would go down as a function of supplier initiated price increases.

This strategy emulates what we collectively accomplished in the 1930s and 1940s. It makes the new jobs good jobs, aligns demand growth with supply growth, triggers a wave of new technology investments, and drives growth in GDP and aggregate profits. That all sounds great; however, we must also acknowledge this would be a radical shock to the economy. It would obviously be implemented in stages, but those would each be a shock. In some ways that's fully intentional. Our economy is seriously off track and needs a fairly dramatic set of changes to get back on course. In the 1930s and 1940s we had a depression and world war to give us a collective kick in the pants. This is intended to achieve the same result through the shifting economic structure and associated incentives. But, it will take an enormous amount of work and innovation across our society to make it all happen.

It's also interesting to contrast this with the 35-hour work week implemented in France. The problem with that is it's too timid. Simply carving an hour off of every day does *not* trigger the kind of wholehearted restructuring of businesses we're looking for. In fact, all it does is introduce new stresses between workers and managers. Everyone still shows up five days a week. Managers want to eke out an extra little bit of work at the end of every day, resenting those who depart on the new schedule. Workers feel entitled to that extra hour, but risk disapproval when they exert that right. Nobody looks at the system and concludes whole new forms of automation or value-creating experiences are needed. They just muddle along with a new source of tension and frustration introduced into the workplace. To achieve the results we seek, we need a far more substantive "shock" to the system.

The bigger question is how this strategy fits into the global context. It would be great if major nations around the world followed our lead, but we can't count on that. Certainly not in the short term and while a number of European nations would probably do so in the long term the rest of the globe is still going to be caught up in the rat race we've all experienced over the last several decades. So how will this really work in the global context?

The first observation is that most of the jobs we're focused on in this category are not subject to global competition. They are inherently localized. Experiences happen in the moment and in the location of the consumer. That's true for bars, restaurants and hotels, as well as brick-and-mortar retail. The wages and working hours for all those can be set based on our national priorities, not those of Beijing or Delhi.

Second, even though our specific focus is on the personal experience category, our wage and work hour structure will bleed over into other areas of the economy, including those focused on global markets. The vast majority of those jobs are not minimum wage and are not hourly. They depend on salaried workers whose work weeks are far more driven by competitive and management dynamics than they are by national labor policies. There will, however, be a very real intention and desire to ensure the bulk of these folks migrate to the 32- and then 24-hour work week.

The first observation on this point is that we may secretly already be nudging close to the 32 hour work week, or at least a four day work week. There are a series of work practices that have slowly and subtly been working their way through corporate America. It started with "casual Fridays." That then evolved into something we called "summer hours" in IBM. The idea behind summer hours is for everyone to work one extra hour a day from Monday through Thursday and then take a half day on Friday. That's the story. Its official. It's also baloney. The hours everybody works during the week aren't rigid enough to even know if anybody works an "extra" one. Sometimes people work 8 hours, sometimes 10, sometimes 12, it's a function of the work on hand not a time clock. The "half day" on Friday is almost always worked at home. My fellow senior executives and I were always careful not to schedule any mandatory meetings or even calls on Friday morning. I never had any trouble reaching someone I needed on those days, but I only sought them out when I truly did need them. The honest truth about this practice is it's a four-day week with a little technology-enabled free time "fuzz" around the edges. In IBM we only did it during the summer, but I've seen the practice used much more flexibly by other global corporations. While everyone would protest the notion vehemently, we're already edging our way toward a four-day work week. That's not 32 hours, but it's the functional equivalent for salaried employees in a globally competitive market.

There's also a fascinating set of work done by the anthropologist, David Graeber. He has been studying the phenomenon of what he calls "bullshit jobs."

These are jobs where the person doing the work believes what they are doing is of little to no purpose and creates no real value to either the institution they're working for or society. I'm not sold on all his examples, but from my own direct executive experience I recognize the reality of many of his assertions. Both his own studies as well as those conducted by independent organizations have found as many as 35–40 percent of the population believe the specific jobs they're doing create no value. That's a huge number. If we force a move to a four- and then three-day work week I suspect that "make-work" will be some of the first to be eliminated.

There are a few other keys to making this a realistic strategy. The first is the aggressive use of all the leading-edge technology we've discussed. We should not underestimate the impact these technologies can have on our global competitiveness. One of the primary objectives of this economic strategy is to establish the United States as the clear global leader in the development and usage of the currently emerging technology generation. We will describe below a set of modern national infrastructure strategies that will aggressively expand our proven digital commons capabilities. These will enable greater productivity leverage than anything yet modeled or estimated. Others can and will attempt to follow that lead, but we should have a decided edge.

One of the specific ways we need to use these technologies is to facilitate and accelerate the blending of work time and leisure time. When done correctly with the right management approach, that blend enables a substantially expanded freedom of when and where work gets done. I know several young individuals and couples who actually live in RVs, traveling the country all while working full time. They spend many hours every week on "work," but also many hours that are "free." Most of them would be hard pressed to count exactly how many hours of each they put in. They aren't paid hourly and many are self-employed entrepreneurs, so their actual hours are determined by what needs to get done and when. They work hard and endure all the stresses young folks do when starting out in life. However, they're using the wonders of our modern technologies to maximize both their free time and the value they get from it.

The final key to this question is to be realistic about when and where to use US labor. For segments driven by global competition and where the primary labor issue is cost, the United States simply will not be able to compete. Trying to do so on too large a scale will just erode the US economy and social contract, not help it.

There is one final piece of the "personal experience economy" puzzle to put in place. When we were dominated by agriculture we created the commodities markets. We described earlier how those institutions helped deal with some of the unique problems associated with the delays between plantings and harvests and the inherent risks from weather, drought, and pests. Our industrial economy equally relies on a robust stock market for the raising and allocation of capital. Those are capital-intense businesses and the stock market addresses those capital needs. Our experience economy has its own problems and needs its own specific market. Commodities markets focus on buying and selling; stock markets focus on raising capital. Our proposed experience market needs a bit of both.

The primary scarce resource to allocate are the people with the talent, creativity, and skill to create high impact experiences. That includes entertainment but encompasses a far wider array of skills. Cooks, hair dressers, artists, guides, stylists, and even personal shoppers are all part of this array. When you include things like Habitat for Humanity we need carpenters and electricians. History professors, philosophers, and priests all have their roles as well. All those resources need to be aligned with venues, participants, and funding sources. Those who are producing experiences need to know who they are doing it for, and whether it will be preplanned or on-demand. Funding sources can range from simple ticket sales to commissions on associated merchandise sales to charitable contributions. This market needs to encompass all of those revenue models.

There are elements of all of this in the market today, but none of it is currently stitched together in such a way as to enable a major new segment of the economy. There's a real danger that the "personal experience economy" can evolve into something often referred to as the "gig economy." The problem with that model is how brutally difficult it is for people to live when there is no certainty about income. We need a model where people have real jobs, with the wages and hours we've outlined, and also have the ability to allocate their time based on opportunities in the market. "Gigs" need to augment and enhance the income of people not be the sole source.

3

TACKLING THE WAGE PROBLEM

W E NOW NEED to deal with the deep historic issue of how to ensure people get paid their full economic value on a sustained basis. Karl Marx was so convinced that this was an unsolvable problem he concluded capitalism itself was fatally flawed. I don't accept that conclusion, but the challenge is nontrivial and finding a workable answer is essential to building a socioeconomic paradigm that will endure. The use of unions to balance the unequal power relationship was fatally flawed because of its deep focus on power, often to the full exclusion of value. We need an answer that brings a shared and aligned focus on value along with the power balance.

One approach used heavily in Germany and to a lesser degree elsewhere in Europe is something referred to as "codetermination." This structure reserves a set of board seats for worker representatives and thereby brings them into more direct participation in top-level decision making. In Germany, where the practice has existed for over a hundred years, there are two different levels of "boards." First is the "executive board," which is comprised of senior executives and is chaired by the CEO. The second is a "supervisory board" comprised of employee and union representatives along with shareholders. Under all these structures the shareholders have the ultimate say in any decisions from the supervisory boards. Other nations have eschewed this two-tier structure, but in all cases the idea is to bring more employee representation into board-level decision making, while keeping that representation inferior to that of the shareholders.

There are many anecdotes suggesting there's merit in this approach. German boards have on several occasions agreed to proposals brought forward by employee representatives and those same representatives have joined in board-level consensus on things like wage cuts and layoffs when competitive dynamics made those moves necessary. However, overall it hasn't been that effective. The problems we've noted around wages failing to track productivity haven't been quite as severe in Germany as elsewhere, but then traditional unions have remained far stronger in Germany than elsewhere. In fact, these codetermination structures have historically been as much about agreements on management methods arising from collective bargaining between unions and corporations as anything else. Finally, almost all of these structures are limited to large corporations and not particularly helpful for the spectrum of employment we need to address.

Part of the problem is a fixation by academics and politicians on the "top of the pyramid," the boards. For those who have lived in the senior executive ranks of large corporations it's a highly distorted set of assumptions about how the world works. Boards, at least the better ones, do provide some level of oversight. However, even the strongest are quite weak compared to the internal senior executive team of the firm. Actual intervention or policy reversal is extremely rare. I was personally responsible for assessing the deepest and most problematic issues faced by IBM for two decades. Many of our conclusions did indeed go to the board in their final stage. However, not once did the board participate in the real evaluation and decision process. Not only did they not know about the answer until it was reached, they frequently didn't even know what those issues were.

As a result, simply adding employee or union representatives to existing board structures may be a useful part of the equation, but on its own it will not achieve what we need. The deeper answer must go back to our earlier observation about the conceptual trap associated with the role of stockholders. Businesses do *not* exist to serve those interests. Businesses exist to create value in the market and the management agenda needs to put that foremost.

The strategic approach to this is something known to management consultants as a "congruence model." Basically, the idea is a company's operational model needs to align, to be "congruent," with the strategic value creation formula of the business. There are a number of these models taught in various business schools and used by consultants. At the core they almost all include four key dimensions. First, managers need to define the key processes and activities associated with the firm's value creation. Those need to be optimized for effectiveness foremost and efficiency second. As noted earlier, everything else can be either outsourced or managed strictly for efficiency. Second, the key measurement and management systems for each of those processes and activities must be defined and tracked with clear definition of responsibilities across the organization.

Those first two are probably pretty intuitive to most readers. Where this gets interesting are the second two focus areas critical to achieving effective strategic alignment. The first of these is around skills and talent. Management must ensure they have people with this right level of capability to execute the company's critical value creating tasks. If they can't directly source those skills, they must institute programs to develop or train their people. The final piece of the alignment process is an organizational culture that supports the specific value creating formula. If the business is focused on customer intimacy, a culture of deep, personal commitment to customers is essential. If the focus is innovation, then everything associated with the innovation process, including an explicit acceptance of the inevitable failures must be built into the culture. If the focus is operational efficiency, then everyone needs to revile expenses and waste.

Two of the four major levers associated with sustaining a company's primary value-creation purpose are directly related to people. We've lost this completely, in large part because of our acceptance of the flawed story about stockholders. We need to restore our collective understanding about what really matters and, in the process, bring everything back into a very different perspective. If we do that, with all its associated management training and processes, then the philosophy behind codetermination can put down roots. If we do not, if we allow the "shareholder first" mind-set to prevail, then code-termination will never be more than a fig leaf.

That's a long-term perspective and while I deeply believe it's where we need to go, we need more immediate answers. There are two measures I think can get us on the right track. The first of these is to mandate far greater employment transparency. One of the many elements that contribute to the historic power imbalance between companies and people is access to information about wages, working conditions, advancement prospects, etc. In our information-driven twenty-first century this needs to become a relic of the past. We need to institute simple, internet-accessible information repositories covering every major aspect of employment practices and every company must keep their specific data up to date. This needs to be managed with the same degree of rigor as any SEC filing. In our fifth paradigm, people matter more than capital. People need to be able to easily see and compare their personal status with the averages of others in their employer, their industry, and their profession or trade. They also need to be able to evaluate potential employers based on all of that data. Any paradigm that puts people at the forefront must empower them with access to the information they need.

There are existing organizations like Glassdoor that currently enable people to post comments on employment practices, but unfortunately these are often little more than forums for disgruntled people to air their complaints. Furthermore, the wage data from those and similar sites are provided by employees and are rarely accurate. These have their uses but fall far short of what's needed. We need data that come directly from the company and that is subject to audit level inspection. This doesn't need to entail any major overhead. It would be a simple matter to develop tools that would automatically extract the necessary data from standard payroll applications like Intuit and others.

The second measure is specific to our new personal experience economy and entails the creation of a trade association for all those people and companies who find themselves working in that important sector. I don't envision this association getting engaged in direct wage negotiations between individuals and companies, but I do see them collecting and propagating information on skills, education opportunities, automation and productivity improvement tools and methods, best practices, job postings, etc. Traditionally these kinds of organizations have relied on membership fees paid by individuals. There can be a place for that, but I'd rather see this primarily paid for by the businesses in these industries. The key objective is to get as much of the potential value alignment as we can while minimizing the power battles and conflicts.

4

Building a Twenty-First-Century National Infrastructure

THESE PROGRAMS FOR our two economic towers will have a huge impact but are not enough. We also need to tackle our national infrastructure. This initiative has three vital objectives. First, our current national asset base has been badly neglected for decades. It represents a criminal mismanagement of trillions of dollars of national wealth that needs to be brought back as a major priority. Second, our modern economy has its own infrastructure needs and opportunities. We can accelerate and ensure our leadership in this next generation by stepping up to those possibilities. Third, rebuilding infrastructure has the potential to put a lot of people to work. Many of those will be people who are being displaced from manufacturing and have no realistic role in either the global innovation market or the new personal experience economy. They need a dignified existence and we need what they are capable of building. This is a crucial point. Without these jobs our overall employment solution is badly incomplete. Modernizing our infrastructure isn't a luxury, it's essential. It's long past time for us to rebuild and modernize our country.

The investment in this effort needs to match its level of importance to our nation. There are two interesting points of comparison to help us calibrate what that might be. If we look at what we spent in the 1930s and 1940s on the WPA, CCC, and RFC programs in current dollars that would be approximately $1 trillion over 5–10 years. The Chinese Belt and Road Initiative is also roughly at that same scale. We are a much stronger economy today than we were back then and if China can spend that much on developing *other nations* we must be able to do the same for ourselves. I'd calibrate this in the range of $200 billion per year on a sustained basis. That's a lot of money, but we've got decades of neglect to recover from and this is about rebuilding our nation. We're worth the investment. As we'll see below, not only are we worth it, but once we clean up some of our failed neoliberal market experiments we'll be able to pay for it with zero increased taxes.

Rebuilding Our Foundations

There are two different broad categories to be addressed. First are all the traditional elements of our infrastructure. That includes roads, bridges, airports, harbors, dams, parks, and public buildings. Many of those have not been addressed since the 1930s. They all need attention. In some cases, they just need maintenance, but in others they need to be rebuilt for the twenty-first century. One of the key twenty-first-century upgrades is the implementation and deployment of Internet of Things (IoT) technologies throughout our infrastructure. IoT technologies basically embed measurement, monitoring, and control instruments into bridges, water mains, and every other major infrastructure component. Those instruments create wireless data feeds that enable many of the next-generation management, maintenance, and optimization capabilities. They will also be included in a new national data strategy described below. Our priorities need to include an extensive modernization of our railroads. The US rail system is a disgrace. In the twenty-first century the focus is less on a coast-to-coast system and more on regional and city systems, but the issues and opportunities are everywhere.

Most of the labor associated with these endeavors is not really subject to global competition. In our earlier jobs analysis, we lumped construction in with our other "foundation" industries. It needs a much more explicit focus than the others in that category. The traditional problem with the construction industry is how sensitive employment is to economic cycles. When the economy is booming everything is great. When it contracts, either locally or nationally, the jobs dry up very, very quickly. A national strategy to rebuild America can help this enormously. The key is to establish a solid baseline of long-term projects with a pipeline of shorter-term ones that can be activated during the down cycles of the economy. We need to design this initiative with a long-term mind-set. The scale and scope of what is needed is enormous. Remember the national highway system alone took decades to unfold. This proposal is probably on at least that scale. Think 50 years or more. It's a national commitment to ourselves and our children.

The beauty of this as a national priority for both government and the private sector is the "double whammy" impact it can have on the economy. The direct jobs along with the ability to smooth out cycles in demand are great for our workforce and the communities that have suffered some of the worst dislocations over the past few decades. Those jobs and the associated infusion of money can help resurrect regional economies all over the country. The process of prioritizing projects should explicitly include linking them to state and regional economic development initiatives. We want to magnify the community development impact of every dollar spent. The second "whammy" is the impact on national productivity. An additional point of improved national productivity, which is reasonable based on history, would easily generate over $200 billion in additional GDP growth every year.

LEADERSHIP IN TWENTY-FIRST-CENTURY GREEN INFRASTRUCTURE

The second investment category is a focus on the new infrastructure possibilities in the twenty-first-century economy. Far and away the most important initiative is to transform our entire energy production, distribution, and consumption paradigm to a green, sustainable future. This is easily the same scale as the efforts aimed at our existing infrastructure and is vitally important to our future as a nation, if not the world. There are projects already under way all over the country, but the scale and urgency are nowhere near where we need it to be. As noted earlier, most of this critical priority is beyond the scope of this book. However, there are several points to note.

Let's start with energy production. Our primary source of energy is currently natural gas which supplies roughly one third of our capacity. This is followed by coal which provides about 30 percent of our needs, and which has been declining in absolute capacity for over a decade. That's still far too much and the ~350 coal plants that remain in operation need to be phased out as quickly as possible. Nuclear provides 20 percent and has seen little growth. Finally, renewables represent 17 percent of our total with most of that split evenly between hydro and wind.

Wind has become the lowest cost source of power and is projected to drop even lower as improved technologies and configurations penetrate the industry. If we added an additional five times as much capacity as we have currently operational we could replace every coal plant in the country and save money in the process. Yes, that would impact the jobs of people in the coal industry, but the wind industry already employs over 5 times as many people as coal.

Small scale solar deployments on homes and commercial sites are also growing rapidly. The total capacity of these installations is not yet a major factor in our overall power consumption, but it has already reached a scale where it has begun to impact the economics of the utility industry. While this is a positive trend for the health of our nation, there is mounting resistance coming from the utilities who are seeing their power forecasts missing their targets.

As these renewable sources become larger components of our overall energy picture they bring impacts on our distribution system. Wind farms need to be placed where there's wind, which may not be where current coal plants are located. Large numbers of small scale solar sources can completely redefine the structure of the grid. Both sources can be intermittent leading to the need for high capacity energy storage and the ability to flexibly shift to stable sources like natural gas and nuclear when needed. All of these will have substantial impacts on our existing power distribution infrastructure.

The two most important aspects on the energy consumption side of the equation are the shift to electric vehicles (EV) and improving the energy efficiency of buildings and homes. Rapidly growing the deployment of high capacity charging stations will be critical to accelerating the EV shift. This profound economic shift may not yet be obvious to most Americans, but it's well under way. One of the biggest economic risks we face from the trend would be a failure of the US auto industry to react effectively to this competitive dynamic. They're well aware of what's happening but have been dangerously slow to respond at the scale we are likely to need. Just as we had to use fuel efficiency targets to prod that sector out of its complacency we may find we need to do something similar around EVs. If we don't do that, we may, unfortunately, find we need yet another government funded industry bailout.

Speed of response to this green imperative is essential. Recent forecasts have indicated we need to materially reduce our carbon emissions by 2030–35 to avoid serious environmental catastrophe. That's not much time given the scale of what we need to transform.

For those who aren't energized by those dire projections there's a compelling economic analysis from the International Renewable Energy Agency (IRENA). In the world of business when an asset becomes obsolete, nonperforming, or a competitive liability it is called a "stranded asset" and must be written off entirely. Many existing assets throughout the energy and commercial world are likely to become stranded once the shift to a green future is complete, and the more we add non-green assets to the nation's capital stock the larger that write-off will be. The folks at IRENA estimated the total size of that write-off under two scenarios. In both cases they assumed we reached the same target levels for emissions by 2050. In the first case, they assumed we started that process immediately and in the second they assumed we waited until 2030 to really ramp up the shift. In the first case their models found we would need to write off $3 trillion in stranded assets. In the second case that goes up to $7 trillion. In both cases the majority of the stranded assets were in buildings, which implies setting energy efficient building codes should be a top priority.

This green initiative needs to be seen and addressed as the national, indeed global, priority that it truly is. Those who worry about what it will cost have their thinking all upside down. This will be a huge stimulus to the economy, creating millions of jobs and enormous growth in GDP. It's also inevitable and unavoidable, and the longer we wait the more we're using our national capital in unproductive ways that will have to be written off in the near future.

New Principles of Digital Economics

These vitally important initiatives must be joined by a focus on our digital infrastructure. The most immediate priority needs to include the deployment of 5G wireless networks around the country. The vast majority of that work will be handled by AT&T, Verizon, and other private sector participants. The zoning and spectrum allocations those organizations require need to be priorities. While most of those are handled by local municipalities, ensuring there are no holdups or gaps should be a national priority.

The overall digital infrastructure opportunity is much more than those simple computing and communications systems. The real frontier is far past that stage. The expanded opportunity is all about enabling the next generation of capabilities we see emerging and includes privacy regulations, intellectual property management, liability laws, and a wide range of investments in new "digital commons."

To begin our journey through all these opportunities we need to first understand why digital assets and digital economics are so unique. The distinct differences can be summarized as:

> All digital assets are non-rivalrous, have near zero marginal cost, can be instantly distributed anywhere in the world and never wear out.

Apologies if that's a mouthful. Let's look at each of those points in turn. Non-rivalrous means that if you have a copy it in no way limits my ability to have a copy. There is no depletion of stock even if every individual in the world has a copy. This means there is inherently no scarcity to be managed through economic exchange. Since that's right at the core of what market economics is all about it calls into question the very nature of how economic value capture can and should work.

Which leads to the next characteristic. *Marginal cost* refers to what it costs to create additional copies of something once you've figured out how to make the first copy. Once you design an automobile there are still tons of costs associated with securing all the raw materials and then manufacturing the auto itself. Those are all *marginal costs*. Digital assets have essentially *zero marginal cost*. That means that not only is there no stock to deplete (non-rivalrous), there is truly no cost associated with making infinite copies. One of the core theories of economics is that in perfect markets price tends to converge with marginal costs. Since that's zero for digital assets, market forces will tend to drive the price to zero, making *value capture* through perfect markets *theoretically impossible*. Since there's no such thing as a perfect market that problem can be alleviated to some degree, but it means it is *only possible to capture value from digital assets in imperfect markets, and the value capture is dependent on the nature of those imperfections.* This is the core economic reality the music industry has struggled to manage. They put the blame on "pirates" which is understandable. However, the reality is the market has been doing its job which is to push prices down to the marginal cost of zero.

Instant global distribution means all aspects of digital markets are by their nature global. That includes production, distribution, and consumption. There are certainly language and cultural stumbling blocks in many categories but those have been steadily diminishing over time. In the long haul the only curbs on the global aspect of digital economics are legal and regulatory. While not all markets are subject to global competitive dynamics, digital markets are inherently global. This means they are subject to full global competition and they can be active participants or victims of the free-flowing global work paradigm.

The fact that *digital assets never wear out* has several deep implications. The biggest will be described below in the discussion on open source. More obviously, once someone has a digital asset they like, there is no reason for them to ever have to replace it. There is no replacement market. This has become a huge issue for the software industry in recent years. Packages that have been around long enough to have all their bugs worked out and that have reached the point of diminishing returns on new functionality struggle to figure out how to get people to buy new releases. This is one of the main economic drivers of all the cloud subscription models. It's the only way software vendors can keep their revenue streams.

DIGITAL COMMONS: ESCAPING THE TRAGEDY

The digital commons story begins with the open-source story. This is an amazing and counterintuitive illustration of the differences between digital and traditional markets. To explain this phenomenon, we need to briefly describe how the traditional software industry works and the challenge to that model that began in the late 1990s. Most software was, and to a large degree still is, distributed in a "compiled" form. This means it has been converted from a format that humans can read and understand into one that only machines can understand. That provides the primary protection for the IP embodied in the code. It is a technology-based "distortion" that helps enable commerce to work around the digital asset. The other key aspect of the model is the internal, hierarchical, development process used to create and maintain that asset. The asset is "closed" in its creation, production, and delivery processes.

A movement began in the late 1990s to challenge this by opening every aspect of this model. Rather than a hierarchical creation and development process driven by a single organization, this movement allowed widely dispersed and otherwise unaffiliated individuals to *freely* participate in the creation and development process. In order for this to work, the code needed to be left in its "open" format, readable and editable by anyone. This is what "open source" means. The resulting asset was then available for distribution to anybody for *free*. The movement referred to both those aspects of "freedom" by distinguishing between "free" as in "free speech" for the first and "free" as in "free beer" for the second. Many in the movement actually preferred to describe it as the "free software" movement, rather than "open source."

At first, nobody in the traditional software industry paid much attention to this movement. They felt certain the model simply wouldn't work. A loose affiliation of developers was going to be unable to build anything of any substantive complexity or value. And, the free delivery meant there would be no sustainable economic model to propel any asset for any length of time. When it began getting traction and was actually able to produce a viable operating system, which is a complex set of code, people began to take notice.

Many software companies began viewing the movement as an existential threat. Microsoft referred to it as a "communist" movement. They also attempted to thwart these innovators by threatening them with IP lawsuits. One of the major problems with that plan was "who to sue?" There was no formal "organization" to target. With a few exceptions the only companies that could be sued were the customers who were using the code. The open-source coders countered the saber rattling by asserting that the IP being developed was theirs, and if they chose to deliver it to the market in open-source form that was their right. That was certainly true, but it was also true that Microsoft and other major software companies had portfolios of patents that were probably being violated. If so, it was completely inadvertent, but they were violated nonetheless. As noted earlier, it is essentially impossible for any single entity in the technology industry to produce anything in the absence of cross-licensing, and nobody had done that for these rebels.

Enter IBM. At the time, IBM had a piece of software that companies could use for their web servers called WebSphere. It wasn't selling very well. There was also a piece of open-source code called Apache, which had a tiny subset of WebSphere's capability, but which was in widespread usage across the industry. The executive in charge of WebSphere decided to see if he could strike a deal with the Apache community to allow IBM to embed Apache inside WebSphere which would then allow IBM to sell its offering as an upgrade to all those users. Technically this could have been done unilaterally, but IBM wanted the full support and consensus from the Apache community. The community had certain demands, including IBM making ongoing contributions to the underlying Apache asset, but all were reasonable. An agreement was struck, and IBM proceeded. WebSphere sales exploded.

Based on this success, IBM drove several other initiatives that collectively drove billions of dollars in both revenue and profits. Analysts and observers found it hard to believe. I personally held hundreds of briefings explaining how it was possible to build big profitable businesses around something that was "free." The rest of the IT industry began realizing open source could be a fruitful means of *capturing* new value by *creating* new value built around the open-source offerings. This simple strategy rippled through the industry. Company after company began using open source as an integral element in their strategies. Decades later the results have been stunning.

A publicly shared collection of assets is referred to by economists as a "commons." Many grandiose utopian visions have centered on the idea of creating a large commons that would create value for all. All of those have failed. They all fall victim to something known as the "tragedy of the commons." Any commons effort faces two historically insurmountable problems. First, in the absence of clear ownership, both of the asset and its value, there is no incentive for the asset to be maintained. Look at any public housing project and see what happens as a result. The initial good intentions almost always evolve into neglect. Second, every commons project suffers from the free-rider problem where people extract value without contributing any. This drives an inevitable dwindling of the shared value along with heated recriminations.

However, a *digital commons* operates differently despite these inescapable market behaviors. Digital assets don't wear out, so maintenance may not be any issue at all. Even in places where ongoing development is needed, the basic asset itself does not erode over time. The fact that digital assets are non-rivalrous and have zero marginal costs means that free riders create no real economic problem. They may create perceptual problems and angry reactions from those who behave better, but they do not cause any actual economic damage. A *digital* commons is basically impervious to the underlying economic causes of the traditional tragedy.

To the astonishment of its critics in the late 1990s, the open-source movement has created the first successful "commons" in history. That isn't because of some sort of limited virtuous behavior, it's because digital assets work differently from physical assets and the old economic rules simply do not apply. These days every major commercial software project starts with an inventory of open-source assets. I personally know the CEO's of several successful start-ups who have been able to jump start their businesses by having 70–80 percent of their initial offerings built from open-source components. The digital commons is not a tragedy, it has become a central wellspring of value for the entire

IT industry. And, it is continuing to grow dramatically, including becoming a major factor in the global development of AI. The existence, success, and power of this new "commons" is already a pillar in one industry and points the way to a new set of economic models for other areas of vital importance in the twenty-first century.

As one consumer segment after another reaches the point of diminishing returns, providers turn to services to find new sources of value and most of those end up rooted in the digital realm. Those roots are put down in soil that is immune to the tragedy of the commons and can be effectively nourished by investments in those commons.

The realization that these digital commons do not suffer from the tragedy of the commons is potentially one of the more important socioeconomic discoveries of the past few decades. It means we can now realistically consider the construction and management of a variety of digital assets as entire new categories of national infrastructure. These investments have the potential to dramatically accelerate our twenty-first-century economy.

Data: A Raw Material Bonanza

The first of these new infrastructure proposals centers on data. Data is probably the most valuable raw material of the coming age. If we go back in history, there was a time when all a company knew about its customers is what they had bought from them and possibly a credit report. Today is completely different. The sources of data have exploded. We all leave a digital trail behind us of every interaction we have with the world. Our purchases, our travel, our credit history, our "likes," our comments and postings, and every other aspect of our lives are now available and for sale to companies and governments all over the world. We are rarely aware of it, but we're an open book.

At one point in my executive career a data company gave me a demonstration of a "proof of concept" they had built for a major auto company. The system they created was intended for use in their dealerships. It showed how as soon as someone walked through their door they could flash a screen in front of a salesperson that showed them the five different vehicles the prospect had been researching over the prior month; the two they had gathered pricing data on the night before; the fact they had just come from their competitor down the street and had taken a test drive . . . along with their name, address, family status, credit score, and income bracket. And, they could do all of that before the person had even offered their name. I knew the sources of data they were using in their system and knew that several of the things they were showing violated licensing and usage terms from those sources, but nonetheless it was a stunning demonstration of what is now technically possible.

As the example illustrates, we are now in an age where privacy issues will be both extremely important and very difficult to manage. We can and should expect to be asked to consent before companies gather data about us. However, the range of data encompassed through explicit acts of consent is already dwarfed by the range of data that is tacitly "consented." When we are asked by a website to register and provide them our address and credit card we set off a chain of events that few ever imagine. Once registered we become an entry in a database. The company then steadily buys data from third parties and adds that material to every entry in that database. At the time of our registration, the company may well have gathered data from our device about every website we've visited in the past and placed a cookie on our device enabling them to track every site we visit in the future. If the process involved an app on our phone they may also be tracking our every movement.

The collection and selling of that data may be done with a variety of usage restrictions. However, as my demo example showed, those are not always followed, and violations can be very hard to detect. One of the techniques commonly employed is to use restricted data to create a new, proprietary "score," like a credit score. The algorithms used to create that score can be kept as a trade secret, never revealing the illicit data usage embodied within the score. When the company that does this then turns around and licenses their new "score" to others the illicit data usage spreads implicitly without anyone's knowledge. Variations on this pattern are everywhere and nearly impossible to thwart.

There is an entire body of new laws, regulations, customs, and expectations we have yet to invent, but will be crucial to our future. The economic value creation potential is enormous, but so too are the risks and potential for societal damage. Many of the abuses will be annoying, embarrassing, infuriating, but ultimately harmless. Others, those with consequential damages, will need laws and protections for citizens and businesses alike. Like all digital economic questions, these are global issues and will need global solutions. There are already countries that require that any data about their citizens be housed on systems within their borders. Debates on tariffs and trade laws have been largely forestalled to date but will be inescapable once the value and privacy risks become more apparent. There's a veritable mountain of work still to be done on this topic.

Part of that work should include our creation of a national digital commons for data. The full range of data we could include in the scope of this proposal is enormous. The US government generates trillions of data points every day, much of which could theoretically be in the public domain. The fully IoT-instrumented infrastructure described earlier would produce data by the truckload. This is another example where the details are beyond the scope of this book. However, there are a few points that should give a feel for the potential dimensions, value, challenges, and issues. There is an existing "open data" movement. Unlike the open software example, the data movement has had trouble getting solid traction. There are numerous issues. These include sourcing and automatically maintaining the data; understanding how to find and interpret the data; being able to join multiple sources together; and, for data about people and companies, how to manage privacy. There are many other issues as well, so this proposal is not simple.

Some of those problems can be addressed through modern data science tools and methods. Many others need more than just technical solutions. The privacy issue is particularly important and complex. In our modern world there is a frightening amount of data being accumulated about every one of us. Most of that is currently being done by companies like Facebook, Amazon, Google, and their compatriots. That's not to mention the credit bureaus and mobile ad placement companies. There's also more of that going on than most of us would like by US law enforcement, the IRS, and the various three-letter intelligence agencies. This is not unique to the United States. India, for example, has begun deploying a nationwide identity system controlled by the government and requiring mandatory involvement for any consumer of any government service. Citizens of China just resign themselves to complete government over-sight. Europe has implemented numerous privacy laws, but they've really only scratched the surface.

None of those sources would be trusted by all of us. Some might prefer that all that data reside under government control, while others wouldn't want the government to have any access at all. Even the most optimistic would have to acknowledge that every one of those sources is likely to abuse their access under certain circumstances. Yet it is happening anyway. This is an area where we as a society have a long way to go before we're ready to even attempt, let alone reach, a consensus.

We need to begin the process by discussing and introducing regulations that establish clear guidelines around privacy and protections from consequential damages. This should probably begin by adopting the General Data Protection Regulation (GDPR) from the EU. We can make a great deal of progress with that step alone, but it will still leave us far short of a full national strategy.

In the long term, I think we should explore a strategy for data about people modeled after the program used to govern the US Federal Reserve. The Fed's leader is appointed through a government review process. However, its operations are removed from any government engagement or oversight. Even the most intrusive presidents have realized the importance of maintaining that arm's-length status. We could potentially create a "citizens data reserve" that could be managed in a similar, or even stricter, arm's-length process. They could be charged with maintaining the security and privacy of all data about our citizens. That could even include a new entry to our bill of rights to encompass our right to privacy and could be enforced by this new organization. They could ensure any data released about us must come with proper authorization by us or through the courts. For this to really work we'd also need a new set of laws limiting companies from gathering data about us that includes our unique personal identities unless it comes through this new "citizens data reserve" and its associated release processes.

This "citizens data reserve" could also be used to address one of the hidden problems lurking in our new digital world. One of the things developed in the uglier parts of the web is the ability to create fake people. The Russian mob for one has built a collection of fake people that can be bought and used for various fraudulent purposes. Some of these fakes are so convincing they have actually been invited to attend closed conferences organized by the US Department of Defense for certified contractors. The process used can include literally years of fake traffic between fake people who are part of fake organizations involved in fake activities. They can be very, very hard to identify. And, through the beauty of digital assets, they can be created in essentially unlimited quantities.

These fake people can be used for all manner of fraud. Everything from fake Yelp reviews to false commentary on public policy issues are now possible. Google, Facebook, and Twitter have become incredibly effective tools to shape public opinion and fake people are being used to distort and magnify those experiences. The Russians, in particular, have been using their armies of fake people to distort commentary and public debate for the purpose of undermining elections all over the democratic world. This is also the basis of one of the most dangerous variants of modern cyberattacks. The simple Nigerian prince ruse can now be elevated to a level where almost nobody can tell whether they're dealing with a serious business opportunity or a total fraud.

If we create and manage an effective "citizens data reserve" we can use it to foil many of these efforts. The Reserve and the processes surrounding it can be used to both ensure privacy for everyone as well as provide identity validation. This is obviously a very complex and sensitive topic to sort out, but something will be needed to ensure we have control as free individuals in the twenty-first century.

ARTIFICIAL INTELLIGENCE: A BOUNDLESS FRONTIER

One of the major things this new digital data commons will enable is the future of AI. Data are the primary fuel for the modern AI development process and having vast amounts from diverse sources as suggested would be a huge boon for that nascent industry. Once again to understand this important opportunity, we need to look at a bit of history. The early AI systems were referred to as "expert systems." The idea was to interview an "expert" and capture their knowledge in a series of "rules" like "if xyz, then do abc." The hope was that if one captured enough of these rules the resulting system would behave the same way the expert would. Essentially all of those efforts were failures. There was simply far too much knowledge needed in any useful domain, the amount of tacit understanding was similarly off the charts, and the systems were unable to adapt to changing parameters or assumptions. The few success stories relied more on sheer computing power than any real intelligence.

Most modern AI works quite differently. Many of them use statistical techniques while others are modeled off the human brain. The latter use simulated neurons connected into networks. Each neuron is capable of emitting a trigger for a set of downstream neurons. There may be one set of neurons that are connected to an array of sensors. There may be another set connected to a set of controls, like a brake pedal or steering wheel. The entire construct is then "trained" through the use of specially structured "training data." That could include movies of streets, traffic, and pedestrians along with "good" and "bad" actions on the controls. The automated training process involves assigning weights to different neurons for different simulated conditions. After thousands, or millions, of training experiences the system "learns" how to properly activate the controls given any set of data that hit its sensors.

This entire development process is radically different from traditional programming. The developer may not even really "know" just exactly what the system has actually "learned." It may react correctly to a range of test data, but that does not mean it's actually doing so for the reasons we think. This lack of certainty and control is inherent to the process. It becomes more a matter of experimental testing than design certification. It also raises a number of important social and IP issues.

First among these is the question of liability. What criteria are appropriate? The builder of the system cannot truthfully certify its performance, because at a very deep level they don't actually know how it works. Should we just insist that the system perform in a way that is equivalent to a human? Is the criterion that it makes no more mistakes than a human? Compared to which humans? An average? The safest? How would we really know? To what degree does the provider of training data have a responsibility? The system actually cannot do anything at all without that data and its performance will largely be based on it. If the data are filled with examples of erratic driving behavior by white drivers will the trained system believe all white drivers are erratic or that the only erratic drivers it encounters will be white? There is evidence of precisely this sort of hidden racial data bias in existing AI systems that have been widely deployed in US courts.

One approach to this problem would be the development of standardized test and certification suites for a wide variety of use cases. These could be used as the basis for a new set of processes for things like authorizing fully automated vehicles as safe for the general roadways. In many ways this is the next generation of safety standards. Getting clarity on this type of certification would definitely help accelerate a number of AI initiatives that would otherwise be at risk due to liability concerns.

The second question goes to the heart of our IP laws. The core social contract of patent law is to grant a limited period of monopoly to an inventor in exchange for a sufficiently detailed disclosure to enable anyone to duplicate the invention once the monopoly expires. The value-creating inventor gets a defined period for maximum value capture. In return, society gets access to the invention for others to use and build on once that period expires. How will that work for these kinds of inventions? The training process is every bit as important as the overall design. More so, in many ways. Is there a data disclosure that goes with the patent filing? Does the granting of a patent carry with it an implied license to that data when the patent expires? If not, then society just got ripped off. If so, then how exactly will that work since the holder of the patent may not actually own most of that data? Even if they do, does it imply a set of licensing terms? Without some sensible arrangement the post-patent data license could be more valuable than the patent-protected monopoly. Is that ok?

Sorting through these regulatory issues will not be trivial nor swift. The inherently global nature of these digital endeavors adds further complexity. The innovation frontier is already racing past our regulatory efforts and will continue to do so. I would not recommend doing anything to hamper those efforts, but I do believe we need to substantially increase our focus on deciding where to put necessary safeguards. At this stage I'm far less worried about "Terminator" systems than I am about privacy and protections against "consequential damages" from poorly trained or biased systems.

THE EXPERIENCE MARKET: A PLATFORM FOR NEW VALUE

The final proposal for our next generation digital infrastructure is related to the proposed new experience marketplace. In addition to enabling the development of the experience economy, we need to address one of the unique problems with digital economics. This problem can be illustrated through the example of YouTube. YouTube makes money through advertising. They are able to do this by providing a *platform* used by content creators to distribute their content. The vast majority of the *value creation* is coming from those creators, but the vast majority of the *value capture* is going to YouTube. Whole books have been written on how digital platform strategies can enable vast new levels of value capture by exploiting the value creation of others while giving them little to nothing in return. The use of those digital platforms is essential to the value creators, but the effective monopoly power of those platforms means the value creators struggle to share in the value capture. That's not an acceptable or sustainable economic model for the twenty-first century.

When the Chicago Board of Trade and New York Stock Exchange were created it was through partnerships among existing participants in the agriculture or industrial sectors. They designed those markets to operate transparently and to enable their businesses, not profit from them. It's possible this new experience market will emerge from existing players in the leisure industry, and, like the other early exchanges, they could design it as a nonprofit to ensure the participating value creators get their due.

However, this may need some sort of catalyst possibly including a regulatory prod. There have been no such regulatory actions to date in this area, but the level of distortion between value creation and capture is alarming. This will need to improve for our twenty-first-century strategy to deliver the sustained value creation we will need.

Most of the activities envisioned in this new marketplace will come from the private sector. Some of that will include things rooted in the leisure industry, but a lot if it will come from other entities using experiences to differentiate their brands and offerings. That's its intent. However, there are also a number of things that can and should be part of this marketplace that are not driven primarily by their economic value. This could include things like our Habitat for Humanity example as well as things supported through the arts. These noneconomic activities enrich our society, but struggle to survive.

I suggest using the proposed experience marketplace to create a new way of allocating and raising funds for all these noneconomic sources of value. In addition to enabling a common process for raising money directly earmarked for specific organizations and/or events this would create a common investment "pool." Anybody could contribute to the pool and all such contributions could be tax deductible. There are various schemes we could potentially use to both attract contributions and enable creative providers greater say in how resources are actually used. By putting the whole activity into the broader context of our experience economy we can bring more cross-pollination between our for-profit and nonprofit spheres.

5

MOVING TO A DEFENSIBLY
FAIR TAX STRATEGY

G ETTING TAXES SET properly is obviously a vitally important part of our
strategy. It's also quite complex, laden with emotions and filled with
incomplete and misleading data. All the various "us versus them," "makers
versus takers" accusations of redistribution, and "tax and spend" hyperbole is
extremely unproductive. This is a case where a careful examination of history
and global comparisons can reveal a great deal, including a highly clarifying
path forward. Once we eliminate the outliers and situations that either historically or geographically don't fit our overall priorities an important set of
findings emerge. After many decades of change, taxes around the world have
reached a fairly stable plateau and have converged to a remarkable degree. This
implies it is now possible to define a strategy that sets an overall budget envelope and tax plan that is defensibly fair to everyone and sustainable for the long
term. Once that is set, it can be locked in and taken off the table. That means
no more tax cuts or increases by either party. That's our objective. It takes the
power dimension of government taxation out of the debate, by establishing a
defensibly fair foundation. Hopefully, then the value dimension of various programs and their alternatives can rise to the top.

To break this down we need to examine four different topics, each with
some level of detail. These are tax rates, tax yields, what services are covered

by those taxes, and specific taxes on capital. Each of these can be quite complex and almost impossibly difficult to understand for any given nation let alone across nations. However, once we boil out the complexities we can see some pretty clear patterns.

GLOBAL BENCHMARKS: POINTERS TO FAIR TAX RATES

Let's start with tax rates. We will look at taxes on corporate profits, individual bottom bracket rates, individual top bracket rates, and value-added/sales taxes. For our global comparison we will use a list of about two dozen countries that include Australia, Canada, China, France, Germany, Ireland, Italy, Japan, Poland, Russia, South Africa, Taiwan, Thailand, Turkey, and the UK. We are completely excluding Denmark, Sweden, and Switzerland from the analysis. We've also excluded Canada and Ireland from the corporate rate analysis because both those nations have adopted "tax haven" strategies. When we get to the analysis of tax yields we will also exclude China and Russia because the heavily state-owned aspect of their economies badly distorts those numbers.

The first observation is that across this whole collection of countries from around the world there is remarkable consistency in tax rates. We've obviously eliminated the true outliers, but still it is clear that on a global basis tax rates have converged enormously. For the corporate rate the low end is 17 percent in Taiwan, the high end is 34 percent in Belgium and the average is 24 percent. To give a further sense of how close these are, there are only two other countries below 20 percent and only one above 30 percent. The global consensus is extremely clear, right around 25 percent.

The low end of the individual rates is messier to disentangle. Most countries have a zero rate for some level of income. However, even those who claim a zero rate usually have some form of mandatory retirement insurance tax that starts at the very bottom of the scale. And, those that have a base rate higher than zero include a variety of important credits or deductions. The consensus for the bottom bracket is a bit less clear but can be summarized as a 0 percent income tax and a 5–7 percent retirement insurance tax.

The individual top bracket isn't quite as tight a pack as the corporate rate, but it is still a very clear consensus. The low end is Poland at 32 percent, the high end is 56 percent in Japan, and the average is 44 percent. To give a sense of the distribution there are six nations with a top bracket below 40 percent, five nations above 50 percent, and ten nations between 40–50 percent. The clear global consensus is 45 percent. As a point of comparison, Denmark and Sweden, two outliers we have excluded from this analysis, have top rates at 60 percent.

The value-added or sales tax is the messiest of the lot. Almost every nation uses these to some degree. Most exclude some list of necessities, like food. Many put their highest tax on services used by travelers, presumably because many of those are paid by people from other nations. The lowest rate is obviously zero, the highest is 24 percent in Finland, and the most common pattern is a range of from 0 to 17 percent across a variety of different categories. Those who rely on a single flat sales tax set the rate at 5–8 percent. There's lots of complexity under the covers, but overall the pattern on rates is also fairly tight.

If we compare these rates to those in the United States, some interesting points emerge. First, the corporate rate had definitely been too high at 35 percent until it was recently reduced to 21 percent. No corporation actually paid the 35 percent rate which is a different problem and one we will cover when we discuss actual yields. The new rate appears to be an overcorrection that amounts to an indulgence for that constituency. We ought to correct that error and aim for 25 percent.

The bottom rate is a bit trickier to compare. The recently updated tax schedule has a tax rate of 10 percent applied to the first $9,500 of income but also includes a deduction of the first $12,000 of income for individuals. If we take our full-time minimum wage worker with the current poverty level income of $14,500, that implies a tax rate of just over 1.7 percent. (10 percent of the 2,500 above the deduction equals $250, which is 1.7 percent of $14,500). However, that does not include Medicare taxes which adds a little more than 1.4 percent. Consequently, the poverty-level US tax rate comes to 3.2 percent income tax plus 6 percent social security. That is much higher than the global norm of 0 percent income and 5–7 percent retirement tax.

The high-end rates the United States used after World War II and up to the Reagan era were also clearly way too high. As we noted earlier, those were in the 90 percent range until 1964 when they dropped, but only to 70 percent. That's substantially above even the outliers we tossed out of the equation. The post-Reagan rates of around 40 percent are on the low end, but much more in line with global norms. The latest cut to 37 percent has dropped us below where we ought to be. There is an "extra tier" that pays an additional premium for the Affordable Care Act, which adds another 3 percent. We'll cover that in more detail in our health care discussion. Even if we add that in, we tax our rich 5–8 points below the global norm and those in abject poverty 3 points above the norm. It's patently unfair and frankly there's no defensible reason our highest rate shouldn't be right at the clear global consensus of 45 percent.

In the United States, sales tax is mainly used by the states. The rates range from 0–12 percent across a very diverse set of goods. That's not far from the global norm. A more consistent set of policies around the United States, even if all paid to the states, would probably be more effective than the patchwork we currently employ. However, the overall rates we are playing with are all well within global standards.

The point of this simple exercise is to demonstrate how the global consensus is remarkably consistent and provides a simple tool to establish tax policies. We need not take these as exact rates, but anyone who wants to assert a major divergence is facing a tall argument. To summarize, a tax rate schedule with corporate rates at 25 percent, bottom bracket individual rates at 0 percent with the addition of 6 percent for social security, top bracket individual rates at 45 percent and a nationally harmonized set of sales taxes in the 0–16 percent range would be defensibly fair based on global norms. Any major deviation from that would need substantial justification and should face considerable challenge. Before we move on to the yields from these rates it is extremely interesting to note that China's tax rates match this schedule exactly. Not only is it defensibly fair on a global basis it would be exactly the same as our top economic competitor.

TAX YIELDS AND INCLUDED SERVICES

Moving on to the actual yields generated by these rates reveals some additional crucial insights. First, we now need to exclude Finland, because even though their rates fall well within the global norms, their yields are much higher, even exceeding Denmark and Sweden. They obviously have far fewer deductions and credits available than others, so we'll drop them out from this point forward. As noted earlier we also need to drop China and Russia for the opposite reason. Their rates fall within the norms, but their yields are far below others because of the dominance of state-owned enterprises.

Yields are not nearly as tightly clustered as rates. The low end of our sample is Turkey who only generates 25 percent of GDP in taxes. The high end, after excluding our extreme outliers, are France and Belgium who are tied at 48 percent of GDP. There's a cluster of six nations in the range of 30–35 percent of GDP and another cluster of five nations in the 40–45 percent range. The overall average is 37 percent. While not nearly as tight a consensus as we saw earlier we can note that there are only two nations below 30 percent and another two above 45 percent. A target yield of something in the mid 30 percent range seems about right for the United States. That would put us squarely in the most common cluster and in the bottom half to third of the distribution. If we added back in the high-end outliers we'd actually be in the bottom quartile with a 34–36 percent of GDP target yield.

This target envisions the United States as a low-tax developed nation. Others might want to place us in the higher cluster and aim for more like 42 percent. That still would put us only in the "medium" tax range. To my mind that's less consistent with our national history and culture, but it's certainly a fair debate and could be productively framed through this collection of benchmarking data.

The yield benchmark isn't nearly as tight a consensus as we had with rates so let's take a look at the United States from both a current and historical perspective. The current tax yield in the United States, including social security and state taxes, is 26–27 percent of GDP. That's way low compared to the global norm. Over 10 points low. The only other countries in our sample that are in that range are South Africa and Turkey. The main reason for that discrepancy will come in a moment, but for now let's examine that US number historically.

First, it has been remarkably consistent. So much so that some economists have tried to assert there's some sort of economic law behind it. Even when tax rates and policies have changed dramatically, the overall yields have been incredibly consistent. In the years when the top bracket was taxed over 90 percent the yield on taxes on individuals ranged from 7.1 percent of GDP to 7.8 percent of GDP. After those rates were dropped to 70 percent the yield ranged from 6.9 percent to 8.9 percent. After Reagan dropped rates even further the yields on individuals ranged from 8.0 percent to 9.1 percent. Since 1960, the total federal tax yields have never fallen below 15 percent of GDP and never exceeded 20 percent of GDP. The vast majority of those years fall in a very tight band around 18 percent for total federal tax yields. When you add in the state taxes with 7–8 percent of GDP yield you get a total that has very consistently hovered in the mid-20-percent range.

The only real shift under the covers is a slight decline in corporate tax yield and a slight increase in social security tax yields. In the 1950s and 1960s corporate taxes usually produced about 4 percent of GDP. In the last two decades that has dropped to 1.5–2.0 percent of GDP. Corporate profits have done the exact opposite, so clearly, we have room to improve our yields on those taxes even if the rates should be in the 25 percent range. The opposite has happened with social security which has gone from 1.5–3.0 percent of GDP in the 1950s and 1960s to 5.5–6.0 percent range the last few decades.

The conclusion is our tax yields are not only very low compared to other nations they have been so for a long time. To understand what's going on we need to now shift our attention to what's being covered by these taxes. The vast majority of the discrepancy is explained by health care. Military spending plays a role as well, but it is health care that dominates the real numbers. In the United States, that 26 percent of GDP covers only about one third of our total health care costs. If you drop two thirds of the health care costs from all the other countries, you find they spend on average ~29 percent of GDP on all other government activities and services. That's more than half the gap between that benchmark and the United States. On average across our sample other nations pay 9.8 percent of GDP on health care. If you were to add two thirds of that to the US tax yield of 26 percent you'd get 32.5 percent of GDP, which would put us close to our target number from our earlier analysis.

This, however, points to two substantial problems. First, the United States doesn't spend 9.8 percent of GDP on health care; we spend closer to 18 percent. If you add two thirds of that to our tax yield of 26 percent you get a total "burden" of 38 percent which puts us right near the average of our sample, but probably 3 points higher than we'd like. This is a crucial point. *Our current overall government and social spending burden is higher than it should be even though our tax yields are much lower than they should be.* Second, we're only getting 26 percent yield out of our taxes even though our rates are not that far off the global norm. Putting a 3 percent excess tax on the poor is not enough to offset under taxing the wealthy by 5–8 percent and we obviously have far too many loopholes. However, if we closed those and *didn't* cover health care we would severely overburden, even cripple, the economy.

As we've indicated earlier and will be covering in the next section we need to shift strategy on health care. That shift will bring it under the overall tax umbrella. The plan will also get those costs down into the 10 percent of GDP range, just as every other nation has done. We then need to tweak our tax rates to hit our defensibly fair ranges and tune the loopholes to get yields up to global standards. When done, we'll have a system exactly in balance and one that will be both fair and economically sustainable. In the process we will not only *not* put an additional burden on the economy, we will be freeing up ~8 percent of GDP for more productive uses. That's up to $1.6 trillion put back into the economy every year. It's defensibly fair and it's big.

IT'S TIME TO TAX CAPITAL

The final piece of the tax puzzle is the handling of capital gains and inheritance. This is considerably trickier to sort out than the material we've covered so far. The global consensus is not nearly as clear and neither the problem diagnosis nor possible solutions are very well understood, let alone tested.

There are essentially two problems we need to tackle, the first of which relates to speculative capital. As we've reviewed several times, some amount of speculative capital is not only good, but essential for our markets to function properly. We've also noted, however, that it can be highly volatile and destructive to those very markets. In the current global economy speculative capital is rampant. One measure of this is the ratio of private capital to GDP. This obviously includes all capital, not just speculative, but when the ratio gets high it's an indication that there's a lot of "excess" capital in the market. Thomas Piketty's book *Capital in the Twenty-First Century* provides a fabulous and detailed analysis of this topic. He observes that in the era of Marie Antoinette's France this ratio hovered around 700 percent. In other words, the amount of capital in private hands was seven times the total GDP of France. In US history that number peaked at around 500 percent twice, once right before World War I and then again right before the great depression.

This ratio collapsed in Europe after World War I and fell again, though not as sharply, after World War II. The United States also dropped slightly through World War II. The ratio was fairly stable at 300–400 percent for both the United States and Europe from the mid-1940s up until the early 1970s. It has been rising steadily in every major country ever since. We've noted several times that the early 1970s was an important inflection point for many key economic factors. Among those was the steady growth in private capital. Italy, Japan, France, Australia, and the UK have all now passed the 500 percent level. Japan and Italy have actually been bumping up against the 700 percent level. The United States briefly hit 500 percent, then dropped down to 400 percent after the 2008 recession, only to begin rising back toward 500 percent. Germany started lower and has been growing more slowly, but they're now passing 400 percent.

There is no magic economic law that indicates 500 percent or 700 percent as being "bad." However, those levels have only been seen in times that did indeed precede bad things happening. What is certain is that these levels indicate there's a great deal more capital in play than can be consumed by the markets and that suggests there's a lot of speculative capital out there. The global economy is also steadily shifting to less capital intense industries, which implies the amount of capital that is actually usable in a productive fashion is almost certainly declining. It's even possible that this underlying economic shift is the root cause of the steady rise in private capital.

In any case, we're entering a period in which the volatility of speculative capital is a definite risk for our sustainable economics. One of the clear steps to deal with this is to reinstitute the laws separating commercial and investment banking. There are also regulations dealing with the amount of leverage banks are allowed which should be carefully inspected. Both of these were addressed to some degree after the 2008 collapse, but both have also been "tampered" with already. Those are important safeguards and need to be fully in place.

The next area to tackle is a modification to our capital gains tax policy. The current system allows individuals to apply a lower tax rate to returns on assets that have been held for over one year. That's specifically to encourage a bit longer investment horizon and treats returns on assets held for less than one year as normal income. We should investigate adding at least two other tiers to this picture. One would be very short-term, like one second or even less. The other would aim for a middle tier, possibly a week or a month.

A version of this idea was originally proposed by the economist James Tobin. His proposal was narrowly aimed at currency trading and was never intended to serve as any substantive revenue generator. He was simply looking to increase transaction "friction" and thereby reduce volatility which is a particular problem in currency markets. I agree that the primary purpose of this change would not be to generate substantial additional tax revenues. We've covered the plan for doing that in our defensibly fair strategy described above. However, we do want to both tamp down volatility and incent longer term investments for more than just the extremely short-term currency markets, which is the reason for the middle tier in the proposal.

Whether my suggested month/week and second tiers are actually "optimal" would require a level of modeling that is outside the scope of this book. Those specific tiers as well as the actual rates would all need to be developed. As noted at the beginning of this section, these are pretty uncharted waters with few data points and essentially no historic or geographic references.

The second major problem to address is the rapidly rising inequality directly associated with this growth in private capital. As we noted earlier, the primary culprit in that problem is the lack of wage growth and we've already described our strategy to address that. However, the steady growth in capital is also contributing to the problem. As was the case for speculative capital, there is no magic economic formula that tells us when inequality becomes destabilizing. However, Marie Antoinette was not sent to the guillotine by people who liked her suggestion to "eat cake." Nor was the tsar of Russia killed because he was insufficiently wealthy.

The most commonly used measure of inequality is something known as the Gini index. While that can be useful, it's not intuitive for most people so for this discussion I will focus on the share of national income going to the top 10 percent of the population. In the United States that peaked in the late 1920s at just below 50 percent. Like many of these measures it dropped after World War II into the mid 30 percent range and remained there until the early 1980s. The ratio has been climbing sharply ever since and has once again exceeded 50 percent. Even more striking is the top 1 percent. Their share of national income also peaked in the late 1920s at 24 percent. It dropped to 10–12 percent after World War II and actually declined slightly up until 1980. They too saw their share skyrocket ever since, once again reaching 24 percent.

It's no coincidence that all these capital metrics are now reaching levels only seen right before the Great Depression. What both of these population groups have in common is that most of their income comes from capital, not wages. This points to another structural problem. We noted earlier that overall GDP growth has been trending back down to the long-term growth of productivity which is right around 2 percent. With population growth in major geographies flattening we are unlikely to see much more than ~3 percent GDP growth for any prolonged period. In contrast, the average annual return on capital is more like 4.5–5 percent and has been for literally a thousand years. The enormous capital destruction by two world wars caused this to drop in the first half of the twentieth century. Then, when economies boomed after the war and capital was recovering, overall GDP growth exceeded capital growth. Now that capital returns have recovered to their historic range and

GDP growth has dropped to its historic average, returns on capital once again are exceeding GDP growth.

This means no matter what happens with wages, the gap between those who rely on work for income versus those who rely on capital will continue to grow. Our wage indexing is useful and in fact critical for aligning demand with production but will not in itself deal with the growing inequality problem. As noted earlier, we are once again in poorly charted waters. The only tools in common use around the world for this problem are real estate/property taxes and inheritance taxes. Neither are really adequate to manage this deep structural shift that threatens to allow inequality to spiral to unheard of levels.

Before we discuss a potential solution lets pause for a moment and decide if this really is a problem. I earlier cited the triggers for the French and Russian revolutions and that form of destabilizing event is what's usually held up as the rationale to keep inequality in check. Those dangers are real, and their depths are hard to determine. Few realized how deep the resentment was in the Soviet Union until Gorbachev opened the doors of dissent through Glasnost. The USSR avoided a second revolution, but the nation itself was in truth ripped asunder. Many believe that all the vehicles for protest in Western democracies provide enough "pressure release" that such an eruption is unlikely here. However, the strong recent growth in nationalism across Europe and the United States are clear indications of deep dissatisfaction. Little of that is currently aimed directly at wealth inequality, but that may just be waiting for the right demagogue to come along and light that particular fuse. Furthermore, the problems do not only come from the disenfranchised. The anti-democracy movement is actually coming from the ultra-wealthy who deeply fear the power of people. Their efforts to undermine the country are one of the larger dangers we face. Since the Citizen's United decision, we've also seen a rapid erosion in the ability of everyday citizens to have their voices heard. Once wealth was equated to speech the wealthy secured a megaphone that has completely drowned out the voices of everybody else. The full solution to money corrupting our politics will obviously take more than a new tax strategy, but the more inequality escalates the harder the problem is to solve. Inequality is also an inescapable addition to the pattern of similarities we've been documenting between today and the period right before the Great Depression and World War II. The exact role of each factor is uncertain, but inequality is unquestionably another destabilizing element. To answer my question, yes, this is a problem we need to care about and deal with in our fifth paradigm.

The most intriguing solution I've come across to deal with this issue is again from Thomas Piketty. He suggests a new "wealth tax," that would work like a property tax only be assessed against an individual's total net worth. His suggestion is to do this at a global level. While I agree on the merits of that point, I'd be happy to just start at a national level, even though the assets and liabilities would need to include all global holdings. Following his lead, it's interesting to look at some of the basic math. Since private capital in the United States is bumping up against 500 percent of GDP that implies we have approximately $100 trillion in wealth. Assuming that's generating 5 percent returns it means we have $5 trillion in annual wealth generation, most of which goes unreported and completely untaxed. That's fully one quarter of the entire economic production of the country that's basically untouched by current tax policies.

These waters are not only uncharted they are more than a little treacherous. Whatever tax was applied would need to be low. It obviously could not exceed 5 percent otherwise we'd be systematically confiscating the principle. Setting the tax so that it put returns on capital in balance with the growth of the economy would be a potential target. That would suggest something in the range of 2 percent. However, that runs the risk of pushing more capital into highly speculative investments, the opposite of what we want. In fact, to offset that particular problem I would recommend setting the capital gains on assets held for more than a year to zero. Deciding on what rates should be set at what asset tiers is also uncertain. And, all of this will create additional incentives for people to move assets into offshore shelters that hide owner identities. If we were to implement such a tax I would also abolish the inheritance tax completely. An annual direct tax on wealth should be more than sufficient.

The other major uncertainty that would need specific modeling would be the income and/or wealth thresholds at which this tax would begin. For most US citizens their homes are their largest asset and those are already subject to real estate taxes. That's not where we want this tax to hit. The real focus would be on the top 1 percent or top 10 percent and defining those specific details would need to be modeled.

Unlike the speculative capital tax this one would generate potentially meaningful tax revenues. If we set the tax at or slightly above 1 percent, for example, it could generate close to $1 trillion per year. I would target all of that toward reducing our national debt, particularly for the first several years. The growth of that debt creates potentially destabilizing risk for precisely the targets of this tax, the holders of substantial capital assets. Using the new tax income to reduce the national debt creates a benefit of direct value to those taxpayers and avoids the risk of setting general government program budgets at levels that might prove unsustainably high.

To summarize this piece of the puzzle, we've reached a point in our overall economic evolution that we need a much more complete and sophisticated set of tax strategies to deal with the growing role of capital in our economy. A restructuring of capital gains to further discourage speculative activities combined with a tax on net worth are proposals aimed at the most pressing aspects of the problems. However, both will need substantial modeling and testing before being worthy of full-scale inclusion in the fifth paradigm.

6

FIXING THE BROKEN HEALTH CARE
AND EDUCATION SYSTEMS

B EGINNING IN THE early 1970s and then accelerating dramatically in the 1980s
the United States embarked on a socio-economic experiment of unprecedented proportions. We attempted to use market forces to the maximum
degree possible to manage health care. This reflected the central neoliberal
belief in the superiority of markets to manage all human endeavors. The results
of this experiment are now crystal clear. It was a complete and utter failure.
By every measure. There are no exceptions. The ongoing excess economic
costs to the nation exceed all our wars in the twentieth century. The human
costs are harder to quantify but easily exceed our losses in Vietnam. Both costs
continue to rise and will not cease until we reverse our disastrous course or
succumb to total socio-economic collapse. The underlying cause of the disaster
will become clear over the next few pages, but at its simplest, harkening back
to Reagan, "the market *is* the problem."

Before we spell out the details, let's take a closer look at the full burden
of the system we broke in the 1980s. In 2015 the US government spent $591
billion on Medicare, including various associated tax benefits. We spent $509
billion on Medicaid which includes both federal and state expenditures. There
were another $331 billion in business and individual health care related tax
deductions, and $61 billion spent on our veterans. That totals $1.49 trillion of

government spending or tax breaks which was 8.3 percent of our GDP. Private enterprises then spent another $1.7 trillion, net of their tax benefits, which adds another 9.5 percent of GDP. The total of $3.2 trillion or 17.8 percent of GDP is at least $1.4 trillion more than what any other health care system in the world would cost. If you also subtract the excess administrative costs associated with the US system, we probably spent $1.6 trillion more on health care than we should have in 2015 alone.

As a simple rule of thumb, everything about the US system is twice the cost of any other system in the developed world. That world gap started in the early 1970s and remained small for most of the following decade. It began to expand dramatically in the early 1980s as we embarked on our grand neoliberal experiment and has grown rapidly ever since.

Staying with our 2015 example, it means our overall society carried 9–10 points of GDP as an economic burden for health care *in excess* of any other nation. The 9.5 percent direct burden on US businesses is also not carried by companies in any other nation. That's the *excess* above and beyond the amounts included in their taxes.

Similarly, US workers carry an 11 percent excess cost burden compared to the workers in any other country. That's the excess, not the total. When a global firm considers hiring people in the United States, not only do they have to consider wage differentials, but every US worker is also carrying an additional 11 percent millstone around their necks. One of the interesting insights from this set of data is that the gap between wage growth in the United States and productivity growth can be almost completely explained by the *excess* growth in health care costs. It is distinctly possible that one of the root causes of our wage growth problem is our failed neoliberal experiment in the use of markets for health care. As we will see shortly, this excess economic burden is also lurking at the root of our cost problems in education. This is a deep, pervasive, and deadly economic cancer caused directly by neoliberal fallacies.

The human costs are much harder to get a handle on. We all either have or know people who have gotten tangled up in the more bizarre and baroque aspects of the US medical market. These experiences themselves take a toll on people and often result in delaying or avoiding treatments that later become far more problematic. None of this can really be quantified even though it's quite real. One area that people have tried to estimate are the number of personal bankruptcies that are directly related to health care costs each year. This too is problematic, but most estimates have concluded it's been over 600,000 families every year since the mid-2000s. That's over ten times our total casualties in Vietnam. Every year. We have no way of knowing how many deaths or permanent disabilities are associated with those 600,000, but it's not zero and even those who don't deal with those physical traumas certainly have their lives upended. The human costs are staggering. In every other developed nation these things just don't happen.

So why are markets so economically destructive in health care? It can be summarized as follows:

> *Health care is an insurance-based market with no substitutes to create natural cost caps and essentially zero price elasticity to its core demand.*

In the early days of our grand market experiment we ignored the implications hidden in that simple statement. As everyone began understanding the issues, various attempts have been made to tinker with the problems, but no amount of tinkering can change the core structural problem. *Any* market with those three features will *always* drive up costs. Like a runaway cancer tumor, a market with that structure will consume every aspect of its host until the host dies or the cancer is removed. That's *not* a market failure. That's what a well-functioning market will do when presented with that set of attributes. *This is a system designed to destroy the overall economy.* It wasn't intentional. It's what happens when neoliberal "belief" in markets is prioritized above "knowledge."

Let's look at each element of that structure, beginning with the insurance model. Some people just have trouble with the idea of insurance. When they hear the phrase "pooling of resources that members draw from based on need" they experience a deep ideological twitch. It sounds like communism. It sounds like "from each according to their ability and to each according to their need." What they fail to see is this is an economic model for the management of risk, not of income or wages. And, as we noted earlier, whenever there is a common risk with large uncertainty in occurrence and economic outcome, insurance is the *only* sensible economic model. Any other model either ties up vastly too much resource or guarantees negative outcomes for most participants. Health care is filled with uncertain risks whose outcome has enormous economic variance. The *only* sensible economic model is insurance.

The "tinkering" of this attribute takes the form of deductibles and co-pays which have shown some value, but at any level that works for the general population has not changed any structural fundamentals. Nor is that even theoretically possible. For those instruments or their companion savings accounts to reach a scale where they changed the fundamental economic structure, we would no longer have an insurance market and we've just outlined why that's essential.

Let's look at the second attribute, the lack of a substitute to create caps on costs. There are lots of insurance markets in the world. House, car, and property insurance all bring the same general numbness to prices we see in health care. However, in those markets there are simple substitutes that cap costs. The repair costs for a car, house, or other piece of property are limited by its replacement value. Financial insurance instruments are often offset by hedging substitutes. But in health care none of that exists. We can't simply decide to "replace" our bodies. We may choose alternative therapies, but as we will see those choices are almost never based on costs, so their ability to put caps on costs are essentially zero.

This is one of the primary focus areas of the more effective systems in other countries. They recognize there are no realistic substitutes and they know that without cost caps prices will naturally escalate. They focus instead on using government negotiations to set caps and treatment definitions throughout the market. These interventions are not "tinkering." They are deliberate steps undertaken at a scale such that the very structure of the market is altered. They create firm pricing boundaries within which everyone must operate. They are specifically there to ensure the market *does not* perform its role. Because, if the market performed properly it would drive up prices to levels we don't want.

The primary reason for this is the third dimension which is actually the most important. This is a market with essentially zero price elasticity. The core demand for health care is not dependent on its cost. The United States performs no fewer heart sonograms per capita than other nations even though they can cost $5,000 in the United States versus $150 elsewhere. In fact, because there is no change in core demand from higher costs, the US system tends to drive everyone to the higher cost options wherever possible. Every part of the system benefits when that happens. It's only the surrounding host economy that suffers.

It's important to note that this is an independent structural element of the market. The insurance payment process and lack of caps magnify its impact but those are separate from the basic zero elasticity aspect of demand. Heart attacks don't go up or down based on prices (other than those triggered by medical bills). Broken arms and car accidents don't change in frequency based on health care costs. The core demand is 100 percent inelastic and every market participant knows that. This is another area where people have tried to tinker with the structure. However, once you step back and think about it you realize how futile those efforts are. The factors that drive changes in the core demand are simply and completely unrelated to prices.

What happens when these three structural elements are combined is that prices go up. And will go up. There are no structural limits beyond consuming every possible resource in its surroundings. That's exactly what the data shows has happened in the United States over the past decades. We don't get sick more often than other nations. We don't go to the doctor more frequently. We don't have more accidents, other than guns. We do have a tendency to choose the most expensive option when there are choices, but that does *not* result in better outcomes. In fact, the system is designed to maximize treatment, not cures, so we often have outcomes that are greatly prolonged compared to other nations. That's our design point, not a bug.

The neoliberal market believers wonder why competition doesn't drive down prices, but that's because they haven't internalized the zero price-elasticity point. *Dropping prices does not increase demand.* All those strategies do is "leave money on the table." Therefore, the most effective competitive strategy is to add frills, add comfort, add tests, add assurances, add, add, add. There's nothing to ratchet it down.

Even from the payer side of the equation there is often far more economic leverage to be had by growing the total bill rather than lowering the cost other than by denying people access to services. There's no price elasticity in core demand. People will get ill and need health care just as often regardless of price. All those people will need to be treated. The more the actuaries say that costs, the more you can charge in premiums. You can potentially raise profits by denying services to get costs below the actuarial estimates, but only if your premiums are based on those higher estimates. Even the payers are economically incented to allow core costs to escalate. And, the core reason is . . . wait for it . . . because there's zero demand elasticity.

Health care costs have become a cancer on our economy. Like any cancer they will grow until they consume every dollar, every resource in the nation. And, like most cancers, the reason can be traced back to a simple "genetic" defect. The gene of zero price elasticity is what transforms a healthy economic sector into a cancerous one.

The United States has made some attempts at setting overall market prices. However, the prime effort was handed over to the AMA to manage, which is a classic case of the fox guarding the henhouse. It's actually quite silly. The industry has even been able to lobby against allowing Medicare to negotiate drug prices. They argued correctly that such intervention would distort the market. That's exactly what's needed. The "undistorted" medical market is structurally designed to only increase costs and thereby grossly distort the overall economy.

The path to fixing all of this is pretty clear, even if fraught with challenges. We have several systems around the world we can examine and draw from. They all have decades of experience getting the right structures in place and they all work vastly better than our own. Just as we did for taxes, we can use them not only to get our structure right, but also to get our initial benchmarks in the right ballpark.

We need to start by having the federal government set prices for all medical services. Note the verb in that sentence. This is *not* a negotiation. This is direct government intervention through nonnegotiable price controls. This is *not* a nationalization of the health care delivery system. However, as any student of economics, business, or markets will tell you, taking control of prices effectively deconstructs the market. That's the deliberate intent. It's also not a temporary intervention. It's a permanent structural change. The government-set prices will need periodic updates. Annual is probably fine for most services, though some might warrant quarterly updates.

The specific prices should be set by benchmarking globally defined treatment protocols and price points. No US lobbyists or medical industry participants can be allowed to engage in the process. Unfortunately, our current political system is dominated by failed neoliberal beliefs and is far too corrupt for us to act on our own. We need to follow the lead of other nations, at least for a while. That's a sad state of affairs, but we must acknowledge it and act accordingly. There is far too much at stake.

Any proposed deviation from the global benchmarks should undergo substantial challenge. Like, presidential approval along with two thirds majorities in both chambers of congress–level challenge. Maybe even throw in governors and statehouses from at least two thirds of the states. And, that should be for the first dollar above the global benchmark. There are *no* credible reasons our costs should be substantially different from global norms.

The usual objection to such a strategy, other than pure and ignorant neoliberal ideology, is that many providers will choose not to offer their services at these price points or that they will be unable to afford crucial R&D expenses. It's utter nonsense. By setting our prices at global levels providers can choose to either offer their services or seek some other planet on which to operate. Some will go out of business, which is fine, in fact probably essential. Even after our massive reset, global spending on health care will exceed $7 trillion which is more than adequate to sustain R&D, particularly once the now unnecessary billions in lobbying expenses are eliminated.

Second, we need to cover all citizens with a basic package of care. It need not be loaded with frills but should be enough to give everyone a solid base and will unload an enormous burden from our workforce and businesses. I'll cover the tax surprise in a moment. The covered services need to include those with "preexisting" conditions. This package must also include all major reproductive care, including female reproductive care. For some odd reason, many current politicians think female reproductive care is something different from human health care. If their constituents object to treating women as humans that's their problem. We can't let that bizarre nonsense enter the system.

Third, we need to provide for a market in optional insurance upgrades for those companies or individuals who want more than the national baseline. This would be a far smaller market than today, and would be strictly optional; however, I suspect there are many who will have an interest in exploring these possibilities. These services will be subject to the same government defined caps as our baseline and can only offer additional services and "perks." We can't allow providers to charge $5,000 to these people for the same sonogram that everyone else gets for $150. If we did they'd withhold service from the general population.

If we did all of the above, we could cut our nationwide health care costs almost in half. And, here's the surprise, we already collect enough taxes and spend enough on health care that there would be practically no increase in government spending. We can have our cake and eat it too. Think back to the outline of 2015 costs. Our estimate of what our total costs should be came to $1.6 trillion and our government already spends $1.5 trillion. We might have to find another $100 billion to cover that gap, but that could quite possibly come from administrative efficiencies alone. And, remember, this is after we've cut $1.6 trillion out of our overall social burden. Based on our tax strategy we'd be targeting $600 billion per year in tax cuts and at least $1 trillion per year to cover the costs of the other fifth paradigm strategies. This isn't magic. It's the reality of just how completely uneconomic the market for US health care has become.

Making these moves would obviously be challenging. Ignoring completely all the political mountains to overcome there's also the reality of radically changing the trajectory of almost 20 percent of our economy. Once completed, every top line economic measure will need to be reported both with and without health care. The capital aspects of the shift will be enormously beneficial to the rest of the economy, adding more to corporate bottom lines than anything in history. It will also provide an incredible improvement to our global competitiveness both for our businesses and our workforce. If we get the constantly growing health care drain removed from labor costs we can also make it much easier to deliver on our promise of aligning wage growth with productivity growth. There are tons and tons of economic benefits here.

The big economic downside is to jobs. We have approximately 16 million people working in the health care industry, many of whom will find themselves looking not just for a new job, but an entire new profession. This adds to the urgency of ensuring that the jobs in our new economy are good jobs. However, that will not be nearly enough. We will need to create a portfolio of retraining programs throughout the transition period to a more sustainable health care system. Budgeting for and providing those opportunities needs to be built into the plan.

Which leads us to the overall education system, which is also unfortunately in need of deep repair. As we hinted in our earlier discussion about the problem, they real key to fixing the system lies in our state subsidized schools. We need to reverse the decades of assault on these institutions by the anti-democracy crowd. Restoring and ensuring sufficient state subsidies to enable them to once again offer tuition to in-state residents at low to zero cost will alter the entire competitive pricing dynamic in the market. The subsidies do need to be restructured to split between fixed costs and variable with only the latter being driven by enrollment rates. The funding for this increase should come from reducing prison spending and achieving the health care cost containment described above. The Medicaid savings alone will be more than enough for what we need. Our fifth paradigm priorities ought to be clear. We want healthy educated citizens for our state tax dollars, not struggling victims of neoliberal driven health care and mass incarceration strategies.

This is a crucial part of our entire national strategy. The reason there is no price elasticity in this market is because of the enormous lifetime value generated through education. That value accrues to both the individual as well as society. Even with all the various economic proposals described in this book, the best and most powerful formula for ensuring that our sustainable economics creates wealth for the bulk of our citizens is through education. It is also the fundamental enabler of the vast majority of our noneconomic value creation. This must be available to everyone for both the basic equality that entails and to ensure our society is enriched by all our citizens, not just a tiny handful. As we spelled out in our fifth paradigm priorities, enabling the full richness of human value creation is core to our social contract.

At the high end of the education market, I'd allow things to continue unfolding as they are. At some point the wealth gap may become so onerous it needs intervention. But for now, I'd worry any cure might be worse than the problem. What's crucial to our overall social contract is not how high the costs of those institutions spiral. What matters is ensuring that solid, high quality, post-secondary education is available to everyone at a low to zero cost. The state programs can once again do that for us and, based on the rest of the competitive dynamics, should pull down costs at the mid-tier private institutions as well.

At the other end of the spectrum the for-profit publicly funded institutions need radical reform. The first step would be to close down the worst offenders, seize their ill-gotten gains, and use it to immediately forgive all student debt for their victims. For those whose fraud is less blatant, they may be redeemable but only if we shift them to a nonprofit status. Even then, the oversight needed is urgent. The need for this entire program should be substantially reduced once we get our state subsidized schools in better financial condition. I don't think they need to be eliminated in total, but there's no sensible rationale to leave them as for-profit organizations with no oversight.

Finally, we need to deal with the veritable mountain of student debt that has accumulated over the past few decades. This is has become a massive "hidden" tax on an entire generation of America. The boldest and far and away best solution would be to simply write it off. The Levy Economics Institute did an in-depth study of the mechanics of how this could be carried out and modeled the potential impact on the overall economy. The mechanics are financially complex involving both federal and private loan sources as well as balance sheet impacts throughout the economy including the federal reserve. Without getting lost in all those complexities it's important to note that the impact on our federal government accounts is limited to the loss of interest payments on the Treasury bills that were issued at the time of the loans, *not* the principle value of the loans. It's still a number in the tens of billions of dollars, but it's not in the trillions. It's completely manageable. Their econometric models concluded the total elimination of student debt would stimulate approximately $100 billion of GDP growth per year. Those models were highly conservative and ignored a substantial number of other benefits. These included things like increasing the number of people getting college degrees and better jobs, changes in household formation, improved consumer credit standings, and increased consumer resilience in the event of future downturns. $100 billion per year is truly a minimum.

There is admittedly a degree of moral hazard associated with this proposal. Frankly, it's far, far less than the hazard associated with our 2008 bank bailout. Still, it really needs to be done in conjunction with the reforms noted above so that we eliminate the original cause of these unnecessary financial burdens. For those who still find that too generous, we could limit the write-off to the overall education costs in excess of inflation since 1980. In any event, it's a crisis that needs urgent intervention. There are no real budgetary costs associated with this. It's merely a loss of a hidden tax stream levied primarily on the lower and middle class. We need those taxes to be set based on our defensibly fair benchmarks, not camouflaged levies on the essential social need for education.

7

REPAIRING THE SOCIAL CONTRACT BREACHES

M OST OF THESE social issues are rooted in our failure to properly manage the judgmental excesses of those who believe in the ethic of power. Just as we needed to excise markets to fix our health care and education system we will need to excise those "strict fathers" from our judicial and social welfare systems. In some ways that's harder. We can fix a broken socio-economic system by replacing it through policy changes. Barring those whose moral beliefs are antithetical to the purpose of a particular program is much harder. Even worse, those individuals are filled with a self-righteous certainty and an uncontrollable desire to mete out punishment. This will require a great deal more political fortitude than just standing behind a clear set of economic analyses.

Let's start with our judicial system. We've already covered the ineffectiveness, immorality, and downright insanity of our mass incarceration and for-profit prison policies. We've also highlighted that our crime problem, which was very, very real for decades, is over. Before we talk about what to do, we need to add a few more diagnoses, starting with the racial problem built into the fabric of our judicial system. In many ways it's actually built into the fabric of our society and just manifests itself in egregious ways in the judicial system. Regardless of the source it's real and unacceptable.

There are those who argue the differential profiling of African Americans is justified. They are wrong. As an expert in data analytics, distinguishing between correlation and causation, and all the other missteps that riddle this discussion, I can appreciate the confusion and uncertainty of those who get misled and just don't know whom to believe. Some of the misinformation is deliberate. Most is just poor or inexperienced work. But it's still wrong.

Adding to this, as was mentioned earlier, we now have AI training data sets with built-in racial biases. Whether that's deliberate or inadvertent is hard to know but it exists. One of the more common tools used by judges to determine sentencing recommendations is an AI system that has been proven to be (mis)trained through biased data. People have an irrational but very real tendency to view the recommendations from systems like these as just one step removed from God. We cannot allow this form of systemic racial biases to enter through the AI door. That would create deep and lasting consequential damage.

When someone says, "black lives matter" we all need to say "yes, they do." If you want or need to add that white lives, and yellow lives, and blue lives, and poor lives, and rich lives all matter too, then "amen, and God bless." None of that takes away from the point that black lives are an integral element of our top value and priority which is people. When our judiciary system brings that into question it must be held to account. Protecting the lives and well-being of the people of this country is the reason the judiciary exists. We do not exist for their benefit, they exist for ours.

One of the more prominent examples of this is the so-called war on drugs. At its peak it was being used in ways that decimated poor black and Hispanic neighborhoods. In many of those places nearly the entire population of black males in their teens and twenties were removed and sent to prison. If we applied the same heartless criteria to today's opioid crisis there would be whole towns in West Virginia and Ohio that would be incarcerated. That's not happening, which is good, but we need to reflect on the fact that a very different set of criteria and judgment is being used. When indignant, self-righteous voices demand harsh treatment of young urban blacks we need to recognize how that same attitude would play in white, rural America.

This leads to the next observation. The purpose of the judicial system is to *protect* people, not *attack* people. The entire "war on . . ." vocabulary and mindset has that upside down. When we frame police work as a "war" we automatically adopt an *attack* posture. When we redeploy weaponry from our military into civilian police forces we're doing the same thing. This attitude comes directly from the ethic of power. Those folks believe that declaring "war" is not only the right strategy, it's actually the moral strategy. All of the data shows that they're deeply wrong. This is certainly not to ignore the fact that police do have to deal with violent and dangerous individuals. They do. However, when they do so with the approach of protecting the community and protecting the innocent the entire dynamic is different and far more effective.

This is also one of the subtle but dangerous aspects of the for-profit prison system. That system automatically orients itself to filling the prisons. When you feel even a subtle influence in that direction you've lost the community protection mind-set and shifted to a "find someone to lock up" mind-set. The deep tragedy is this trend is happening at a time when the actual crime rate is so low. We should be naturally shifting to more of a *protect* posture, and yet in far too many cases we are not. There are too many of these kinds of subtle pressures and far too many "ethic of power" demagogues and indignant self-righteous voices.

Hand in hand with these issues are a related pair of attitudinal and behavioral realities. We proclaim that everyone is innocent until proven guilty, but we do not believe it, nor do we act that way. In fact, for far too many these days guilt is just assumed. This holds true for both urban blacks and southern farmers. The former gets stopped, frisked, and frequently thrown in jail and the latter has their truck and possessions seized and then sold to generate revenue for the local police. When this happens, it is the police that are the ones people need protection from. Many of our highest law officials these days have outright contempt for the entire notion of due process. As far as they're concerned it's a total waste. The danger of that cannot be overstated. When the Attorney General proclaims a preference for Guantanamo tribunals because of his mistaken belief that that would allow for the elimination of the rights to representation and discovery, we are in a dangerous place.

When these kinds of assaults are perpetrated by the very forces that are supposed to protect us our primary protection is the courts. Unfortunately, that's been one of the major targets of the anti-democracy movement. They have worked tirelessly, particularly at the federal appeals court level, to place judges who will consistently favor those in power over their victims. They've even attempted to place radio commentators with literally no legal background into those lifetime positions, strictly on the merits of their consistently hostile commentary toward the poor and vulnerable.

Among the most vulnerable populations in America are the current generation of immigrants. We will cover immigration policy in considerable depth in a later chapter. Here I only want to observe a few important points. We have declared war on immigrants. Technically we're only at war with undocumented immigrants, but in the "uncivil" court of opinion where everyone is guilty until proven otherwise, we've effectively declared war on all immigrants. Also, technically, being in the country without proper authorization is a civil misdemeanor, a "parking ticket" violation, not a criminal offense. The average penalty for that offense along our southern border is a fine of $10. But, once you declare war those kinds of niceties get tossed out the window. Back in that "uncivil" court, immigration is a crime, not a parking ticket. In fact, for far too many people it's considered a crime of literally monstrous proportions deserving of kidnapping or even capital punishment.

This power ethic war mentality has led us into many dangerous slippery slopes. First, when ICE descends with officers to violently seize old women and children we are displaying an enormous excess of force. If you notice, they almost always have four officers per victim. In those rare instances when the individual being apprehended is actually a dangerous criminal, that may well be justified. But, it is used everywhere and is frequently utterly out of proportion to the civil offense in question and the real risk to the officers. They are well aware of this reality. They do it deliberately as a quite conscious effort to generate terror in certain communities. We recently orchestrated a set of deliberate shifts that allowed us to kidnap children from their parents and then use them as ransom to drop asylum pleas and negotiating pawns for political purposes. We have allowed the ethic of power and psychology of "war" to turn us into a nation of terrorists.

What we have also done is to largely repeal the Fourth Amendment to the Constitution. Current laws allow immigration officers and the police to conduct unlimited searches and property seizure for anyone trying to enter the country. They may do this to anyone they even suspect may be guilty of that crime. And, that extends 100 miles inland from the border around the entire periphery of the country. Approximately 200 million Americans or 57 percent of our population fall within that scope. Since the same rules apply to any airport that has international arrivals, the actual extent is far greater than that. The Supreme Court has consistently upheld this law. We have allowed ourselves to become a country where the police may stop anyone and demand to "see their papers."

We reassure ourselves that these indignities don't apply to us, only those evil immigrants. However, once we begin allowing these deep erosions to our system of justice we've embarked on the wrong path. The reality is absolutely any one of us can be searched and assaulted in this fashion in the name of "protecting our borders." When we decide that's acceptable we're only a small step from ever more intrusive violations of the very liberties we so cherish.

The dangerous realities we've just reviewed are not universal. In fact, more effective police work is among the most important factors in the reduction of crime in America. In 1994, New York City pioneered an approach to policing known as CompStat, an abbreviation of compare statistics. What this essentially does is apply solid, modern management techniques to policing. As its name suggests, it begins with very detailed, neighborhood by neighborhood data on criminal activities. It's updated constantly and used in weekly meetings to identify priority areas for intervention. The whole set of city resources are available for those interventions, including social workers and community activists. The interventions themselves are swift and consistent. Whatever technique seems best suited to the specific problem is used. The results are then measured, and the effective techniques retained while the ineffective are discarded. Local commanders hold their officers accountable for getting steady improvement.

This has proven to be effective and has been adopted in over 40 different cities around the country. What's most notable is how far removed it is from a "war" mind-set. It's the opposite. It's a "management" mind-set. Measure what you want, communicate the results, use all available resources, engage the community in the process, reward those who produce steady improvements . . . good old Management 101. This isn't to say there aren't instances where the "right technique" is pretty aggressive. There are. But, they are not used for the purpose of being aggressive, they're used pragmatically, where needed. It's a management process, not a military campaign.

As a society we know how to do this. The reality is, crime *is* way down and we have cities all over the country whose police efforts and dedication are a big part of the reason. A prominent example is New York City where the crime rate has dropped to levels not seen since 1952. However, we've allowed a whole series of dangerous and destructive practices to infect our justice system. For-profit prisons have to go. The destruction of civil liberty in the name of border protection has to end. We have to focus on reducing our prison population dramatically. We need to stop declaring war on ourselves. We need our courts to protect the vulnerable, not target them as victims. And, we need to purge every hint of racism from our judicial system.

The second major social contract breach is how we handle the poor. We covered the utter failure of the 1996 reform earlier. We also reviewed how endemic this tragedy is all over the world. Getting the minimum wage up to a living standard instead of abject poverty will definitely help. Almost all current recipients of things like food stamps do indeed have jobs. Those jobs just don't pay enough to survive. Wages are always a problem but so are the available hours. Many are only able to find part-time or seasonal work while others struggle as day laborers who never know whether anything will materialize. The minimum wage adjustment will help, but it won't solve the problem.

A major part of our social challenge are those people whose ethic-of-power belief causes them to conclude that poverty is a moral failing of the poor. These people feel the answer is to improve what they perceive as moral character defects. The tools they think are appropriate to accomplish this goal are forms of punishment up to and including outright starvation. If we whip them hard enough, steal from them, spit on them, treat them like filth, and call them animals, that will "cure" them of their moral failings. It's sick. However, the ethic of power is deeply believed by many and no matter how much it fails, punishment will be demanded from those voices again and again. As long as poverty still exists they are convinced we just need more punishment. The reality is no matter how much punishment we inflict, poverty will continue. For those believers, their only answer to that truth will be more escalation. Their ethical system offers no other options.

Part of the problem is deciding for whom and how our programs should be designed. The vast majority of people caught in these desperate situations are looking for a hand *up*, not a hand *out*. To be clear, they do need direct help. Without it mere survival becomes a struggle. But what they really seek is a way out of their situation. I've known many of these folks and to a person they will willingly, even eagerly, work harder than most. If we give them what they need to survive and assist them in finding jobs that provide a living wage, those who can will do so. They need no added incentives, nor is punishment at all appropriate. They are not "evil." They just need help.

That help is not trivial. It's far more than just money and access to possible jobs. There are real issues around family stability, child development, depression, substance abuse, and many more sources of derailment. These issues need persistent focus and resources from the people who really care about providing the help these people need. For those who do, the personal rewards can be deeply soul satisfying, but the inevitable failures are every bit as wrenching. We are blessed as a society to have so many who are willing to put themselves on the line in this fashion. For them, this is a formula for value based on people that transcends so much of what consumes the rest of us. It's a great example of why we are so much more than just "economic" actors.

The remainder of those who need our help fall into two other categories. Some are simply unable to work. They suffer from either physical or mental impairments that make work an unrealistic goal. There are some charitable organizations that create "jobs" designed for some of these disabled people, but there's not nearly enough of that, nor is it realistic to create enough of this sort of "make work" to make a difference. These people do need a hand out and will need it permanently. There are not a lot of them, but there are enough that we need programs that will work for them. Loading those programs with unrealistic work demands or punishments is silly, senseless, and in the end simply insulting. Most of these people also rely on our health care system. It's important that both of these support systems operate with a sensible degree of consistency around things like qualification criteria and management processes.

The final category are those people who could work, but don't want to. There really aren't that many of those folks. These are the people our "punishment is the answer" crowd fixates on. However, punishment has never been effective with these people. Are they "freeloaders"? Yes, I'm sure they are. But there truly aren't that many of them and designing the entire social welfare system around the anger certain people feel toward them is not productive. All that does is punish the other people described above for whom our assistance and compassion could truly make a difference in their lives and for our society.

Once again, looking at global norms can help us get in the right ballpark. Our outliers in this case are Luxembourg, Denmark, and Iceland, all of whom have programs significantly above the norms. When they are excluded the average spending on "noncontributory" assistance programs of all types is 3 percent of GDP. In the United States, if you count both federal and state expenditures and budgets we also average right around 3 percent. As we noted earlier, much of that comes in the form of food stamps, and housing assistance, not direct cash. In total, we're spending about the right amount.

However, as we saw in the TANF program, the key is how much of what spend reaches those in need and how much gets siphoned off. From the recipient's standpoint most countries look at cash contributions relative to average industrial wages. The low end of that range is 11 percent in Germany where industrial wages are pretty high. The high end is 30 percent in both Norway and the Netherlands. The global average is right around 20 percent and is fairly consistent. Our sample has ten nations between 16 and 20 percent and five between 21 and 25 percent. There are only two nations below 15 percent and three above 26 percent. The United States sits at 5 percent and nearly half of that gets siphoned off by the anti-abortion crowd. It really is disgraceful. We do allocate money for the poor, it just doesn't get to them.

Most of these nations make their assistance available to anyone who needs it and put no caps on lifetime need. The United States only provides assistance to families with children and has a lifetime cap of five years. Most nations also recognize the difference between those who need temporary help and those who are permanently disabled. The norm is to provide enough additional assistance to the disabled to ensure they can live without ever working since they never will. All common sense.

A major bipartisan study focused on steps to reduce child poverty completed their work in early 2019. After studying dozens of programs around the world they came to some pretty straightforward and unsurprising conclusions. All the "moralizing" programs from around the world that focus on behaviors and job requirements have been failures and counterproductive. They end up creating bureaucracies dedicated to denying people access to the very resources nations have allocated for their assistance. What works best is simply providing financial assistance to people directly and in proportion to the size of the family. The consensus conclusion from their work is that a target of $3,500 per child per year would yield dramatic reductions in child poverty. They also concluded those costs would be dwarfed by the returns to society in the form of reduced health problems, crime, and increased taxes from those who are able to lift themselves into better earnings over time.

The "generosity" of civilized nations does not result in higher levels of dependence or poverty. Those statistics are driven by economic realities, not social policies. The mean-spiritedness of the United States does not reduce our levels of poverty, nor does it save any money. All we do with our current policies is magnify the human suffering and tragedy that already exists in this world. We are long overdue for redesigning our programs to actually focus on helping people up and out of poverty rather than hatefully sneering at them or tricking them into unwanted pregnancies. Our fifth paradigm priority is clear—our most important value is people and these folks are included in what we value as a society. The assistance we provide is a direct reflection of those values.

8

GLOBAL CONSIDERATIONS

ECONOMIC VALUE CREATION AND TRADE

THE GLOBAL ECONOMY is four to five times the size of the United States and will be the key to economic growth in the twenty-first century. That's an unavoidable fact. No amount of "head in the sand" or alternate stories will change that. It was made possible through the alignment and agreement around key principles of open markets and currency exchange. We've tinkered with it a bit over the years, but most of the key pillars had their roots in Bretton Woods. At this point we know a lot about how it works. We also know there are several flaws that urgently need to be addressed.

The first of these was noted earlier. Harmonizing currency, trade, and property laws has missed completely the need to harmonize workers' rights and working conditions. That's long overdue and needs to be a crucial global priority. This will not be simple tinkering. This needs its own Bretton Woods–like convention and is something the United States should lead. Our own house is not really in order here, so we should not be surprised when the global norms demand we make changes too. As we discussed in the section on our health care strategy, our current system creates an enormous unfair burden on American workers and any company that wants to employ them. We need to fix that for our own reasons and can expect that to be part of any global norm coming out of this proposed future "Bretton Woods."

The second area that needs attention is intellectual property. There are already a number of multilateral agreements and processes in place around IP. However, none of those are really designed for the modern world. As described earlier, the modern innovation process is almost always deeply collaborative, and that collaboration is increasingly global. None of our agreements or legal standards are designed around that reality. This is another nontrivial task and one that will need its own Bretton Woods.

The third area of focus should be on the rights and responsibilities associated with data, particularly about people. Privacy needs to become a global priority and the definition of the rights and responsibilities associated with that priority are in desperate need of clarification. The recent work by the EU around General Data Protection Regulation (GDPR) should be the starting point. We may be able to simply get a global ratification of those rights. That would be a great start and give us a foundation on which to build. However, it will only be a start and we will need a process to manage and adjust as technology and practices evolve.

The fourth focus is climate change. We need to rejoin the Paris Accords and get back on track to meet our commitments. That's essential, but more is needed. The full scope of the issue and possible actions would fill an entire book. I won't attempt to cover all of that here but do want to highlight one important element that must be done through global coordination. It's vitally important that we establish regulatory, tax, and accounting laws that build carbon costs and other externalities into business expense and liability standards. No nation can do that on its own. To do so would create unmanageable economic penalties. However, if we establish externality accounting standards globally, then we will finally begin harnessing market forces to solve climate change. Once established, any nation that fails to comply with the new global accounting rules needs to be faced with corrective economic tariffs from every nation that does so comply. Ironically, our current global trade laws have actually been used to threaten lawsuits against nations attempting to use government incentives aimed at accelerating our global transition to clean energy. Those laws have made national sovereignty a bit of a sham.

The fifth area that needs attention is actually one that dates back to the original Bretton Woods as well as the changes made in the early 1970s. Currency exchange is probably the most fundamental pillar of our global economy, but unfortunately it needs repair. Global currency markets have become havens for speculative capital and have turned into Blitzkrieg machines assaulting sovereign markets all over the globe. When nations the size and maturity of France discover they are no longer able to manage their own currency something has gone badly wrong. These excesses were one of the problems the Tobin tax was intended to address. The very short-term capital gains tax we've proposed could help. However, this is unquestionably a global issue and one that will need global coordination to tackle. Our original Bretton Woods needs another Bretton Woods.

The other original pillar is the principle of open and tariff free trade. From the very beginning every nation in the world has put selective tariffs in place to protect local agriculture. Many of these reflect the various national policies and practices that emerged out of the turmoil rooted in the shift from agrarian societies to industrial societies. It's easy for economists to prove how inefficient these are, but they are integral elements of the social contracts of every nation. Nobody really challenges or disputes these. It's time we begin to examine the same carefully selective tariff strategies for different industrial sectors.

The national economic strategy we outlined earlier made the point that in areas where the principle economic driver of labor is cost we should not expect to source that work from the United States. No matter how much we normalize working terms and conditions, wages will remain vastly different between geographies. Attempting to mask this broadly through tariffs will just render our businesses globally uncompetitive and perversely accelerate the movement of work elsewhere. We also outlined strategies to drive growth in sectors that are basically immune from global wage competition and we created strategies for all the new value creating sectors of the future. Nothing that follows changes those core principles.

That set of principles needs to guide the vast majority of what we do. However, we also need to recognize they won't encompass everything and there will almost certainly be places where we want to retain a core set of national capabilities, resources, and jobs, despite their being subject to global competition and cost driven wages. Some of these could be driven by concerns for national defense. Others will be driven by concerns for the potential damage done to our communities and our social cohesion. Whenever we set down this path we are likely to create measurable inefficiencies and may sacrifice our ability to compete globally. It should be rare, but where it's the right thing to do, we need to do so.

I expect every nation will go through a similar process. Some of our decisions will harmonize with those made by others and some will not. There will be disputes along the way. We need to manage this process patiently recognizing we're not embarked on a battle of principles but rather something more akin to what we all accept in the agriculture sector. Each nation will be accepting some form of economic inefficiency in return for an improved social contract. Those will be sovereign choices based on each nation's history, culture, and social needs. Over time they should sort themselves out just as we've done in the past. We need to keep our well-intentioned ideologues out of these particular skirmishes. We're seeking practicality, not purity.

The final set of global economic strategies is the incredible opportunity to build traditional and modern infrastructures around world. We obviously need to start with our own but as we look outward there are opportunities to replicate what we did with Europe through the Marshall Plan and what China is doing today across Asia and Africa. In the areas of traditional infrastructure, the most obvious starting places are in our own backyard with Mexico, as well as Central and South America. Developing coordinated economic development strategies with all those nations would create enormous value in both the short and long terms. It would also go a long way toward easing the immigration pressures along our southern border. Mexico and Central America in particular scream out for a different strategy. Our past ideological interventions have been utter failures proving the flaws in that approach. NAFTA has good intentions, but as a stand-alone agreement misses most of what would really enrich all of our nations. Some of these nations are at risk of total failure, an event we certainly do not want in our backyard. We need to focus on joint economic development, including the essential foundations of safety and security.

We should also look for opportunities to do similar work across Africa and even potentially India. In Africa, we will find that China is already established

and has been systematically pursuing projects with the most promising economic returns. However, there's still a vast continent to develop and opportunities are ample. India is more complex but could be even more lucrative in the
long term. Much of their infrastructure dates from the early British colonial
days and is badly in need of modernization. However, they have their own plans
and the local family power structure may make it difficult to find mutually
valuable working arrangements. Nonetheless, the opportunities are enormous
and well worth exploring.

The opportunities in the area of modern infrastructure are also considerable. The digital opportunities can be pursued as direct extensions of our own
strategies. The inherent global reach and non-rivalrous nature of these initiatives make them easy to extend globally. Proactive outreach to other nations
can be done for very little expense and can create substantial returns both for
us and for the nations who join our efforts.

Our national data strategy can be extended to other nations who have
embarked on similar initiatives. While I'm sure there would be many areas of
mutual value, I'm also sure there would also be areas of concern for some. For
example, our "citizens data reserve" might prove incompatible with other national
strategies and our internal protections would need to apply globally. Many of
these deals could easily entail usage and/or data placement restrictions that would
add to all the complexities we described for our own initiative. Nonetheless, this
is a promising area that is worth exploring even if it's slow to bear fruit.

Our plan to create training and testing data to enable certification standards for AI systems would be easily extended globally. It would also help
establish the kind of common standards necessary to drive global growth in
these technologies. It costs us nothing for others to use these kinds of digital
assets and when they do it can directly expand the market for our leadership
technologies.

Last, but not least, expanding our experience market globally would also
be a fabulous win-win opportunity. In addition to the direct expansion of the
resources in the market it can become a major element in driving growth for
the tourism industry, both here and abroad. It can also be one of the prime elements in a global strategy around noneconomic value creation.

China and the Thucydides Trap

Over the last 150–200 years China has evolved from its nineteenth-century struggles with Western powers to the crippling rise of communism and to their reemergence as a global economic power. The fundamental details of their rapidly modernizing economy almost mathematically guarantee their growth will continue to the point where they will eventually dwarf the United States. While less mathematically certain, they fully intend to begin leading the world in many of the next generation technologies. They are no longer content to remain contained within the borders of the "middle kingdom." The external initiatives they already have under way will reshape 65–70 percent of the globe. They've only just begun modernizing their military, but we should fully expect that process to follow. Anybody who doesn't realize they fully intend and expect to become a superpower with the same sort of 3–4x advantage over the United States that we have had over other powers over the past 50 years hasn't been paying attention.

None of this is anything we can stop or even slow. If they were a society that shared our freedoms and values we could adopt the same sort of posture the British did toward the United States as we followed our own stratospheric and unstoppable rise over the past 100 years. However, they are not and as such our path is a bit more complex.

The Thucydides Trap is a theory that asserts the transition between a major established national power and an emerging rising power almost always leads to war. There are probably over a dozen examples historians can cite going all the way back to the Peloponnesian War between Sparta and Athens. The key strategic question is how we avoid this trap now that China's rise to global rivalry has become inevitable.

Over the course of this book we've described or hinted at almost all of the elements we will need to employ. In my mind, these can be organized under five major priorities.

First, we need to implement our own national strategy. Our house is not in order right now and our deep structural flaws must be repaired. That strategy can provide a fabulous leadership example, one that can rekindle our "shining beacon" both for ourselves and for the world, regardless of our relative size. It's also a strategy that will build a substantial and rewarding socioeconomic foundation that is largely immune from global competitive dynamics.

Second, we need to energetically and enthusiastically engage with China across the board. Our people, companies, economy, and culture will all benefit. The vast majority of what China and her people are bringing to the world are things we can embrace and enjoy. We just need to ensure as we do so that we do not allow the dark aspects of their totalitarian society to infect our own.

Third, we need to follow through on the various potential leadership initiatives around the world that we've outlined above. In the process we need to deepen our engagement with the EU and India, sharing the stage with them and allying with them to address global opportunities and challenges.

Fourth, we need firm policy of containment when China tests boundaries. The trick to this is avoiding any direct power escalation. We might win those confrontations in the short term, but in the long term we can't count on that and we don't want to make that the basis of conflict resolution. We need to establish as early as possible where boundaries exist and that their violation will receive a firm response.

Fifth, we need to remind ourselves of the inherent "rightness" of our values. It may take time, even whole generations, but eventually the importance of people as people, with inalienable rights to life, liberty, and the pursuit of happiness, will prevail. This connects with the first point above. If we renew our national commitment to the compass headings and strategies outlined in this book, if we begin creating a true instantiation of the fifth paradigm, we will do more to lead the world than all the tanks and bombs ever built.

9

IMMIGRANTS AND OUR NATIONAL FABRIC

I T'S A CLICHÉ, but a true one: we are a nation of immigrants. It was true from the beginning when our founders declared our independence and severed our ties with Britain. The slaves who were so central to our early population and economy came unwillingly, in chains. They can't really be called immigrants, but they too arrived here from abroad, and under duress. It was the work of immigrants that drove our transition from an agricultural nation to an industrial nation. They populated and built our cities and filled our factories. The clichéd Irish policeman from Boston stands alongside the Jewish deli owner in New York and the Scotch-Irish steelworker in Pittsburgh. In the late nineteenth century roughly one third of our total immigrant population had arrived from Ireland and another 25–30 percent had come from Germany. Our simple economic formula where GDP growth is equal to population growth plus productivity growth was propelled by both factors right up until we closed our borders in the 1920s and the population component slowed.

Once we reopened our borders in 1965 the immigration cycle began anew. Our population has now been renewed, joined by roughly 45 million new immigrants over the last 50 years. Once again, there's a dominant source. In this case it's Mexico, comprising about 28 percent of the total, followed by China, India, and the Philippines. That 45 million consists of 21 million naturalized citizens, 13 million lawful permanent residents, and 11 million who are unauthorized.

Of those 11 million there are 3 million who would fully qualify as residents but have been procedurally blocked from the application process. There are another 3.6 million brought in before their eighteenth birthday and 4 million parents caring for children who are full US citizens. The total number has been basically stable for over a decade. The combination of the 2008 recession and the ramped-up enforcement under Obama caused the number of newly arrived unauthorized immigrants to plummet. The mix has also changed and is now led by people fleeing violent gangs in Central America many of whom would qualify as asylum seekers.

Over the last 50 years, our immigrant population has climbed to 13 percent of our total which is the low end of the 13–15 percent range we saw from the 1850s up until the 1920s. Since 1970, immigrants have accounted for over 50 percent of our total population growth. The rate of new arrivals reached a peak in the early 2000s and has stabilized at roughly 1–1.2 million per year, about three-fourths of whom will likely become long-term residents. Once again, immigrants are becoming a meaningful force driving our economic growth. We have reclaimed our heritage.

We have also, unfortunately, refueled discomfort, fears, and, in some cases, outright racial bigotry. Those have always been present, and, again, like the 1920s, have become fertile ground for demagogues who want to stir those ingredients into a hatred for "others." The fears are real, but for most they are rooted, not in bigotry, but in ignorance. The greatest traction for the demagogues are in sectors of the country with very few immigrants. The regions with large immigrant populations have their own stresses, frustrations, and anger, but generally have not been receptive to the demagogues. They want better answers and solutions to real problems, not a descent into the quagmires of hate. Still, there are far too many being enticed and goaded into those pits and that leads only to destruction and despair.

FALSE DEBATES AND FEARS

The demagogues have been hard at work. Our airwaves are filled every day and night with false statements and fearmongering. Immigrants are not murderers, rapists, and criminals, they do not "steal jobs," they do not create an undue social burden, and they are not an "invasion" of our sovereign nation. They are part of our national fabric, part of who we are.

Let's just run through the facts. In early 2018 four new studies were published that reconfirmed decades of similar findings. The first focused on violent crime and looked specifically at communities and periods in which immigration, specifically undocumented immigration, increased substantially. There were no changes in incidents of violent crime in any of those areas during or following the period of increased immigration. The same team then went and looked at changes in nonviolent crimes, including drug and alcohol arrests, overdoses, and DUI incidents. No change. A different group published their findings from a detailed analysis of data from Texas in 2015. Texas is a bit of an outlier in its hostility to the vulnerable in general and immigrants in particular. They make a specific point to log people's immigration status during every arrest hoping to find proof to justify their biases. Their own probably biased data conclusively indicates native born Americans are much more likely than immigrants to commit crimes including larceny, sexual assault, rape, and murder. Finally, a study from a group in the UK focused on a younger US cohort and found the exact same things. The least likely group to commit a crime are undocumented immigrants followed by documented immigrants followed by native born Americans. The same findings have emerged from essentially every study done for decades. There simply is no room for debate on this topic. Immigrants are less likely to commit crimes than native born Americans—period.

The next bugaboo is jobs. Here one needs to begin injecting a bit of quality control on the data. There are those who assume a completely static market. They then measure the amount of employment among immigrant populations, discover it's quite high, and then assume every one of those jobs was one lost to a "real" American. These analysts are often surprised that their data show such high employment rates for immigrants. That's part of the twisted bias that exists on this topic. If those analysts found low employment they would accuse the immigrants of being lazy grifters. Nothing could be further from the truth. As every study has proven, immigrants work. They work a lot and they work hard.

Furthermore, our economy is not a static thing. Working immigrants spend money and create their own economic demand. The jobs they take are not lost jobs for others. When immigrant jobs increase so do non-immigrant jobs. In lockstep. They rise and fall together. When immigrant populations rise in a community, non-immigrants do not suddenly lose jobs. The jobs go up and down together. Communities with very high levels of employment for immigrants have high employment levels for non-immigrants. In fact, communities with high levels of unemployment for non-immigrants tend to have very low immigrant populations. Jobs are driven by economic conditions, not population distribution.

The closely related worry is around wages. These are more complicated studies because the measured variations are small and hard to tease out. They also only impact small slices of the population. The best studies have found that high immigrant populations do tend to reduce wages for certain groups during economic downturns by a maximum of about 2 percent. However, during economic upticks those same populations can be credited with about a 2 percent increase in wages. The effects are small and basically accentuate the deeper underlying economics. The minimum wage plan included in our proposed national economic strategy would dwarf this whole dynamic.

Which leads finally to the cruelest cut of all, our social programs and taxes. Immigrants, both documented and not, have lower participation rates in our minuscule and embarrassing programs than non-immigrants. On average, the 17 percent of immigrants who qualify get about 9 percent of their income from aid while similarly qualifying non-immigrants get 15 percent. Undocumented immigrants are completely prohibited from essentially all of those programs. In a sad and deep irony, undocumented immigrants are estimated to contribute $12 billion per year to the Social Security Trust fund even though they will never be able to receive any benefits from that program. The only substantive program through which undocumented immigrants benefit are the K–12 education programs which are open to all. Of course, they only represent 1.3 percent of that population so calling them a huge burden on society is absurd.

A 2009 study on Medicare found that immigrants contributed $33 billion to the program and consumed only $19 billion for a net addition of $14 billion.

The balance for non-immigrants was a negative $31 billion. Immigrants basically subsidized nearly half the net costs of Medicare in that study.

Another study examined the overall balance of all benefits versus tax contributions across the total immigrant population. They concluded that first generation immigrants on balance took $57 billion per year more than they contributed (which excluded the positive $12 billion to social security), the second generation paid $30 billion more in taxes than they got in benefits, and the third generation paid $224 billion more than they received. The bias of the authors is evident when they conclude that data indicates immigrants need to pay more taxes.

I see something different in those numbers. The total US federal and state spending is roughly $6 trillion. The net burden of first generation immigrants in this data is $45 billion which is less than one percent of that budget. The second generation actually covers two thirds of that minimal amount. That means the net burden of first and second-generation immigrants is less than one quarter of one percent of our total government spending. And, from that point on they become net contributors.

What's more, almost all the benefits they receive flow right back into their communities. Those benefits don't go into some black hole. They get spent on food, clothing, rent, gas, and countless other needs. All of that helps drive economic growth for the businesses where they live. None of that is any "burden" at all. In reality it's a highly targeted stimulus for our poorest communities.

IMMIGRANTS' ROLE IN OUR SOCIETY AND ECONOMICS

I've hinted at it, but it's an important point to render explicit which is the special place immigrants play in our national culture. Throughout our history the people who come here are almost always in flight. It may be from economic distress, from gangs, from war, or from famine, but they come out of need. For every one that arrives at our door there are millions who remained behind. The ones who come are the ones with the courage, vision, hope, and faith to dream about a better life. The truly indolent are not those who take that kind of leap. They come as individuals and they come with deep ties to families. They are often being forced to abandon their communities and nations and are seeking to replant themselves here to find new communities and a new nation as their home. Many will work literally for decades, even entire generations, to reassemble their families and establish their new roots. They work, build, and grow for themselves, their families, and their new communities. They also, laugh, dance, cry, and struggle. Underneath all of that you will find courage, dignity, and most of all hope—the very character attributes that drove them to lift themselves up and come to our shores. These are people with the moral sinews that enrich our American heritage. They are the same sinews that forged this nation.

Immigrants make up 13 percent of our population, 15 percent of our total economic output, 16 percent of our workforce, and over 22 percent of small business owners. They represent roughly $1 trillion in consumer spending. Nobody would be surprised to know that they represent 27 percent of our agricultural workforce and 22 percent of our construction workers, but did you realize they represent 31 percent of US software developers? How about the fact that 40 percent of the Fortune 500 were founded by first or second-generation immigrants? One-third of all the venture capital–backed firms that went public in the period from 2006 to 2012 were founded by immigrants as are one-half the startups with current valuations over $1 billion. In 2016, 76 percent of the new patent grants and 100 percent of the Nobel Prizes awarded to US citizens went to immigrants. These are sinews of high-tensile economic steel.

Those "sparklers" are examples of the American dream we all cherish. Not everybody achieves that kind of success, but immigrants are disproportionate contributors to our economy. Recall again our simple economic formula that GDP growth is equal to population growth plus productivity growth. We've documented extensively that productivity growth has been slowing since the early 1970s. The birth rate of our non-immigrant population has also been slowing. The 50-percent growth in our overall population coming from immigrants is now one of the major factors driving our entire GDP growth.

Immigrants come with hopes and dreams. Many of them also come with distinct challenges. Their character may have hidden depths, but their initial resources are often limited and their knowledge of what lies ahead practically nonexistent or filled with misinformation. They are vulnerable both to those who prey on their journey as well as those who prey on their arrival. Their ignorance and language barrier can be mistaken as a lack of intelligence, or as attempts to deceive. In the early waves of European immigration, Ellis Island served as a way station both to provide a quarantine period for disease and an entry period to get oriented. Today's immigrants have the same vulnerabilities and face the same challenges. In the chapter on changing our attitudes toward policing we emphasized the psychology of "protecting the community" instead of a "war on crime." This truth is magnified a hundredfold for immigrants. We need to see them as a vulnerable community that deserves and needs protection, not as evil invaders to be contained and assaulted.

In many ways immigrants are model citizens. They are sometimes poor, and they do struggle, but the strong moral character that brought them here helps them survive and steadily grow. They don't commit crimes, they work hard, they pay taxes even for benefits they'll never receive, and they lift themselves out of poverty to be net contributors to our overall tax base. They not only do this, they do it amid an atmosphere that is the opposite of what they deserve. Were we to truly treat them with the welcome and protection described above, they would thrive even more.

A BASIC IMMIGRATION STRATEGY

There are three major elements to the fifth paradigm strategy and it begins by dusting off our welcome mat. We need a national "renewal of vows," a recommitment to the words on the Statue of Liberty. There will be limits that will be spelled out below, but our core attitude needs to be shaped by our welcoming, not our limiting, to those who wish to join our collective journey. We need to welcome those with dreams and hopes. We need to welcome those with family roots. We need to welcome the best and brightest from every nation. And, we need to openly welcome our fair share of the refugees whose plight is a global problem that we need to help manage along with other global leaders.

We need to calibrate our total intake so that the immigrant share of our population remains in the 13–15 percent range. We've proven through history that that's a manageable level. We've also learned that the upper end of that range can generate social stresses that give birth to demagogues. There's no need for us to test that boundary any more than we have. It's important to note that we're currently nowhere near the upper end of that range. We could easily absorb another 5 million new immigrants before we'd need to begin tamping down arrivals. That's what has happened in the past. We ebbed and flowed and absorbed and grew. Periods of 15 percent would slowly subside to 13 percent and then regrow to 15 percent. A 13–15 percent range on a sustained basis is plenty. We currently settle around 60,000 asylum seekers each year from around the world. That's barely even a rounding error on our 13–15 percent target. It's well within the error range of the tools we use just to measure these statistics. We need not shut our doors to these desperate people.

We do want to shape and mold the composition of those arriving. We will always have people arriving from Mexico and Latin America just because of proximity and all of the family ties that now exist. If we embark on the kind of updated Marshall Plan outlined in our global economic strategy this should ease a bit, though I doubt it will ever really stop. In recent years there have actually been slightly more immigrants returning to Mexico than there have been new arrivals. It's far too early to conclude we've reached some sort of balance point, but we may not be far from that.

More important to the rest of our global strategy would be an explicit welcome to immigrants from China, India, and across sub-Saharan Africa. In the long term, we want to knit deeper ties with all those regions. Probably our most enduring strategic edge to counter the economic rise of China will be our cultural ability to generate trust and relationships with the full diversity of the planet. That will be nowhere more important over the next 50 years than with India and Africa to balance China herself. Current immigrants from these regions are among the highest educated of all our new arrivals. In many instances their education levels exceed those in the United States. These are people with both moral character and intellectual skills.

Finally, we need to celebrate the strength of our national fabric, not our borders. We are not weak, nor at risk. We need not act like frightened children cowering behind Lady Liberty's skirt. We are not defined by what we are not. We are defined by our shared values and identity and the virtues and strength of those who have joined our incredible national journey.

We will always have more people arriving than we are ready to receive. That's just reality, and it carries with it the need to enforce the limits we set as a society. Most of this actually happens in cities and consists of those overstaying their visas. Some happens at the border either openly or illicitly. None of that needs to be dealt with harshly or with a punitive mind-set. After all, none of the arrivals know what our quotas are nor where we are against them. They just arrive with hope and need to be sent home with their hopes intact for the future. In the vast majority of cases their violations are technically civil misdemeanors. The crime is no more than a parking ticket, and the actual fine is often as small as ten to twenty dollars. It may also entail a deportation to resolve the situation, but that's not actually the civil penalty. There's no need or place for anger in any of this.

The exceptions are those who truly are dangerous and a threat. Many of them are known to the rest of the immigrant community. In fact, other immigrants are often the primary victims of the "bad guys." We do want to weed these people out as our top targets and the best way to do so is in partnership with other immigrants. When we demonize people based on race or country of origin we lose the most important policing tool of all. When we adopt a "protect the immigrant community" instead of a "war on immigrants" mind-set the solutions fall in our laps. The so called "sanctuary city" trend simply represents mature communities recognizing how unproductively destructive the current "war on immigrants" strategy truly is. They're doing what needs to be done in the context of an immoral and ultimately ineffective national agenda.

It's also worth pausing a moment to calibrate just what we're talking about. In all of fiscal year 2017, out of the nearly 527,000 people either apprehended or deemed inadmissible at the border, there were three people who had prior convictions for murder or manslaughter. That's right, three. If we add in those with prior convictions for rape or any form of sexual assault there were 140. Go further and add those with any convictions for assault, battery, or domestic violence and you get 832. Add in priors for drug possession or smuggling and you get roughly 2,000 total criminals. That's about 0.4 percent of the total. To be clear, we do want to find these people and weed them out. The best way to find those needles in the haystack is to enlist the help of the 99.6 percent who do not have these kinds of serious prior convictions.

We also need to calibrate what amounts to overall enforcement success. We will set our targets and aim to remain within them. However, they are not handed to us on stone tablets. The level of precision in both the target and the measured result is low. After all, our 13–15 percent target range gives us an error band of 6–8 million people. Even having tens of thousands that we "should" have caught, but "miss," is utterly irrelevant to achieving our national strategy. We need to manage for the safety and security of our existing citizens *and* new arrivals far more than we need to hit a specific arrest or deportation number.

The judicial process itself is badly broken. Civil misdemeanors don't normally rise to the level where our full legal protections come into play. Among other things the right to representation in particular is waived. This leads poor people, often children, with zero understanding of the law being confronted by a complex bureaucracy that, in some instances is effectively ruling on a life or death decision. The results can be disastrous. The courts themselves are hopelessly backlogged. The more we declare war on these vulnerable people, the more our full judicial protections are needed, a resource demand of ridiculous proportions. Yet, without those protections we are committing grave ethical offenses every single day.

The entire process needs to be de-escalated and redesigned to deliver on its purpose. A simple apprehension for an expired visa can be handled like the misdemeanor it is. Give people a court date, a social worker to contact, and, where appropriate, an ankle bracelet, and let them proceed. Studies have found 99.6 percent of those who are handled in this fashion show up for their court dates. Every city in the country knows how to handle parking tickets.

For those situations that truly are life or death decisions or that involve actual criminal, instead of civil, offenses, we ought to be using our full legal processes. People have a right to representation in those situations. Every city in the country knows how to manage this as well.

OUR NATIONAL TAPESTRY

Real assimilation is a process on all sides. It takes time and leadership. It happens in fits and starts. It happens when people live alongside one another and their fears evolve into the normal human mix of delight and frustration. When there are no "others," just people. We are a nation of immigrants, with a culture that is incredibly rich in its ability to absorb and evolve. But, as amazing as we are, we are also a nation of humans with human fears and limits. Our strategy must recognize this reality—in fact, we need to embrace it. We need to realize that the assimilation and integration process is as rich, rewarding, and important as the infusion of new energy, ideas, and culture. In truth, our American heritage comes only when immigrants and their distinct threads are woven deeply into our shared fabric, our American tapestry.

The Latin phrase we put on all our currency is "E pluribus unum." It means "out of many, one." It was adopted by the Founding Fathers as part of the Great Seal of the United States. Our national flag is another symbol of our purpose to join one people from disparate sources. The stripes representing the original colonies and the stars representing our states are all held within our common national symbol. We did not choose a family crest from one of our founders. We chose a symbol that incorporated all of us as distinct elements in a single whole. E pluribus unum. It's at the heart of our deepest symbols.

We are proud of our history. It is deep and rich. However, compared to the cultures of China, India, or most of Europe, we're still quite young. We may no longer be babes in diapers, but our cultural development is in its early stages. Our greatest days are in front of us. We will continue to gain depth and strength from our steady evolution as well as our ongoing embrace and infusion of the new. We are nowhere near any sort of cultural plateau. If anything, we're still finding our stride, finding our national soul, finding our own cultural depths, finding our voice. We're still weaving our national tapestry, not cutting it from the loom.

As we do this there are core elements that hold us together, that provide our cohesion. These are our values and our sources of identity and placement in the world. We outlined our values earlier. It started with people and freedom. It included our phenomenal ability to create new value, both economic and noneconomic. It recognized the need for truth, civility, and respect in our engagements with each other. And, it recognized that each of us as free individuals are part of our families, our communities, and this nation. These are the elements that bind the threads of our diverse fabric together and are at the heart of what enables us to be a nation carried on waves of immigration. We are defined by our values and what we do, not where we come from nor the color of our skin. Any of us can rise to any stature regardless of where we were born.

All of those binding threads are open for new arrivals to join and embrace. For the vast majority it is the inspiring strength of those values that bring them to our shores. They don't arrive here in the millions because of our bombs and certainly not for our charity programs. They come because the threads that bind us can bind them as well into a common whole propelled by the power of those values. Yes, that includes economics and jobs. But it also includes freedom, dignity, and an explicit place for family and community. They come for our whole incredible American tapestry and they come to join, not unravel.

This is a civilized strategy. However, we're operating amid a stoked-up atmosphere of fear. One of the crucial tools used by demagogues is language, often very specific words. These are intended to put people in the kind of conceptual traps that ensnared us in Vietnam. They are not simple, trivial ploys. As the Vietnam example illustrated, extremely sophisticated and worldly people can be led to devastatingly bad decisions framed by bad choices created by simple concepts and words. It's only a slight exaggeration to argue the word "domino" killed millions of people.

In the case of immigration there are two of these. The first is to simply dehumanize immigrants. Whether they are called illegals, invaders, or animals, they become "others," and human decency need no longer apply. This phenomenon is found everywhere in immigration debates. It's used to deny people access to legal help. It's used to forcibly separate mothers from infant children. It's been used by demagogues throughout history as a prelude to violence, mass killings, and genocide. Every leader must oppose this at every moment. Those words must not be allowed to enter the discussion without confrontation and challenge.

The other deadly word is "amnesty." Its very connotation creates a false set of decisions. Like Vietnam, it creates a frame within which every path is rooted in false choices. It's a completely erroneous frame. People come to this country. At some point they become integral elements of the community and have become Americans. This path has been trod by literally millions of Americans. In fact, it is the family heritage of practically every American. That is what defines us, not whether we got a parking ticket somewhere on our journey.

CONCLUSION

CHOOSING A VISION TO
GUIDE OUR JOURNEY

THIS BOOK HAS highlighted the strong parallels between where we are today and the period right before the Great Depression, the rise of Fascism, and the eruption of World War II. The parallels are not superficial, nor limited to a single sphere. They span the full depths of our economics, including data that is not often in our public eye. They include the repercussions of those issues on people, communities, and the social fabric. In Madeleine Albright's book, *Fascism: A Warning*, she notes that fascism arose in the 1920s and 1930s as a direct result of the failures of capitalism. We're experiencing the exact same failures today with the same consequences. Nationalism is in full bloom and the signs of its progression to fascism are abundant. We should not be surprised that the same dynamic is under way. However, we do need to be alarmed.

We need to be specifically alert to the emergence and rise of demagogues, particularly fascist demagogues. Unlike your garden-variety autocrat, a fascist demagogue does not rely solely on a secret government security apparatus to maintain power. Fascists do have and use those resources, but most of their power comes from their ability to incite and rally a significant segment of the general public. They do this by exploiting fear and aiming it at a target, at "others." The philosophical dimension of *identity* is central to their power. In the absence of fear the demagogue has no raw material. It's the demonization of an "other" as the cause of fear that creates the fascist power dynamic. There is no need for their reach to encompass a majority of the population. All they need are enough to create a complete, self-reinforcing social dynamic. The demagogue can point the finger at the "other," make them a target, dehumanize them, and then let people's fears grow to hate and eventually violence.

The current demagogue's chosen targets are immigrants and racial minorities, particularly Hispanic and African Americans. They no longer seek to unite us based on our common journeys or shared beliefs. Instead they divide us based on where we were born, the color of our skin, and the language of our parents. Those who don't fit the demagogue's mold have been made into targets with sustained efforts to dehumanize them. Using language that refers to immigrants as illegals, vermin, or animals and referring to family efforts to remain intact as "chain migration" are all classic demagogic techniques to dehumanize people. Once the targets are dehumanized, other people's fears can be stoked into hate. No amount of lying or harm is too excessive. Ripping infants from their mother's arms is treatment immigrants should just expect. It's what was done by Nazis when they forced Jews into concentration camps. It's happening today in America and supported by millions, maybe even hundreds of millions.

Demagogues play a dangerous symbiotic role for those who substitute stories for reality. The only thing those folks need to convert a complete fabrication into an accepted "truth" is the endorsement by a social authority figure. The demagogue plays that role. It allows for the rapid creation of ever expanding distortions of reality. It allows the demagogue to take full control of reality itself. "Truth" loses all objective foundation and becomes only what the demagogue and his followers decide to assert. All other voices become irrelevant. The power of reality itself is placed in the hands of the demagogue.

The leverage of the power-based ethical system is equally devastating. The demagogue becomes the supreme leader those people hunger for, and his willingness to inflict "punishment" on the vulnerable appeals to their desire for "justice." The demonized and dehumanized "others" can be subjected to essentially unlimited harm. "Injustices" can be made up at random and punishments created on a whim. This is the dynamic that killed millions in Europe in the 1940s and is steadily growing in America today. Strict loyalty to the desires, whims, and demands of the demagogue is not just acceptable; it actually defines morality.

In this atmosphere, identity, truth, and ethics all become centered on the supreme leader. Words can lose their meaning, become twisted into their exact opposites. "Freedom" means the power to oppress the vulnerable. Logic gets turned inside out. The demagogue embodies the law and is therefore above the law. Legal arguments are constructed that literally claim the demagogue can commit murder and remain untouched because he "is" the law. Morality includes forcing juvenile immigrant rape victims to carry a fetus to term and then rip the nursing infant from the mother. It includes celebrating police who shoot innocent black people and then declaring as unpatriotic anyone who protests. It includes referring to white supremacists as the "good people on both sides."

We become a society of Orwellian speech, pretzelian logic, and reptilian morals.

That is not a great American future.

This is the vision painted by the contemporary conservatives. It is based on fear. It seeks to hide from the world, to erect borders, and treat friends with suspicion. It envisions a nation that is insular, cocooned in fear from the incredible vibrancy and uncertainty of the modern global landscape. There's loud and insistent muscle-flexing but it is primarily aimed at the small, the weak, and our friends. The volume and bullying are actually covering a heart of timidity and cowardice. It is a land of the free and the brave only in stories, in false bravado. In truth, it is America alone.

I offer a different vision, a fifth paradigm, one that places people and the creation of value by people for people at the top. It's a paradigm for society where value creation and people can flourish. It's a society that treats people as people, not labor and not interest groups. It's a society that enables all of us to maximize the personal value of our time. It's a society where our wealth of time is equal to the wealth in our wallets. It's a society that has climbed that economic Maslow hierarchy with food, health, and material abundance and a renewed focus on global innovation and personal value enrichment. It's a society where life, liberty, and the pursuit of happiness are inalienable rights of all, not some, and not only a few. It is America, home to people who really *live* as people.

In the nineteenth century we as a nation were driven by a "manifest destiny" to expand our territory. In the twentieth century we were the global leaders of democracy and freedom powered by an unmatched economic engine. In the twenty-first century we can become the greatest creators of value for people as people. It's a potential shining beacon—a better paradigm for society and a better way to live for all Americans.

Achieving that vision is well within the reach of this country. What it takes is leadership. Proud leadership. Leadership that is able to confront and roll back the anti-democratic forces. Leadership that puts people at the top of our priorities. Leadership that realizes helping people is *not* in conflict with building a sustainable economic engine. That realizes the error in that neoliberal conceptual frame and understands that when people thrive the demand side of the economy thrives, and then, and only then, is the economy on a truly sustainable trajectory.

We need to reject those who seek to lead through fear, doubt, ideological traps, and a vision of a society ruled through a hierarchy of power. We need leadership based on confidence in our history and a vision of a society rooted in the value of people as people.

We are once again at one of those points "in the course of human events" when leadership really matters. It's time for all of them—for all of us—to step forward. A fifth paradigm awaits.

INDEX